Continuous Integration

Continuous Integration

Improving Software Quality and Reducing Risk

Paul M. Duvall

with

Steve Matyas and Andrew Glover

Addison-Wesley

Upper Saddle River, NJ • Boston • Indianapolis • San Francisco
New York • Toronto • Montreal • London • Munich • Paris • Madrid
Capetown • Sydney • Tokyo • Singapore • Mexico City

Library of Congress Cataloging-in-Publication Data

Duvall, Paul M.
Continuous integration : improving software quality and reducing risk / Paul M. Duvall, with Steve Matyas and Andrew Glover.
p. cm.
Includes bibliographical references and index.
ISBN 978-0-321-33638-5 (pbk. : alk. paper) 1. Computer software—Quality control. 2. Computer software—Testing. 3. Computer software—Reliability. I. Matyas, Steve, 1979- II. Glover, Andrew, 1976- III. Title.

QA76.76.Q35D89 2007
005—dc22

2007012001

ISBN 13: 978-0-321-33638-5
ISBN 10: 0-321-33638-0

Text printed in the United States on recycled paper at RR Donnelley in Crawfordsville, Indiana.
Seventh printing, May 2012

I have been blessed with a wonderful family.
To my parents, Paul and Nona, and to my
brothers and sisters, Sue, Joan, John, Mary,
Sally, Tim, Pauline, and Evie.

—P.M.D.

Contents

Foreword by Martin Fowler*

In my early days in the software industry, one of the most awkward and tense moments of a software project was integration. Modules that worked individually were put together and the whole usually failed in ways that were infuriatingly difficult to find. Yet in the last few years, integration has largely vanished as a source of pain for projects, diminishing to a nonevent.

The essence of this transformation is the practice of integrating more frequently. At one point a daily build was considered to be an ambitious target. Most projects I talk to now integrate many times a day. Oddly enough, it seems that when you run into a painful activity, a good tip is to do it more often.

One of the interesting things about Continuous Integration is how often people are surprised by the impact that it has. We often find people dismiss it as a marginal benefit, yet it can bring an entirely different feel to a project. There is a much greater sense of visibility because problems are detected faster. Since there is less time between introducing a fault and discovering you have it, the fault is easier to find because you can easily look at what's changed to help you find the source. Coupled with a determined testing program, this can lead to a drastic reduction in bugs. As a result, developers spend less time debugging and more time adding features, confident they are building on a solid foundation.

Of course, it isn't enough simply to say that you should integrate more frequently. Behind that simple catch phrase are a bunch of principles and practices that can make Continuous Integration a reality. You can find much of this advice scattered in books and on the Internet

*Martin Fowler is series editor and chief scientist at ThoughtWorks.

(and I'm proud to have helped add to this content myself), but you have to do the digging yourself.

So I'm glad to see that Paul has gathered this information together into a cohesive book, a handbook for those who want to put together this best practice. Like any simple practice, there's lots of devil in the details. Over the last few years we've learned a lot about those details and how to deal with them. This book collects these lessons to provide as solid a foundation for Continuous Integration as Continuous Integration does for software development.

Foreword by Paul Julius

I have been hoping someone would get around to writing this book—sooner rather than later. Secretly, I always hoped it would be me. But I'm glad that Paul, Steve, and Andy finally pulled it all together into a cohesive, thoughtful treatise.

I have been knee-deep in Continuous Integration for what seems like forever. In March 2001, I cofounded and began serving as administrator for the CruiseControl open source project. At my day job, I consult at ThoughtWorks, helping clients structure, build, and deploy testing solutions using CI principles and tools.

Activity on the CruiseControl mailing lists really took off in 2003. I had the opportunity to read descriptions of thousands of different CI scenarios. The problems encountered by software developers are varied and complex. The reason developers go to all this work has become clearer and clearer to me. CI advantages—like rapid feedback, rapid deployment, and repeatable automated testing—far outweigh the complication. Yet, it is easy to miss the mark when creating these types of environments. And I never would have guessed when we first released CruiseControl some of the exciting ways that people would use CI to improve their software development processes.

In 2000, I was working on a large J2EE application development project using all the features offered in the specification. The application was amazing in its own right, but a bear to build. By build, I mean compile, test, archive, and conduct functional testing. Ant was still in its infancy and had yet to become the de facto standard for Java applications. We used a finely orchestrated series of shell scripts to compile everything and run unit tests. We used another series of shell scripts to turn everything into deployable archives. Finally, we jumped through some manual hoops to deploy the JARs and run our functional test suite. Needless to say, this process became laborious and tedious, and it was fraught with mistakes.

So started my quest to create a reproducible "build" that required pressing "one button" (one of Martin Fowler's hot topics back then). Ant solved the problem of making a cross-platform build script. The remaining piece I wanted was something that would handle the tedious steps: deployment, functional testing, and reporting of the results. At the time, I investigated the existing solutions, but to no avail. I never quite got everything working the way I wanted on that project. The application made it successfully through development and into production, but I knew that things could be better.

Between the end of that project and the start of the next, I found the answer. Martin Fowler and Matt Foemmel had just published their seminal article on CI. Fortuitously, I paired up with some other ThoughtWorkers who where working on making the Fowler/Foemmel system a reusable solution. I was excited, to say the least! I knew it was the answer to my prayers lingering from the previous project. Within a few weeks, we had everything ready to go and started using it on several existing projects. I even visited a willing Beta test site to install CruiseControl's precursor in a full-scale objective enterprise. Shortly after that, we went open source. For me, there has been no looking back.

As a consultant at ThoughtWorks, I run into some of the most complicated enterprise deployment architectures out there. Our clients are frequently looking for a quick fix based on a high-level understanding of the advantages promised by the industry literature. As with any technology, there exists a fair bit of misinformation about how easy it will be to transform your enterprise. If years of consulting have taught me anything, it is that nothing is as easy as it looks.

I like to talk to clients about practically applying CI principles. I like to stress the importance of shifting the development "cadence" to truly leverage the advantages. If developers only check in once a month, lack focus around automated testing, or have no social imperative to fix broken builds, there are big issues that must be addressed to reap the full benefits of CI.

Does that mean that IT managers should forget about CI until these practices have been shifted? No. In fact, using CI practices can be one of the fastest motivators for change. I find that installing a CI tool like CruiseControl prompts software teams to be proactive instead of reactive. The change does not happen overnight and you have to set your expectations appropriately—including those of the IT managers involved. With persistence and a good understanding of the underlying principles, even the most complicated environments can be made simpler to understand, simpler to test, and simpler to get into production quickly.

The authors have leveled the playing field with this book. I find this book to be both comprehensive and far-reaching. The book's in-depth coverage of the most important aspects of CI will help readers make well-informed decisions. The broad range of topics covers the vast array of approaches that dominate the CI landscape today and helps readers weigh the tradeoffs they will have to make. Finally, I love seeing the work that so many have strived to achieve in the CI community become formalized as the basis for further innovation. Because of this, I highly recommend this book as a vital resource for making sense of complicated geography presented by enterprise applications by using some CI magic.

Preface

Early in my career, I saw a full-page advertisement in a magazine that showed one keyboard key, similar to the Enter key, labeled with the word "Integrate" (see Figure P-1). The text below the key read, "If only it were this easy." I am not sure who or what this ad was for, but it struck a chord with me. In considering software development, I thought, surely that would *never* be achievable because, on my project, we spent several days in "integration hell" attempting to cobble together the myriad software components at the end of most project milestones. But I liked the concept, so I cut out the ad and hung it on my wall. To me, it represented one of my chief goals in being an efficient software developer: to automate repetitive and error-prone processes. Furthermore, it embodied my belief in making software integration a "nonevent" (as Martin Fowler has called this) on a project—something that just happens as a matter of course. Continuous Integration (CI) can help make integration a nonevent on your project.

FIGURE P-1 Integrate!

What Is This Book About?

Consider some of the more typical development processes on a software project: Code is compiled, and data is defined and manipulated via a database; testing occurs, code is reviewed, and ultimately, software is deployed. In addition, teams almost certainly need to communicate with one another regarding the status of the software. Imagine if you could perform these processes at the press of a single button.

This book demonstrates how to create a virtual Integrate button to automate many software development processes. What's more, we describe how this Integrate button can be pressed continuously to reduce the risks that prevent you from creating deployable applications, such as the late discovery of defects and low-quality code. In creating a CI system, many of these processes are automated, and they run every time the software under development is changed.

What Is Continuous Integration?

The process of integrating software is not a new problem. Software integration may not be as much of an issue on a one-person project with few external system dependencies, but as the complexity of a project increases (even just adding one more person), there is a greater need to integrate and ensure that software components work together—early *and often*. Waiting until the end of a project to integrate leads to all sorts of software quality problems, which are costly and often lead to project delays. CI addresses these risks faster and in smaller increments.

In his popular "Continuous Integration" article,[1] Martin Fowler describes CI as:

> . . . a software development practice where members of a team integrate their work frequently, usually each person integrates at least daily—leading to multiple integrations per day. Each integration is

1. See www.martinfowler.com/articles/continuousIntegration.html.

verified by an automated build (including test) to detect integration errors as quickly as possible. Many teams find that this approach leads to significantly reduced integration problems and allows a team to develop cohesive software more rapidly.

In my experience, this means that:

- All developers run private builds[2] on their own workstations before committing their code to the version control repository to ensure that their changes don't break the integration build.
- Developers commit their code to a version control repository *at least* once a day.
- Integration builds occur several times a day on a separate build machine.
- 100% of tests must pass for every build.
- A product is generated (e.g., WAR, assembly, executable, etc.) that can be functionally tested.
- Fixing broken builds is of the highest priority.
- Some developers review reports generated by the build, such as coding standards and dependency analysis reports, to seek areas for improvement.

This book discusses the automated aspects of CI because of the many benefits you receive from automating repetitive and error-prone processes; however, as Fowler identifies, CI is the process of integrating work frequently—and this need not be an automated process to qualify. We clearly believe that since there are many great tools that support CI as an automated process, using a CI server to automate your CI practices is an effective approach. Nevertheless, a manual approach to integration (using an automated build) may work well with your team.

2. The Private (System) Build and Integration Build patterns are covered in *Software Configuration Management Patterns* by Stephen P. Berczuk and Brad Appleton.

Rapid Feedback

Continuous Integration increases your opportunities for feedback. Through it, you learn the state of the project several times a day. CI can be used to reduce the time between when a defect is introduced and when it is fixed, thus improving overall software quality.

A development team should not believe that because their CI system is automated, they are safe from integration problems. It is even less true if the group is using an automated tool for nothing more than compiling source code; some refer to this as a "build," which it is not (see Chapter 1). The effective practice of CI involves much more than a tool. It includes the practices we outline in the book, such as frequent commits to a version control repository, fixing broken builds immediately, and using a separate integration build machine.

The practice of CI enables faster feedback. When using effective CI practices, you'll know the overall health of software under development *several times a day*. What's more, CI works well with practices like refactoring and test-driven development, because these practices are centered on the notion of making small changes. CI, in essence, provides a safety net to ensure that changes work with the rest of the software. At a higher level, CI increases the collective confidence of teams and lessens the amount of human activity needed on projects, because it's often a *hands-off* process that runs whenever your software changes.

A Note on the Word "Continuous"

We use the term "continuous" in this book, but the usage is technically incorrect. "Continuous" implies that something kicks off once and never stops. This suggests that the process is constantly integrating, which is not the case in even the most intense CI environment. So, what we are describing in this book is more like "continual integration."

Who Should Read This Book?

In our experience, there is a distinct difference between someone who treats software development as a *job* and someone who treats it as a *profession*. This book is for those who work at their profession and find themselves performing repetitive processes on a project (or we will help you realize just how often you are doing so). We describe the practices and benefits of CI and give you the knowledge to apply these practices so that you can direct your time and expertise to more important, challenging issues.

This book covers the major topics relating to CI, including how to implement CI using continuous feedback, testing, deployment, inspection, and database integration. No matter what your role in software development, you can incorporate CI into your own software development processes. If you are a software professional who wants to become increasingly effective—getting more done with your time and with more dependable results—you will gain much from this book.

Developers

If you have noticed that you'd rather be developing software for users than fiddling with software integration issues, this book will help you get there without much of the "pain" you thought would be involved. This book doesn't ask you to spend more time integrating; it's about making much of software integration a nonevent, leaving you to focus on doing what you love the most: developing software. The many practices and examples in this book demonstrate how to implement an effective CI system.

Build/Configuration/Release Management

If your job is to get *working* software out the door, you'll find this book particularly interesting as we demonstrate that by running processes *every time* a change is applied to a version control repository, you can generate cohesive, working software. Many of you are managing builds while filling other roles on your project, such as development. CI will do some of the "thinking" for you, and instead of waiting until the end of the development lifecycle, it creates deployable and *testable* software several times a day.

Testers

CI offers a rapid feedback approach to software development, all but eliminating the traditional pain of reoccurring defects even after "fixes" were applied. Testers usually gain increased satisfaction and interest in their roles on a project using CI, since software to test is available more often and with smaller scopes. With a CI system in your development lifecycle, you test *all along the way,* rather than the typical feast or famine scenario where testers are either testing into the late hours or not testing at all.

Managers

This book can have great impact for you if you seek a higher level of confidence in your team's capability to consistently and repeatedly deliver working software. You can manage scopes of time, cost, and quality much more effectively because you are basing your decisions on working software with actual feedback and metrics, not just task items on a project schedule.

Organization of This Book

This book is divided into two parts. Part I is an introduction to CI and examines the concept and its practices from the ground up. Part I is geared toward those readers not familiar with the core practices of CI. We do not feel the practice of CI is complete, however, without a Part II that naturally expands the core concepts into other effective processes performed by CI systems, such as testing, inspection, deployment, and feedback.

Part I: A Background on CI—Principles and Practices

Chapter 1, Getting Started, gets you right into things with a high-level example of using a CI server to continuously build your software.

Chapter 2, Introducing Continuous Integration, familiarizes you with the common practices and how we got to CI.

Chapter 3, Reducing Risks Using CI, identifies the key risks CI can mitigate using scenario-based examples.

Chapter 4, Building Software at Every Change, explores the practice of integrating your software with every change by leveraging the automated build.

Part II: Creating a Full-Featured CI System

Chapter 5, Continuous Database Integration, moves into more advanced concepts involving the process of rebuilding databases and applying test data as part of every integration build.

Chapter 6, Continuous Testing, covers the concepts and strategies of testing software with every integration build.

Chapter 7, Continuous Inspection, takes you through some automated and continuous inspections (static and dynamic analysis) using different tools and techniques.

Chapter 8, Continuous Deployment, explores the process of deploying software using a CI system so that it can be functionally tested.

Chapter 9, Continuous Feedback, describes and demonstrates the use of continuous feedback devices (such as e-mail, RSS, X10, and the Ambient Orb) so that you are notified on build success or failure as it happens.

The Epilogue explores the future possibilities of CI.

Appendixes

Appendix A, CI Resources, includes a list of URLs, tools, and papers related to CI.

Appendix B, Evaluating CI Tools, assesses the different CI servers and related tools on the market, discusses their applicability to the practices described in the book, identifies the advantages and disadvantages of each, and explains how to use some of their more interesting features.

Other Features

The book includes features that help you to better learn and apply what we describe in the text.

- Practices—We cover more than forty CI-related practices in this book. Many chapter subheadings are practices. A figure at the beginning of most chapters illustrates the practices covered and lets you scan for areas that interest you. For example, *use a dedicated integration build machine* and *commit code frequently* are both examples of practices discussed in this book.
- Examples—We demonstrate how to apply these practices by using various examples in different languages and platforms.
- Questions—Each chapter concludes with a list of questions to help you evaluate the application of CI practices on your project.
- Web site—The book's companion Web site, www.integratebutton.com, provides book updates, videos, code examples, and other material.

What You Will Learn

By reading this book, you will learn concepts and practices that enable you to create cohesive, working software many times a day. We have taken care to focus on the practices first, followed by the application of these practices, with examples included as demonstration wherever possible. The examples use different development platforms, such as Java, Microsoft .NET, and even some Ruby. CruiseControl (Java and .NET versions) is the primary CI server used throughout the book; however, we have created similar examples using other servers and tools on the companion Web site (www.integratebutton.com) and in Appendix B.

As you work your way through the book, you gain these insights:

- How implementing CI produces *deployable software* at every step in your development lifecycle.
- How CI can *reduce the time* between when a defect is introduced and when that defect is detected, thereby lowering the cost to fix it.
- How you can *build quality into your software* by building software often rather than waiting to the latter stages of development.

What This Book Does Not Cover

This book does not cover every tool—build scheduling, programming environment, version control, and so on—that makes up your CI system. It focuses on the implementation of CI practices to develop an effective CI system. CI practices are discussed first; if a particular tool demonstrated is no longer in use or doesn't meet your particular needs, simply apply the practice using another tool to achieve the same effect.

It is also not possible, or useful, to cover every type of test, feedback mechanism, automated inspector, and type of deployment used by a CI system. We hope that a greater goal is met by focusing on the range of key practices, using examples of techniques and tools for database integration, testing, inspection, and feedback that may inspire applications as different as the projects and teams that learn about them. As mentioned throughout the book, the book's companion Web site, www.integratebutton.com, contains examples using other tools and languages that may not be covered in the book.

Authorship

This book has three coauthors and one contributor. I wrote most of the chapters. Steve Matyas contributed to Chapters 4, 5, 7, 8, and Appendix A, and constructed some of the book's examples. Andy Glover wrote Chapters 6, 7, and 8, provided examples, and made contributions elsewhere in the book. Eric Tavela wrote Appendix B. So when sentences use first-person pronouns, this should provide clarity as to who is saying what.

About the Cover

I was excited when I learned that our book was to be a part of the renowned Martin Fowler Signature Series. I knew this meant that I would get to choose a bridge for the cover of the book. My coauthors and I are part of a rare breed who grew up in the Washington, D.C., area. For those of you not from the region, it's a very transient area. More specifically, we are from Northern Virginia and figured it would be a fitting tribute to choose the Natural Bridge in Virginia for the cover. I had never visited the bridge until early 2007—after I had chosen it for the book cover. It has a very interesting history and I found it incredible that it's a functioning bridge that automobiles travel on every day. (Of course, I had to drive my car over it a couple of times.) I'd like to think that after reading this book, you will make CI a natural part of your next software development project.

Acknowledgments

I can't tell you how many times I've read acknowledgments in a book and authors wrote how they "couldn't have done it by (themselves)" and other such things. I always thought to myself, "They're just being falsely modest." Well, I was dead wrong. This book was a massive undertaking to which I am grateful to the people listed herein.

I'd like to thank my publisher, Addison-Wesley. In particular, I'd like to express my appreciation to my executive editor, Chris Guzikowski, for working with me during this exhaustive process. His experience, insight, and encouragement were tremendous. Furthermore, my development editor, Chris Zahn, provided solid recommendations throughout multiple versions and editing cycles. I'd also like to thank Karen Gettman, Michelle Housley, Jessica D'Amico, Julie Nahil, Rebecca Greenberg, and last but definitely not least, my first executive editor, Mary O'Brien.

Rich Mills hosted the CVS server for the book and offered excellent ideas during brainstorming sessions. I'd also like to thank my mentor and friend, Rob Daly, for getting me into professional writing in 2002 and for providing exceptionally detailed reviews throughout the writing process. John Steven was instrumental in helping me start this book's writing process.

I'd like to express my gratitude to my coauthors, editor, and contributing author. Steve Matyas and I endured many sleepless nights to create what you are reading today. Andy Glover was our clutch writer, providing his considerable developer testing experience to the project.

Lisa Porter, our contributing editor, tirelessly combed through every major revision to provide edits and recommendations which helped increase the quality of the book. A thank you to Eric Tavela, who wrote the CI tools appendix, and to Levent Gurses for providing his experiences with Maven 2 in Appendix B.

We had an eclectic cadre of personal technical reviewers who provided excellent feedback throughout this project. They include Tom Copeland, Rob Daly, Sally Duvall, Casper Hornstrup, Joe Hunt, Erin Jackson, Joe Konior, Rich Mills, Leslie Power, David Sisk, Carl Tallis, Eric Tavela, Dan Taylor, and Sajit Vasudevan.

I'd also like to thank Charles Murray and Cristalle Belonia for their assistance, and Maciej Zawadzki and Eric Minick from Urbancode for their help.

I am grateful for the support of many great people who inspire me every day at Stelligent, including Burke Cox, Mandy Owens, David Wood, and Ron Wright. There are many others who have inspired my work over the years, including Rich Campbell, David Fado, Mike Fraser, Brent Gendleman, Jon Hughes, Jeff Hwang, Sherry Hwang, Sandi Kyle, Brian Lyons, Susan Mason, Brian Messer, Sandy Miller, John Newman, Marcus Owen, Chris Painter, Paulette Rogers, Mark Simonik, Joe Stusnick, and Mike Trail.

I also appreciate the thorough feedback from the Addison-Wesley technical review team, including Scott Ambler, Brad Appleton, Jon Eaves, Martin Fowler, Paul Holser, Paul Julius, Kirk Knoernschild, Mike Melia, Julian Simpson, Andy Trigg, Bas Vodde, Michael Ward, and Jason Yip.

I want to thank the attendees of CITCON Chicago 2006 for sharing their experiences on CI and testing with all of us. In particular, I'd like to acknowledge Paul Julius and Jeffrey Frederick for organizing the conference, and everyone else who attended the event.

Finally, I'd like to thank Jenn for her unrelenting support and for being there through the ups and downs of making this book.

Paul M. Duvall
Fairfax, Virginia
March 2007

About the Authors

Paul M. Duvall is the CTO of Stelligent Incorporated, a consulting firm and thought leader in helping development teams reliably and rapidly produce better software by optimizing Agile software production. He has worked in virtually every role on a software development project, from developer and tester to architect and project manager. Paul has consulted for clients in various industries including finance, housing, government, health care, and large independent software vendors. He is a featured speaker at many leading software conferences. He authors a series for IBM developerWorks called *Automation for the People,* is a coauthor of the *NFJS 2007 Anthology* (Pragmatic Programmers, 2007), and is a contributing author of *UML 2 Toolkit* (Wiley, 2003). He is a co-inventor of a clinical research data management system and method that is patent pending. He actively blogs on www.testearly.com and www.integratebutton.com.

Stephen M. Matyas III is the vice president of AutomateIT, a service branch of 5AM Solutions, Inc., which helps organizations improve software development through automation. Steve has a varied background in applied software engineering, including experience with both commercial and government clients. Steve has performed a wide variety of roles, from business analyst and project manager to developer, designer, and architect. He is a contributing author of *UML 2 Toolkit* (Wiley, 2003). He is a practitioner of many iterative and incremental methodologies including Agile and Rational Unified Process (RUP). Much of his professional, hands-on experience has been in the Java/J2EE custom software development and services industry with a specialization in methodologies, software quality, and process improvement. He holds a bachelor of science degree in computer science from Virginia Polytechnic Institute and State University (Virginia Tech).

Andrew Glover is the president of Stelligent Incorporated, a consulting firm and thought leader in helping development teams reliably and rapidly produce better software by optimizing software production. Andy is a frequent speaker at various conferences throughout North America as well as a speaker for the No Fluff Just Stuff Software Symposium group; moreover, he is the coauthor of *Groovy in Action* (Manning, 2007), *Java Testing Patterns* (Wiley, 2004), and the *NFJS 2006 Anthology* (Pragmatic Programmers, 2006). He also is the author of multiple online publications including IBM's developerWorks and O'Reilly's ONJava, ONLamp, and Dev2Dev portals. He actively blogs about software quality at www.thediscoblog.com and www.testearly.com.

About the Contributors

Lisa Porter is the senior technical writer for a consulting team providing network security solutions to the U.S. government. Lisa provided technical editing prior to the production of this book. Her early years were spent supporting a large software development project with multiple applications, where she gained a great appreciation for requirements determination and project maturity/capability activities. She has also applied the principles of technical writing in the world of foreign language translation and the architectural/engineering industry. Lisa has been editing books and online publications since 2002.

Eric Tavela is the chief architect for 5AM Solutions, Inc., a software development company that focuses on applying software engineering best practices to serve the life sciences research community. Eric's principal background is in designing and implementing Java/J2EE applications and in mentoring developers in object-oriented software development and UML modeling.

Part I

A Background on CI: Principles and Practices

Chapter 1
Getting Started

Build Software at Every Change

First, master the fundamentals.
—LARRY BIRD (AMERICAN PROFESSIONAL BASKETBALL PLAYER)

The founder of javaranch.com, Kathy Sierra, said in her blog, "There's a big difference between saying, 'Eat an apple a day' and actually eating the apple."[1] The same goes for following fundamental practices on a software project. Seldom will you hear people say that "Testing is ineffective" or "Code reviews are a waste of time" or that frequent software builds is a bad practice to follow. But these seemingly fundamental practices must be tougher to practice than to preach, because the frequency of these practices on projects is miserably low.

If you would like to run frequent integration builds so that it becomes a *nonevent* on your project—including compilation, rebuilding your database, executing automated tests and inspections, deploying software, and receiving feedback—**Continuous Integration (CI)** can help. In this chapter, we show you the common features available to CI systems that build upon these fundamental software practices.

1. From http://headrush.typepad.com/.

Understanding the fundamentals of CI is quite easy, and in no time you'll be integrating these fundamental practices of software development into your builds.

Build Software at Every Change

When reading books, I like to see an example first and then learn the "why" behind the example afterward, as I find that an example provides a context for learning the "why." We describe a CI scenario based on a typical implementation. You'll find there are various ways to implement a CI system, but this should get you started in understanding the parts of a typical system.

What Is a *Build*?

A **build** is much more than a compile (or its dynamic language variations). A build may consist of the compilation, testing, inspection, and deployment—among other things. A build acts as the process for putting source code together and verifying that the software works as a cohesive unit.

A CI scenario starts with the developer committing source code to the repository. On a typical project, people in many project roles may commit changes that trigger a CI cycle: Developers change source code, database administrators (DBAs) change table definitions, build and deployment teams change configuration files, interface teams change DTD/XSD specifications, and so on.

Keeping Examples Up to Date

The risk of writing a "hands-on" example in a book is that it quickly becomes outdated, especially with a dynamic topic like CI. To offset changes that may occur after this book is published, we will update the book's companion Web site, www.integratebutton.com, with examples on not just CruiseControl and Ant, but many other CI servers and tools as well.

The steps in a CI scenario will typically go something like this.

1. First, a developer commits code to the version control repository. Meanwhile, the CI server on the integration build machine is polling this repository for changes (e.g., every few minutes).
2. Soon after a commit occurs, the CI server detects that changes have occurred in the version control repository, so the CI server retrieves the latest copy of the code from the repository and then executes a build script, which integrates the software.
3. The CI server generates feedback by e-mailing build results to specified project members.
4. The CI server continues to poll for changes in the version control repository.

Figure 1-1 illustrates these parts of the CI system.

The following sections describe the tools and players identified in Figure 1-1 in more detail.

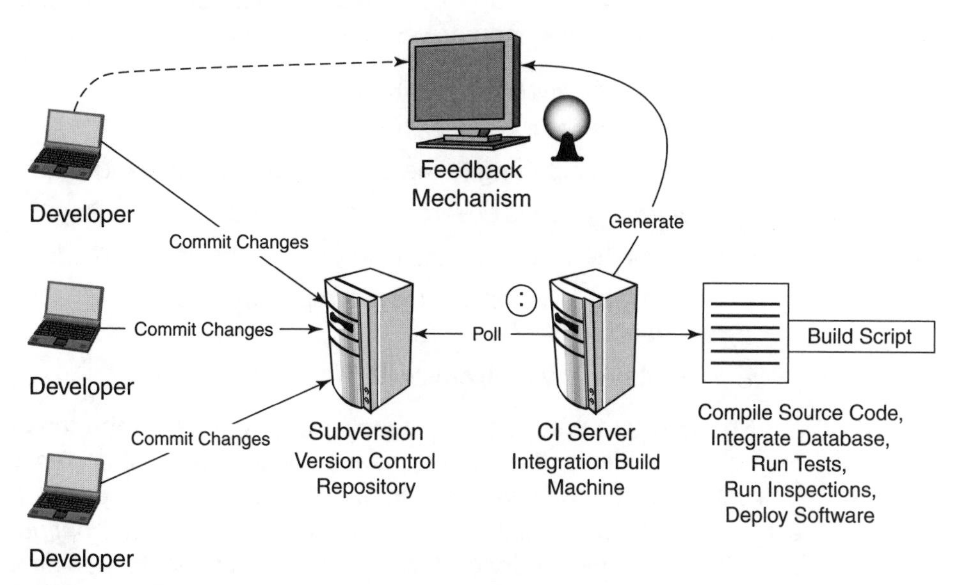

FIGURE 1-1 The components of a CI system

Developer

Once a developer has performed all of the modifications related to the assigned task, she runs a private build (which integrates changes from the rest of the team) and then commits her changes to the version control repository. This step may occur at any time and does not affect the subsequent steps of the CI process. An integration build does not occur unless there are changes applied to the version control repository.

Listing 1-1 demonstrates an example of executing a private build by calling an Ant build script from the command line. Notice that this script retrieves the latest updates from the Subversion version control repository.

Find Problems Earlier by Building Often

Once you've automated your build and it can be run via a single command, you are ready to perform CI. By running this automated build whenever a change is committed to your project's version control system, teams can answer questions like:

- Do all the software components work together?
- What is my code complexity?
- Is the team adhering to the established coding standards?
- How much code is covered by automated tests?
- Were all the tests successful after the latest change?
- Does my application still meet the performance requirements?
- Were there any problems with the last deployment?

Knowing that software was successfully "built" with the latest changes is valuable, but knowing that software was built *correctly* is invaluable, as software defects will undoubtedly creep into a code base at some point. The reason you want to build *continuously* is to get rapid feedback so that you can find and fix problems throughout the development lifecycle.

LISTING 1-1 Running a Private Build Using Ant

```
> ant integrate
Buildfile: build.xml
clean:
svn-update:
all:
compile-src:
compile-tests:
integrate-database:
run-tests:
run-inspections:
package:
deploy:
BUILD SUCCESSFUL
Total time: 3 minutes 13 seconds
```

After running a successful private build, you can check in new and modified files to the repository. Most version control systems provide simple commands to perform these processes, as shown in Listing 1-2 using Subversion.

LISTING 1-2 Committing Changes to a Subversion Repository

```
> svn commit -m "Added CRUD capabilities to DAO"
Sending src\BeerDaoImpl.java
Transmitting file data .

Committed revision 52.
```

You can execute your build script and commit changes to your repository using your Integrated Development Environment (IDE) as well. Just make sure you can perform both activities from the command line so that you don't have tightly coupled dependencies with your IDE or version control system.

Version Control Repository

Simply put, you must use a version control repository in order to perform CI. In fact, even if you don't use CI, a version control repository should be standard for your project. The purpose of a version control repository is to manage changes to source code and other software assets (such as documentation) using a controlled access repository. This provides you with a "single source point" so that all source code is available from one primary location. A version control repository allows you to go back in time and get different versions of source code and other files.

You run CI against the mainline of the version control repository (e.g., the Head/Trunk in systems like CVS and Subversion). There are different types of version control systems you can use too. We use Subversion for most of the examples in the book because of its feature set—and it's freely available. Other Software Configuration Management (SCM)/version control tools include CVS, Perforce, PVCS, ClearCase, MKS, and Visual SourceSafe. To learn effective techniques of software configuration management, see *Software Configuration Management Patterns* by Stephen Berczuk and Brad Appleton.

CI Server

A CI server runs an integration build whenever a change is committed to the version control repository. Typically, you will configure the CI server to check for changes in a version control repository every few minutes or so. The CI server will retrieve the source files and run a build script or scripts. CI servers can also be hard-scheduled to build on a regular frequency, such as every hour (but note that this is not CI). In addition, CI servers usually provide a convenient dashboard where build results are published. Although it is recommended, a CI server isn't required to perform continuous integration. You can write your own custom scripts. Moreover, you can manually run an integration build whenever a change is applied to the repository. Using a CI server[2] can reduce the number of custom scripts that you would otherwise need to write. Many CI servers are freely available and open source. Listing 1-3 shows an example of using the CruiseControl config.xml to poll a Subversion repository looking for changes.

LISTING 1-3 CruiseControl config.xml Polling Subversion Repository

```
<project name="brewery" >
  <listeners>
    <currentbuildstatuslistener file="logs/${project.name}/status.txt"/>
```

2. For more information on CI servers, see Appendix B.

```
  </listeners>
  <modificationset quietperiod="30">
    <svn RepositoryLocation="http://build.ib.com/trunk/brewery"
      username="bfranklin"
      password="GOFly@Kite"/>
  </modificationset>
  <schedule interval="300">
    <ant anthome="apache-ant-1.6.5" buildfile="bld-{project.name}.xml"/>
  </schedule>
  <log dir="logs/${project.name}">
    <merge dir="projects/${project.name}/impl/logs/junit"/>
    <merge dir="projects/${project.name}/impl/logs/cobertura"/>
  </log>
  <publishers>
    <artifactspublisher dir="projects/${project.name}/impl/logs"
dest="artifacts/${project.name}"/>
    <artifactspublisher dir="projects/${project.name}/impl/logs"
dest="artifacts/${project.name}"/>
  </publishers>
</project>
```

In Listing 1-3, the `interval` attribute of the `schedule` task indicates how often CruiseControl will check for changes in the Subversion repository (in this example, 300 seconds). If CruiseControl finds any modifications, it executes a delegating build (called using the `buildfile` attribute in Listing 1-3). The delegating build (not shown) retrieves the latest source code from the repository and executes the project build file, such as the one in Listing 1-3. Other CI servers may use a Web-based configuration or other interface for administration. CruiseControl comes with a Web application so that you can view the results of the latest build and view build reports (such as test and inspection reports). Figure 1-2 illustrates an example of CruiseControl build results for a project.

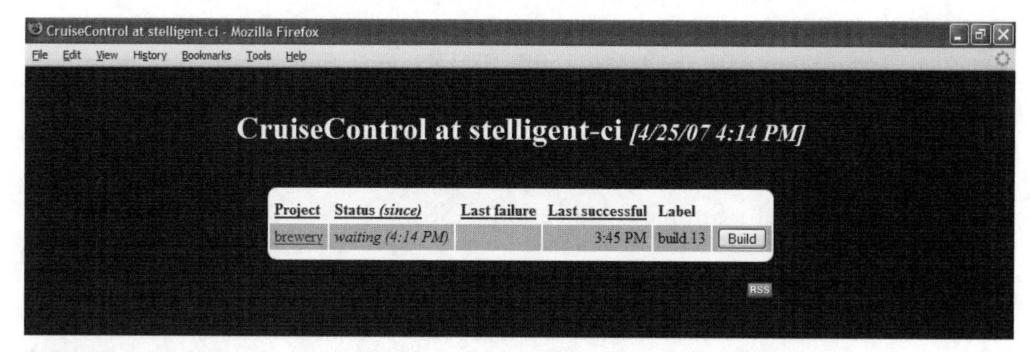

FIGURE 1-2 CruiseControl dashboard displaying the latest build status

Build Script

The **build script** is a single script, or set of scripts, you use to compile, test, inspect, and deploy software. You can use a build script without implementing a CI system. Ant, NAnt, make, MSBuild, and Rake are examples of build tools that can automate the software build cycle, but they don't provide CI by themselves. Some may use an IDE to build software; however, since CI is a "hands-off" process, solely using IDE-based builds won't cut it for CI. To be clear, using an IDE to run a build is appropriate as long as you can run the same build *without* using the IDE as well. Listing 1-4 shows an example of the shell of an Ant script that runs through the type of processes typically performed as part of a private build.[3]

LISTING 1-4 Shell of an Ant Script to Perform a Build

```
<?xml version="1.0" encoding="iso-8859-1"?>
<project name="brewery" default="all" basedir=".">
  <target name="clean" />
  <target name="svn-update" />
  <target name="all" depends="clean,svn-update"/>
  <target name="compile-src" />
  <target name="compile-tests" />
  <target name="integrate-database" />
  <target name="run-tests" />
  <target name="run-inspections" />
  <target name="package" />
  <target name="deploy" />
</project>
```

Feedback Mechanism

One of the key purposes of CI is to produce feedback on an integration build, because you want to know as soon as possible if there was a problem with the latest build. By receiving this information promptly, you can fix the problem quickly. Figure 1-3 shows an e-mail as a feedback mechanism. We demonstrate more feedback devices in Chapter 9. Other feedback mechanisms include Short Message Service (SMS) and Really Simple Syndication (RSS).

3. A more detailed example is provided at www.integratebutton.com.

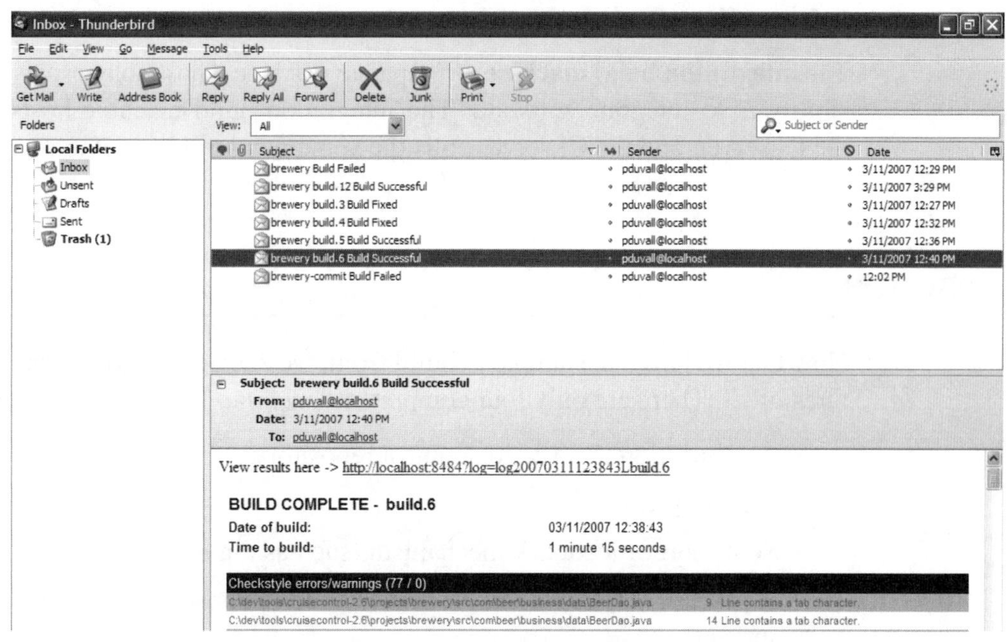

FIGURE 1-3 E-mail messages from the CI server

Listing 1-5 contains an example of using the CruiseControl CI server to send an e-mail to project members.

LISTING 1-5 CruiseControl config.xml Configured to Send E-mail

```
<project>
  …
  <publishers>
    <htmlemail
      css="./webapps/cruisecontrol/css/cruisecontrol.css"
      mailhost="localhost"
      xsldir="./webapps/cruisecontrol/xsl"
      returnaddress="pduvall@localhost"
      buildresultsurl="http://localhost:8080"
      mailport="225"
      username="pduvall"
      password="password"
      reportsuccess="always"
      spamwhilebroken="true">
      <always address="pduvall@localhost"/>
      <always address="aglover@localhost"/>
    </htmlemail>
  </publishers>
  …
</project>
```

Integration Build Machine

The **integration build machine** is a separate machine whose sole responsibility is to integrate software. The integration build machine hosts the CI server, and the CI server polls the version control repository.

Features of CI

Now that we have an example to build from, we can delve into the features of CI. There are only four components *required* for CI.

- A connection to a version control repository
- A build script
- Some sort of feedback mechanism (such as e-mail)
- A process for integrating the source code changes (manual or CI server)

This "bare-bones" behavior is the key to an effective CI system. Once an automated build is run with every change to your version control system, you can add other features to your CI system.

By performing automated and continuous database integration, testing, inspection, deployment, and feedback, your CI system can reduce common risks on your project, thus leading to better confidence and improved communication. Some features depend on other features; for instance, automated testing depends on source code compilation.

This repeatable process can help reduce risks throughout the development lifecycle. These subprocesses are described in detail next.

Source Code Compilation

Continuous source code compilation is one of the most basic and common features of a CI system. In fact, it's so common that it has almost become synonymous with CI. Compilation involves creating executable code from your human-readable source. CI is much more than source code compilation, though; with the proliferation in the use of *dynamic* languages—Python, PHP, Ruby, and so on—compilation is

The Integrate Button

The **Integrate button** (see Figure 1-4) is a visualization of a fully functioning and automated integration build—making the build a *nonevent.* Include many of the processes to ensure that your software works as intended. You can compile, rebuild a database with test data, run tests, inspect, deploy, and provide feedback. By automating your build, you can run many of the processes at the *push of a button.*

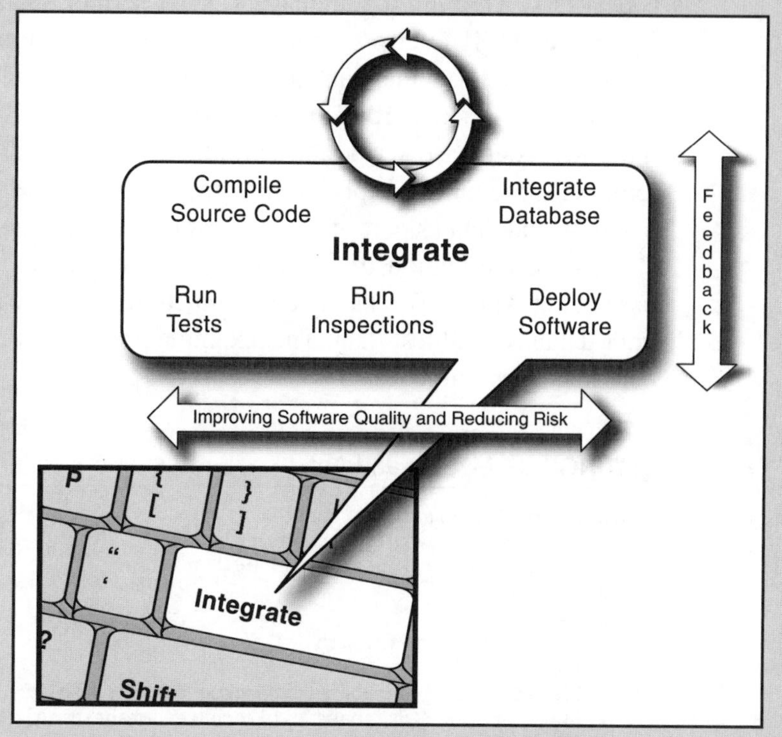

FIGURE 1-4 Visualization of the Integrate button

slightly different in these environments. Although you are not generating binaries using dynamic languages, many provide the capability to perform strict checking, which you can think of as compilation in the context of these languages. Despite this subtlety, dynamic language environments benefit from the other activities executed during a CI build.

Database Integration

Some people consider the source code integration and integration of the database as completely separate processes—*always* performed by different groups. This is unfortunate because the database (if you are using one on your project) is an integral part of the software application. By using a CI system, you can ensure the integration of a database through a single source: your version control repository.

Figure 1-5 demonstrates enabling continuous database integration in the build process of a CI system. We treat the database source code—Data Definition Language (DDL) scripts, Data Manipulation Language (DML) scripts, stored procedure definitions, partitioning, and so on—in the same manner as any other source code in the system. For instance, when a project member (developer or DBA, for instance) modifies a database script and commits it to the version control system, the same build script that integrates source code will rebuild the database and data as part of the integration build process.

Listing 1-6 demonstrates how to drop and create a MySQL database using Ant's `sql` task. There is much more you will do to rebuild your database and test data. This example hard-codes many values for demonstration purposes.

LISTING 1-6 MySQL and Ant

```
<target name="db:create-database">
  <sql driver="com.mysql.jdbc.Driver"
    url="jdbc:mysql://localhost:3306/"
    userid="root"
    password="sa"
    classpathref="db.lib.path"
    delimiter=";">
    <fileset file="${database.dir}/drop-database.sql"/>
    <fileset file="${database.dir}/create-database.sql "/>
  </sql>
</target>
```

We demonstrate examples, approaches, and the benefits of database integration in Chapter 5.

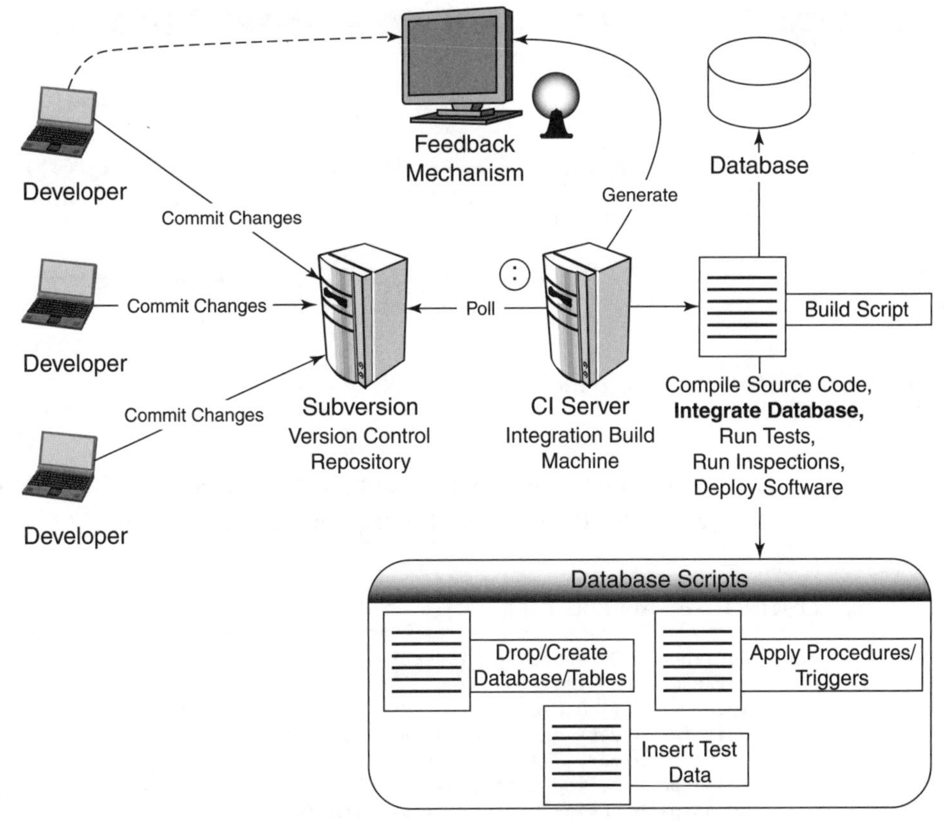

FIGURE 1-5 Database integration design

Testing

Many consider CI *without* automated, continuous testing not to be CI. We couldn't agree more. Without automated tests, it is difficult for developers or other project stakeholders to have confidence in software changes. Most developers on projects that use a CI system use unit-testing tools such as JUnit, NUnit, or other xUnit frameworks to run tests. Furthermore, you can run different categories of tests from a CI system to speed up your builds. These categories may include unit, component, system, load/performance, security, and others. Many of these tests are discussed in more detail in Chapter 6. Figure 1-6 shows an example of a JUnit report that CI servers such as CruiseControl may display as part of an integration build.

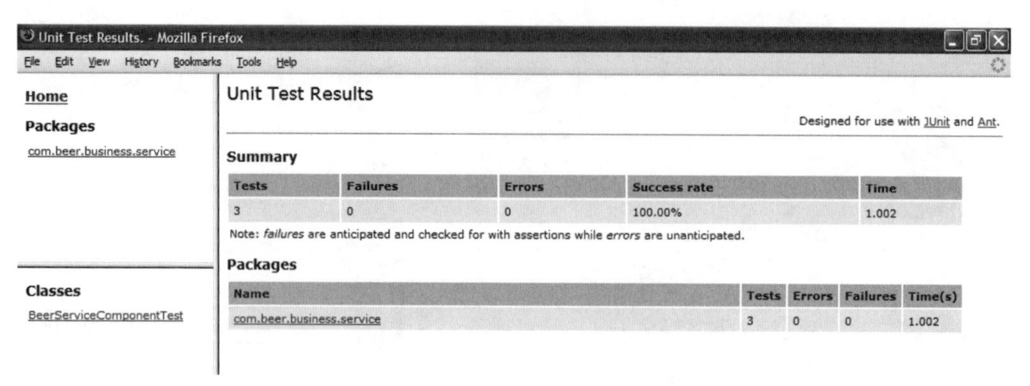

FIGURE 1-6 Unit test regression report using JUnit

Listing 1-7 demonstrates an example that runs a batch of JUnit tests and generates the report in Figure 1-6 using Ant tasks.

LISTING 1-7 Ant and JUnit

```
<?xml version="1.0" encoding="iso-8859-1"?>
  <target name="run-tests">
    <mkdir dir="${logs.junit.dir}" />
    <junit fork="yes" haltonfailure="true" dir="${basedir}"
         printsummary="yes">
      <classpath refid="test.class.path" />
      <classpath refid="project.class.path"/>
      <formatter type="plain" usefile="true" />
      <formatter type="xml" usefile="true" />
      <batchtest fork="yes" todir="${logs.junit.dir}">
        <fileset dir="${test.unit.dir}">
          <patternset refid="test.sources.pattern"/>
        </fileset>
      </batchtest>
    </junit>
    <mkdir dir="${reports.junit.dir}" />
    <junitreport todir="${reports.junit.dir}">
      <fileset dir="${logs.junit.dir}">
        <include name="TEST-*.xml" />
        <include name="TEST-*.txt" />
      </fileset>
      <report format="frames" todir="${reports.junit.dir}" />
    </junitreport>
  </target>
</project>
```

Inspection

Automated code inspections (e.g., static and dynamic analysis) can be used to enhance the quality of the software by enforcing rules. For instance, a project might have a rule that no class may be longer than 300 lines of noncommented code. You can use your CI system to run these rules automatically against a code base. We discuss and demonstrate various tools and techniques in Chapter 7.

The sample software inspection report shown in Figure 1-7 was generated using Checkstyle, which inspects Java code. Using a report like this can enable continuous monitoring of coding standards and quality metrics.

Listing 1-8 shows an example using the Checkstyle static code analysis tool with Ant. This example generates the report in Figure 1-7.

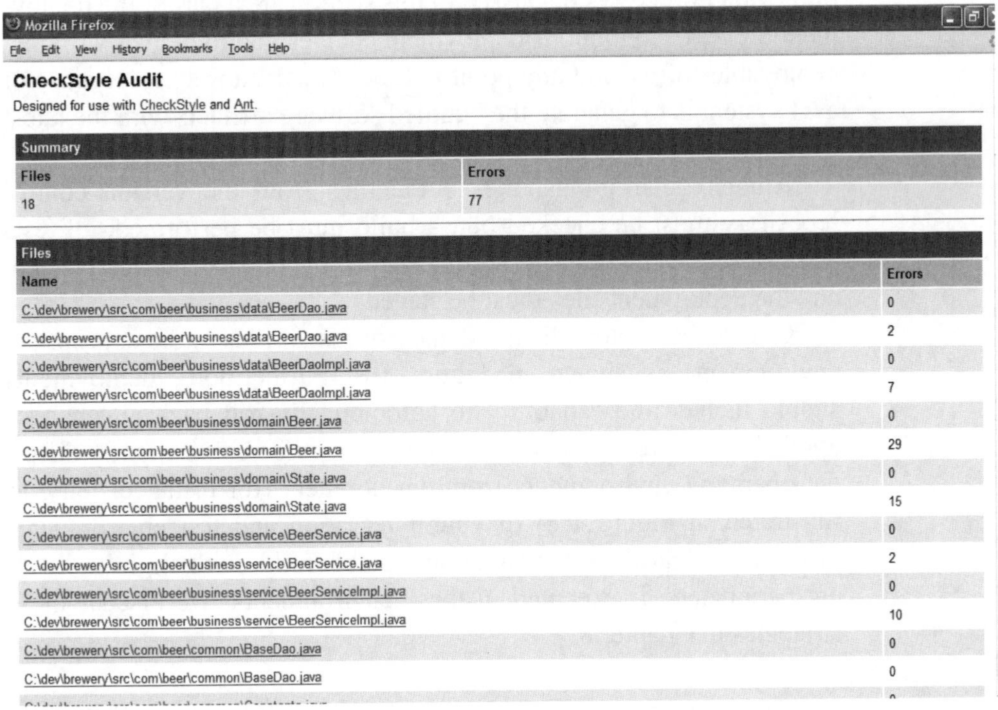

Mozilla Firefox

File Edit View History Bookmarks Tools Help

CheckStyle Audit

Designed for use with CheckStyle and Ant.

Summary

Files	Errors
18	77

Files

Name	Errors
C:\dev\brewery\src\com\beer\business\data\BeerDao.java	0
C:\dev\brewery\src\com\beer\business\data\BeerDao.java	2
C:\dev\brewery\src\com\beer\business\data\BeerDaoImpl.java	0
C:\dev\brewery\src\com\beer\business\data\BeerDaoImpl.java	7
C:\dev\brewery\src\com\beer\business\domain\Beer.java	0
C:\dev\brewery\src\com\beer\business\domain\Beer.java	29
C:\dev\brewery\src\com\beer\business\domain\State.java	0
C:\dev\brewery\src\com\beer\business\domain\State.java	15
C:\dev\brewery\src\com\beer\business\service\BeerService.java	0
C:\dev\brewery\src\com\beer\business\service\BeerService.java	2
C:\dev\brewery\src\com\beer\business\service\BeerServiceImpl.java	0
C:\dev\brewery\src\com\beer\business\service\BeerServiceImpl.java	10
C:\dev\brewery\src\com\beer\common\BaseDao.java	0
C:\dev\brewery\src\com\beer\common\BaseDao.java	0

FIGURE 1-7 Automated inspection report using Checkstyle

LISTING 1-8 Checkstyle Example Using Ant[4]

```
<target name="run-inspections">
  <taskdef resource="checkstyletask.properties"
classpath="${checkstyle.jar}"/>
  <checkstyle config="${basedir}/checkstyle-rules.xml"
failOnViolation="false">
    <formatter toFile="${checkstyle.data.file}" type="xml" />
    <fileset dir="${src.dir}" includes="**/*.java" />
  </checkstyle>
  <xslt taskname="checkstyle"
    in="${checkstyle.data.file}"
    out="${checkstyle.report.file}"
    style="${checkstyle.xsl.file}" />
</target>
```

Deployment

Many processes encompass what is considered *deployment*. In fact, most of the other processes discussed in this section are a part of the deployment process. Continuous deployment enables you to deliver working, deployable software at any point in time. This means a key purpose of a CI system is to generate the bundled software artifacts with the latest code changes and make it available to a testing environment.

Among other things, the source files from the version control repository must be checked out, a build must be performed, all tests and inspections must successfully execute, the release must be labeled, and the deployment files must be staged.

CI can even automatically deploy or install files to the appropriate environment, as shown in Figure 1-8. Furthermore, deployments should include the capability to automatically roll back all changes applied in the deployment. Note that you may be using slightly different operating environments from development (for instance, Jetty, as illustrated in Figure 1-8) to your integration and test environments (Tomcat). Regardless, the same automated build, with slightly different parameters, is executed in these environments. We discuss these strategies in Chapter 8.

---

4. From "Automation for the People: Continuous Inspection," by Paul Duvall. From IBM developerWorks, August 2006, at http://www-128.ibm.com/developerworks/java/library/j-ap08016/.

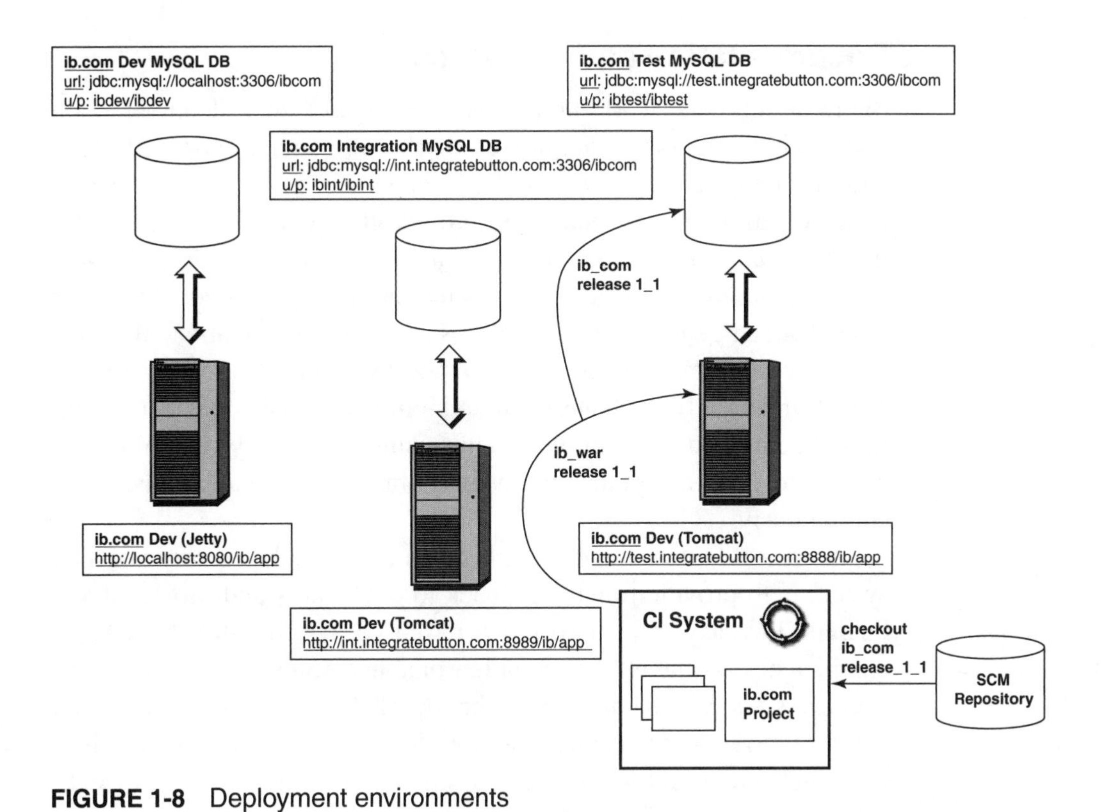

FIGURE 1-8 Deployment environments

Listing 1-9 demonstrates the use of a tool called Cargo, which provides an interface between Ant and a Web container. In this case, we are deploying to a Tomcat server. Cargo provides interfaces to many of the popular Web containers on the market.

LISTING 1-9 Deploy to Tomcat Using Ant and Cargo

```
<target name="deploy">
  <cargo containerId="tomcat5x" action="start"
    wait="false" id="${tomcat-refid}">
    <zipurlinstaller installurl="${tomcat-installer-url}"/>
    <configuration type="standalone" home="${tomcatdir}">
      <property name="cargo.remote.username" value="admin"/>
      <property name="cargo.remote.password" value=""/>
      <deployable type="war" file="${wardir}/${warfile}"/>
  </configuration>
  </cargo>
</target>
```

Documentation and Feedback

Many developers work under the firm belief that documentation belongs in the source code, in fact, that clear, concise code with well-chosen class, variable, and method names (for instance) is the best documentation. A CI system can provide the benefits of documentation without some of the hassles. You can use tools such as Maven, Javadoc, or NDoc to generate documentation. Moreover, there are tools that can generate class diagrams and other information, all based on the committed source code in your version control repository. You'll find significant benefits in obtaining near-real-time documentation of source code and project status using your CI system. You may choose to generate your document artifacts periodically rather than continuously.

A critical feature to good CI systems is *speed*. The essence of a CI system is to provide timely feedback to developers and project stakeholders. It's easy to load so much into a CI system—for the sake of completeness—that it takes an unreasonable amount of time to finish a cycle. As such, a balance must be struck between the breadth and depth of a CI process against the need to provide rapid results. This is especially important when using continuous testing. We discuss techniques for creating fast builds in Chapters 4 and 6.

Summary

This chapter has given you a simple overview of the features of Continuous Integration. It also has shown how you can incorporate additional processes into your CI system, such as comprehensive database integration, testing, inspection, deployment, and feedback. The rest of this book explores the details of each of these processes associated with developing software using CI.

Questions

How do you know you are doing CI correctly? These questions can help you decide what's missing on your projects.

- Are you using a version control repository (or SCM tool)?
- Is your project's build process automated and repeatable? Does it occur entirely without manual intervention?
- Are you writing and running automated tests?
- Is the execution of your tests a part of your build process?
- How do you enforce coding and design standards?
- Which of your feedback mechanisms are automated?
- Are you using a separate integration machine to build software?

Chapter 2
Introducing Continuous Integration

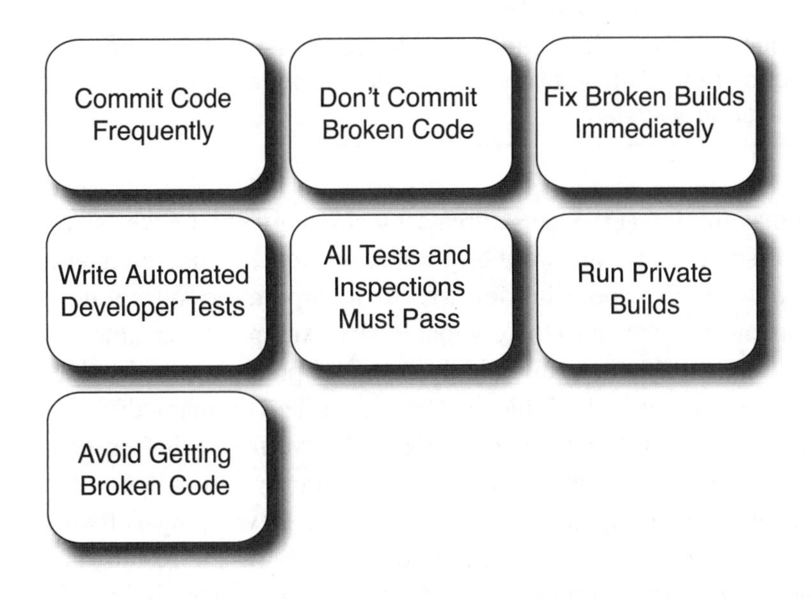

Assumption is the mother of all screw-ups.
—WETHERN'S LAW OF SUSPENDED JUDGMENT

Early in my career, I learned that developing good software comes down to consistently carrying out fundamental practices *regardless of the particular technology.* In my experience, one of the most significant problems in software development is *assuming.* If you assume a method will be passed the right parameter value, the method will fail. Assume that developers are following coding and design standards and the software will be difficult to maintain. Assume configuration files haven't changed, and you'll spend precious development hours needlessly hunting down problems that don't exist. When we make assumptions in software development, we waste time and increase risks.

Reducing Assumptions

Continuous Integration can help reduce assumptions on a project by rebuilding software *whenever a change is applied* to a version control system.

We may think that the latest, greatest technology will be the "silver bullet" to solve all of our problems, but it will not. At one company, one of my initial responsibilities was to incorporate good software development practices into the company—by example. Over time, we were able to implement many widely accepted practices for developing good software into the projects. Having worked on many different projects that used different methodologies, I have found that, in general, iterative projects—using Agile practices, in my case—work best, because risks are mitigated all along the way. Developing software requires planning for change, continuously observing the results, and incrementally course-correcting based on the results. This is how CI operates. CI is the embodiment of tactics that gives us, as software developers, the ability to make changes in our code, knowing that if we break software, we'll receive *immediate feedback.* This immediate feedback gives us time to course-correct and adjust to change more rapidly.

CI is about the fundamentals. It may not be the most glamorous activity in software development, but integrating software is vitally important in today's complex projects. Seldom do the *users* of the software say to me, "Wow, I really like the way you integrated the software in the last release." And since that doesn't happen, it may seem like it isn't worthwhile to make these efforts behind the scenes. However, anyone who has developed software using a practice such as CI is empowered by a consistent and repeatable build process kicked off when a change occurs to the version control repository.

CI as a Centerpiece for Quality

Some see CI as a process of simply putting software components together. We see CI as the centerpiece of software development, as it ensures the health of software through running a build with every change. Determining the quality of software can be as easy as checking the latest integration build.

Spending *some* time on the nonglamorous fundamental activities in software development means there is *more* time to spend on the challenging, thought-provoking activities that make our jobs interesting and fun. If we don't focus on the fundamentals, such as defining the development environment and building the software, we'll be forced to perform low-level tasks later, usually at the most inconvenient times (immediately before software goes to production, for example). This is when mistakes happen as well. The discipline involved in keeping the build "in the green" frees you from worrying about whether everything is still working. It's like exercising—yes, it takes self-discipline; yes, it can be painful work—but it keeps you in shape to play in the big game, when it counts.

This chapter attempts to answer the questions that you may have when making the decision to implement the practices of CI on a project. It provides an overview of the advantages and disadvantages of CI, and covers how CI complements other software development practices. CI is not a practice that can be handed off to a project's "build master" and forgotten about. It affects every person on the software development team, so we discuss CI in terms of what all team members must practice to implement it.

What's a day of work like using CI? Let's examine Tim's experiences.

A Day in the Life of CI

As Tim opens the door to his company's suite, he views the widescreen monitor displaying real-time information for his project. The monitor shows him that the last integration build ran successfully a few minutes ago on the CI server. It shows a list of the latest quality metrics, including coding/design standard adherence, code duplication, and so on. Tim is one of 15 developers on a Java project creating management software for an online brewery. See Figure 2-1 for a visualization of some of the activities in Tim's day.

Starting his day, Tim refactors a subsystem that was reported to have too much duplicate code based on the latest reports from the CI server. Prior to committing his changes to Subversion, he runs a **private build,** which compiles and runs the unit tests against the newest source code. After running this build on his machine, he commits his changes to Subversion. All the while, the CruiseControl CI server is polling the Subversion repository. A few minutes later, the CI server discovers the changes that Tim committed and runs an integration build. This integration build runs automated inspection tools to verify that all code adheres to the coding standard. Tim receives an e-mail about a coding standard violation, quickly makes the changes, and checks the source code back into Subversion. The CI server runs another build and it is successful. By reviewing the Web reports generated by the CI server, Tim finds that his recent code refactoring successfully reduced the amount of duplicate code in his subsystem.

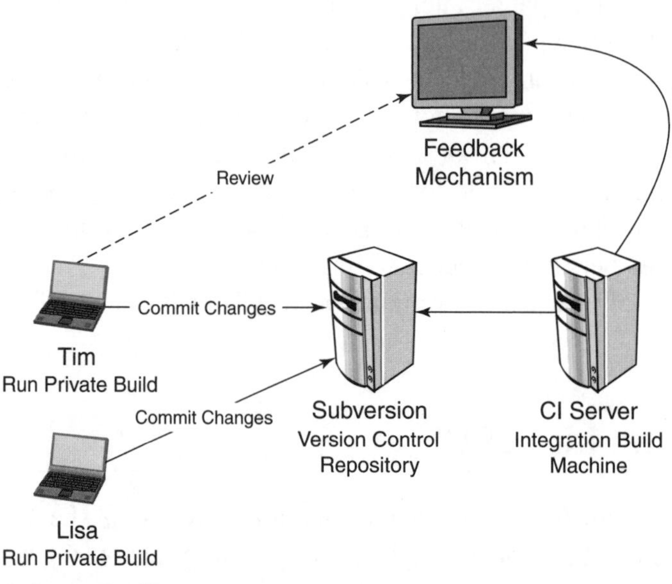

FIGURE 2-1 A day in the life

Later in the day, another developer on the project, Lisa, runs into Tim's office.

Lisa: I think the changes you made earlier today broke the last build!

Tim: Hmm...but, I ran the tests.

Lisa: Oh, I didn't have time to write tests.

Tim: Are you following the code coverage metric we have established for the project?

Because of this discussion, they decided to fail the integration build if their code coverage was below 85%. Furthermore, Lisa wrote a test for the defect and fixed the problem she discovered because of her conversation with Tim. The integration build continued to stay "in the green."

Terms of the Trade

automated—A "hands-off" process. Once a *fully automated* process begins, no user intervention is required. Systems administrators call this a "headless" process.

build—A set of activities performed to generate, test, inspect, and deploy software.

continuous—Technically, *continuous* means something that, once started, never stops. This would mean the build runs all the time; however, this isn't the case. Continuous, in the context of CI, is more like *continual,* and in the case of CI servers, a process continually runs, polling for changes to the version control repository. If the CI server discovers changes, it executes a build script.

Continuous Integration—"A software development practice where members of a team integrate their work frequently, usually each person integrates at least daily—leading to multiple integrations per day. Each integration is verified by an automated build (including test) to detect integration errors as quickly as possible. Many teams find that this approach leads to significantly reduced integration problems and allows a team to develop cohesive software more rapidly."[1]

1. From www.martinfowler.com/articles/continuousIntegration.html.

development environment—The environment in which software is written. This can include the IDE, build scripts, tools, third-party libraries, servers, and configuration files.

inspection—Analysis of source code/bytecode for the internal quality attributes. In the context of this book, we refer to the automated aspects (static and runtime analysis) as **software inspection.**

integration—The act of combining separate source code artifacts together to determine how they work as a whole.

integration build—An integration build is the act of combining software components (programs and files) into a software system. This build includes multiple components on bigger projects or only low-level compiled source files on smaller projects. In our everyday life, we tend to use the terms *build* and *integration build* interchangeably, but for the purposes of this book we make the distinction that an *integration build* is performed by a separate integration build machine.

private (system) build—Running a build locally on your workstation before committing your changes to the version control repository, to lessen the chances that your recent changes break the integration build.[2]

quality—The Free On-Line Dictionary of Computing[3] defines quality as "an essential and distinguishing attribute of something..." and "superior grade." The term *quality* is often overused, and some seem to think it is based on perception. In this book, we take the stance that quality is a measurable specification just like any other. This means you can identify specific metrics of quality, such as maintainability, extensibility, security, performance, and readability.

release build—Readies the software for release to users. It may occur at the end of an iteration or some other milestone, and it must include any acceptance tests and may include more extensive performance and load tests.

---

2. Based on *Software Configuration Management Patterns* by Stephen Berczuk and Brad Appleton.

3. At www.thefreedictionary.com.

risk—The potential for a problem to occur. A risk that has been realized is known as a **problem.** We focus on the higher-priority risks (damage to our interests and goals) that have the highest likelihood of occurring.

testing—The general process of verifying that software works as designed. Furthermore, we define developer tests into multiple categories, such as unit tests, component tests, and system tests, all of which verify that objects, packages, modules, and the software system work as designed. There are many other types of tests, such as functional and load tests, but from a CI perspective, all unit tests written by developers, at a minimum, are executed as a part of a build (although builds may be staged to run fast tests first followed by slower tests).

What Is the Value of CI?

At a high level, the value of CI is to:

- Reduce risks
- Reduce repetitive manual processes
- Generate deployable software at any time and at any place
- Enable better project visibility
- Establish greater confidence in the software product from the development team

Let's review what these principles mean and what value they offer.

Reduce Risks

By integrating many times a day, you can reduce risks on your project. Doing so facilitates the detection of defects, the measurement of software health, and a reduction of assumptions.

- **Defects are detected and fixed sooner**—Because CI integrates and runs tests and inspections several times a day, there is a greater chance that defects are discovered *when they are introduced* (i.e., when the code is checked into the version control repository) instead of during late-cycle testing.

- **Health of software is measurable**—By incorporating continuous testing and inspection into the automated integration process, the software product's health attributes, such as complexity, can be tracked over time.
- **Reduce assumptions**—By rebuilding and testing software in a clean environment using the same process and scripts on a continual basis, you can reduce assumptions (e.g., whether you are accounting for third-party libraries or environment variables).

CI provides a safety net to reduce the risk that defects will be introduced into the code base. The following are some of the risks that CI helps to mitigate. We discuss these and other risks in the next chapter.

- Lack of cohesive, deployable software
- Late defect discovery
- Low-quality software
- Lack of project visibility

Reduce Repetitive Processes

Reducing repetitive processes saves time, costs, and effort. This sounds straightforward, doesn't it? These repetitive processes can occur across all project activities, including code compilation, database integration, testing, inspection, deployment, and feedback. By automating CI, you have a greater ability to ensure all of the following.

- The process runs the same way *every time.*
- An ordered process is followed. For example, you may run inspections (static analysis) before you run tests—in your build scripts.
- The processes will run every time a commit occurs in the version control repository.

This facilitates

- The reduction of labor on repetitive processes, freeing people to do more thought-provoking, higher-value work

- The capability to overcome resistance (from other team members) to implement improvements by using automated mechanisms for important processes such as testing and database integration

Generate Deployable Software

CI can enable you to release deployable software at *any point in time.* From an outside perspective, this is the most obvious benefit of CI. We could talk endlessly about improved software quality and reduced risks, but deployable software is the most tangible asset to "outsiders" such as clients or users. The importance of this point *cannot* be overstated. With CI, you make small changes to the source code and integrate these changes with the rest of the code base on a regular basis. If there are any problems, the project members are informed and the fixes are applied to the software *immediately.* Projects that do not embrace this practice may wait until immediately prior to delivery to integrate and test the software. This can delay a release, delay or prevent fixing certain defects, cause new defects as you rush to complete, and can ultimately spell the end of the project.

Enable Better Project Visibility

CI provides the ability to notice trends and make effective decisions, and it helps provide the courage to innovate new improvements. Projects suffer when there is no real or recent data to support decisions, so everyone offers their best guesses. Typically, project members collect this information manually, making the effort burdensome and untimely. The result is that often the information is never gathered. CI has the following positive effects.

- **Effective decisions**—A CI system can provide just-in-time information on the recent build status and quality metrics. Some CI systems can also show defect rates and feature completion statuses.
- **Noticing trends**—Since integrations occur frequently with a CI system, the ability to notice trends in build success or failure, overall quality, and other pertinent project information becomes possible.

Establish Greater Product Confidence

Overall, effective application of CI practices can provide greater confidence in producing a software product. With every build, your team knows that tests are run against the software to verify behavior, that project coding and design standards are met, and that the result is a functionally testable product.

Without frequent integrations, some teams may feel stifled because they don't know the impacts of their code changes. Since a CI system can inform you when something goes wrong, developers and other team members have more confidence in making changes. Because CI encourages a single-source point from which all software assets are built, there is greater confidence in its accuracy.

What Prevents Teams from Using CI?

If CI has so many benefits, then what would prevent a development team from continuously integrating software on its projects? Often, it is a combination of concerns.

- **Increased overhead in maintaining the CI system**—This is usually a misguided perception, because the need to integrate, test, inspect, and deploy exists regardless of whether you are using CI. Managing a robust CI system is better than managing manual processes. *Manage the CI system or be controlled by the manual processes.* Ironically, complicated multiplatform projects are the ones that need CI the most, yet these projects often resist the practice as being "too much extra work."
- **Too much change**—Some may feel there are too many processes that need to change to achieve CI for their legacy project. An incremental approach to CI is most effective; first add builds and tests with a lower occurrence (for example, a daily build), then increase the frequency as everyone gets comfortable with the results.
- **Too many failed builds**—Typically, this occurs when developers are not performing a private build prior to committing their code to the version control repository. It could be that a devel-

oper forgot to check in a file or had some failed tests. Rapid response is imperative when using CI because of the frequency of changes.

- **Additional hardware/software costs**—To effectively use CI, a separate integration machine should be acquired, which is a nominal expense when compared to the more expensive costs of finding problems later in the development lifecycle.
- **Developers should be performing these activities**—Sometimes management feels like CI is just duplicating the activities that developers should be performing anyway. Yes, developers should be performing some of these activities, but they need to perform them *more effectively and reliably in a separate environment.* Leveraging automated tools can improve the efficiency and frequency of these activities. Additionally, it ensures that these activities are performed in a clean environment, which will reduce assumptions and lead to better decision making.

How Do I Get to "Continuous" Integration?

It's often surprising to learn the level of automation of most development organizations. Developers spend most of their time automating processes for their users, yet don't always see ways to automate their own development processes. Sometimes teams believe their automation is sufficient because they've written a few scripts to eliminate some steps in the development process. The following is a typical scenario.

Joan (Developer): ...I already automated that. I wrote some batch scripts that drop and recreate the database tables.

Sue (Technical Lead): That's great. Did you apply it to the CVS repository?

Joan: No.

Sue: Did you make it a part of the build script?

Joan: No.

Sue: So, if it's not a part of the CI system then it's not really automated yet... right?

CI is not just the process of gathering a few scripts together and running them all the time. In the preceding scenario, it's great that Joan wrote those automation scripts, but in order for them to actually add value to the end product, they must be added to the version control repository and made a working part of the build process. Figure 2-2 illustrates the steps to making a process continuous.

These steps can be applied one by one to virtually every activity you conduct on a project.

- **Identify**—Identify a process that requires automation. The process may be in the areas of compilation, test, inspection, deployment, database integration, and so on.
- **Build**—Creating a build script makes the automation repeatable and consistent. Build scripts can be constructed in NAnt for the .NET platform, Ant for the Java platform, and Rake for Ruby, just to name a few.
- **Share**—By using a version control system such as Subversion, you make it possible for others to use these scripts/programs. Now the value is being spread consistently across the project.
- Make it **continuous**—Ensure that the automated process is run with every change applied, using a CI server. If your team has the discipline, you can also choose to manually run the build with every change applied to the version control system.

Here is an acrostic to help you remember and communicate this: "**I** **B**uild **S**o **C**onsistently"—for **I**dentify, **B**uild, **S**hare, and **C**ontinuous.

Aim for incremental growth in your CI system. This is simple to implement, the team gets more motivated as each new item is added, and you can better plan what you need next based on what's working

FIGURE 2-2 Getting to CI— "**I** **B**uild **S**o **C**onsistently"

Is It Continuous Compilation or Continuous Integration?

I've worked with a number of organizations on implementing CI, and on several occasions I've heard the reply, "Yes, we do CI." Of course, I think, "Great!" and then ask a few questions. How much code coverage do you have with your tests? How long does it take to run your builds? What is your average code complexity? How much code duplication do you have? Are you labeling your builds in your version control repository? Where do you store your deployed software?

I discover that what they've been doing all along is more like a "continuous compilation," in which they've set up a tool like CruiseControl to poll their version control repository (e.g., CVS) for changes. When it detects changes, it retrieves the source code from CVS, compiles the code, and sends an e-mail if anything goes wrong. Automatically compiling the software system on a separate machine is better than nothing at all, but doing that isn't going to provide all of the benefits of a full-featured CI system.

so far. Often, attempting to throw everything into a CI system immediately can be a bad move, just like refactoring a lot of code at once isn't the best approach when writing software. Get it to work first, get developers using it, and then add other automated processes as needed based on the project risks.

When and How Should a Project Implement CI?

It is best to implement CI early in the project. Although possible, it is more difficult to implement CI late in a project, as people will be under pressure and more likely to resist change. If you do implement CI later in a project, it is especially important to start small and add more as time permits.

There are different approaches to setting up the CI system. Though you eventually want a build to run on every change to the system, you can start by running a build on a *daily* basis to get the practice going in your organization. Remember: *CI is not just a technical implementation; it is also an organizational and cultural implementation.* People often resist change, and the best approach for an organization may be to add these automated mechanisms to the process piece by piece.

At first the build can just compile the source code and package the binaries without executing the automated regression tests. This can be effective, initially, if the developers are unfamiliar with an automated testing tool. Once this is in place and developers have learned the testing tool, you can move closer to the benefits of CI: running these tests (and inspections) with every change.

The Evolution of Integration

Is CI the newest, latest, "whiz-bang" approach to software development? Hardly. CI is simply an advance in the evolution of integrating software. When software programs consisted of a few small files, integrating them into a system was not much of a problem. The practice of performing nightly builds has been described as a best practice for years. Similar practices have been discussed in other books and articles. In the book *Microsoft Secrets*, Michael A. Cusumano and Richard W. Selby discuss the practice of daily builds at Microsoft. Steve McConnell, in *Software Project Survival Guide,* discusses the practice of the "Daily Build and Smoke Test" as part of a software development project.

In *Object Solutions: Managing the Object-Oriented Project,* Grady Booch writes, "The macro process of object-oriented development is one of 'continuous integration'… At regular intervals, the process of 'continuous integration' yields executable releases that grow in functionality at every release... It is through these milestones that management can measure progress and quality, and hence anticipate, identify, and then actively attack risks on an ongoing basis." With the advent of XP and other Agile methodologies, and with the recommended practice of CI, people began to take notice of the concept of not just daily, but "continuous," builds.

The practice of CI continues to evolve. You'll find the practice in almost every XP book. Often, when people discuss the practice of CI, they refer to Martin Fowler's seminal "Continuous Integration" article.[4]

As hardware and software resources continue to increase, you'll find that more processes will become a part of what is considered to be CI.

How Does CI Complement Other Development Practices?

The practice of CI complements other software development practices, such as developer testing, adherence to coding standards, refactoring, and small releases. It doesn't matter if you are using RUP, XP, RUP with XP, SCRUM, Crystal, or any other methodology. The following list identifies how the practice of CI works with and improves these practices.

- **Developer testing**—Developers who write tests most often use some xUnit-based framework such as JUnit or NUnit. These tests can be automatically executed from the build scripts. Since the practice of CI advocates that builds be run any time a change is made to the software, and that the automated tests are a part of these builds, CI enables automated regression tests to be run on the entire code base whenever a change is applied to the software.
- **Coding standard adherence**—A coding standard is the set of guidelines that developers must adhere to on a project. On many projects, ensuring adherence is largely a manual process that is performed by a code review. CI can run a build script to report on adherence to the coding standards by running a suite of automated static analysis tools that inspect the source code against the established standard whenever a change is applied.
- **Refactoring**—As Fowler states, refactoring is "the process of changing the software system in such a way that it does not alter

4. See www.martinfowler.com/articles/continuousIntegration.html.

the external behavior of the code yet improves its internal structure."[5] Among other benefits, this makes the code easier to maintain. CI can assist with refactoring by running inspection tools that identify potential problem areas at every build.

- **Small releases**—This practice allows testers and users to get working software to use and review as often as required. CI works very well with this practice, because software integration is occurring many times a day and a release is available at virtually *any time.* Once a CI system is in place, a release can be generated with minimal effort.
- **Collective ownership**—Any developer can work on any part of the software system. This prevents "knowledge silos," where there is only one person who has knowledge of a particular area of the system. The practice of CI can help with collective ownership by ensuring adherence to coding standards and the running of regression tests on a continual basis.

How Long Does CI Take to Set Up?

Implementing a *basic* CI system along with simple build scripts for a new project may take you a few hours to set up and configure (more if you don't have any existing build scripts). As you expand your knowledge of the CI system, it will grow with the addition of inspection tools, deployments that are more complex, more thorough testing, and many other processes. These additional features tend to be added a little at a time.

For a project already in progress, it can take days, weeks, or even months to set up a CI system. It also depends upon whether people have been dedicated to work on the project. Usually you must complete many tasks when moving to a continuous, automated, and headless system such as when using a CI server. In some cases, you may be moving from batch or shell scripts to a build scripting tool such as Ant

5. Fowler, et al. *Refactoring: Improving the Design of Existing Code* (Reading, MA: Addison-Wesley, 1999).

or managing all of the project's binary dependencies. In other cases, you may have previously used your IDE for "integration" and deployment. Either way, the road map to full CI adoption could be quite a bit longer.

CI and You

In order for CI to work effectively on a project, developers must change their typical day-to-day software development habits. Developers must commit code more frequently, make it a priority to fix broken builds, write automated builds with tests that pass 100% of the time, and not get or commit broken code from/to the version control repository.

The practices we recommend take some discipline, yet provide the benefits stated throughout this chapter. The best situation is one where most project members agree that there is an exponential payback to the time and attention they pay to the practices of CI.

There are seven practices that we've found work well for individuals and teams running CI on a project.

- Commit code frequently
- Don't commit broken code
- Fix broken builds immediately
- Write automated developer tests
- All tests and inspections must pass
- Run private builds
- Avoid getting broken code

The following sections cover each practice in greater detail.

Commit Code Frequently

One of the central tenets of CI is integrating *early and often*. Developers must commit code frequently in order to realize the benefits of CI.

Waiting more than a day or so to commit code to the version control repository makes integration time-consuming and may prevent developers from being able to use the latest changes. Try one or both of these techniques to commit code more frequently.

- **Make small changes**—Try not to change many components all at once. Instead, choose a small task, write the tests and source code, run your tests, and then commit your code to the version control repository.
- **Commit after each task**—Assuming tasks/work items have been broken up so that they can be finished in a few hours, some development shops require developers to commit their code as they complete each task.

Try to avoid having everyone commit at the same time every day. You'll find that there are usually many more build errors to manage because of the collisions between changes. This is especially troublesome at the end of the day, when people are ready to leave. The longer you wait to integrate with others, the more difficult your integration will prove to be.

I Just Can't Commit

A friend runs a 25-developer project and he'd like to incorporate many CI practices, but he is experiencing challenges in getting the developers to commit code frequently. I've found that the main reason that changes are not committed frequently is because of the project culture. Sometimes developers do not want to commit their code until it is "perfect." This usually happens because their changes affect too many components. Committing code frequently to the version control repository is the only effective way to implement CI, and this means that all developers need to embrace this development practice by grabbing smaller chunks of code and breaking up their tasks into smaller work items.

Don't Commit Broken Code

A dangerous assumption on a project is that everyone knows not to commit code that doesn't work to the version control repository. The ultimate mitigation for this risk is having a well-factored build script that compiles and tests the code in a repeatable manner. Make it part of the team's accepted development practice to always run a private build (which closely resembles the integration build process) before committing code to the version control repository. See the later section, Run Private Builds, for additional recommendations before committing your code.

Fix Broken Builds Immediately

A **broken build** is anything that prevents the build from reporting success. This may be a compilation error, a failed test or inspection, a problem with the database, or a failed deployment. When operating in a CI environment, these problems must be fixed immediately; fortunately, in a CI environment, each error is discovered incrementally and therefore is likely very small. Some projects have a penalty for breaking the build, such as throwing some money in a jar or placing the picture of the last developer to break the build on the company's large-screen monitor (just kidding; hopefully no one is doing this). The project culture should convey that fixing a broken build is a top project priority. That way, not just some but every team member can then get back to what they were doing.

Write Automated Developer Tests

A build should be fully automated. In order to run tests for a CI system, the tests must be automated. Writing your tests in an xUnit framework such as NUnit or JUnit will provide the capability of running these tests in an automated fashion. Chapter 6 provides details on writing automated tests.

All Tests and Inspections Must Pass

In a CI environment, 100% of a project's automated tests must pass for your build to pass (this is a technical criterion, not an expectation that all workers or all work should be perfect). Automated tests are as important as the compilation. Everyone accepts that code that does not compile will not work; therefore, code that has test errors will not work either. Accepting code that does not pass the tests can lead to lower-quality software.

An unscrupulous developer may simply comment out the failing test. Of course, this defeats the purpose. Coverage tools assist in pinpointing source code that does not have a corresponding test. You can run a code coverage tool as part of an integration build.

The same goes for running automated software inspectors. Use a general rule set of coding and design standards that all code must pass. More advanced inspections may be added that don't fail the build, but identify areas of the code that should be investigated.

Run Private Builds

To prevent broken builds, developers should emulate an integration build on their local workstation IDE after completing their unit tests. This build allows you to integrate your new working software with the working software from all the other developers,[6] obtaining the changes from the version control repository and successfully building locally *with* the recent changes. Thus, the code each developer commits has contributed to the greater good, with code that is less likely to fail on the integration build server.

---

6. Some configuration management tools, such as ClearCase, have an option to automatically update your local environment with the changes from the version control repository (called "dynamic views" in ClearCase).

Keep Builds in the "Green"

I find that there are two measures of using CI effectively: number of commits and build status. Each developer (or pair) should have at least one commit to the repository per day, and the number of checkins usually demonstrates the size of the changes (more commits usually means smaller changes—and this is good). Your build status should be "green" (pass) a large percentage of the day; set this value for the team. We all get a "red" build status sometimes, but what's important is that it's changed back to green as soon as possible. Never let your team get used to waiting in the red status until this or that other project task is done. The willingness to leave the status at red for other criteria defeats much of the strength of CI.

Avoid Getting Broken Code

When the build is broken, don't check out the latest code from the version control repository. Otherwise, you must spend time developing a workaround to the error known to have failed the build, just so you can compile and test your code. Ultimately, it's the responsibility of the team, but the developers responsible for breaking the build *should* already be working on fixing their code and committing it back to the version control repository. Sometimes a developer may not have seen the e-mail on the broken build. This is when a passive feedback mechanism such as a light or sound can be useful for colocated developers. We consider it critical that all developers know the state of the code in the version control repository. For more information on continuous feedback mechanisms, see Chapter 9. An alternative, but not preferable, approach to avoiding a checkout is to use the version control system to roll back any changes since the most recent commit.

Summary

Now you have the ammunition to go talk to others about CI. This chapter covered some of the basics of CI, discussed how to get to a continuous process, and pointed out all the other areas that get explored in detail in subsequent chapters. Table 2-1 summarizes seven practices to follow when using CI. The next chapter delves into the software risks that CI can help mitigate to improve quality.

TABLE 2-1 CI Practices Discussed in This Chapter

Practice	*Description*
Commit code frequently	Commit code to your version control repository at least once a day.
Don't commit broken code	Don't commit code that does not compile with other code or fails a test.
Fix broken builds immediately	Although it's the team's responsibility, the developer who recently committed code must be involved in fixing the failed build.
Write automated developer tests	Verify that your software works using automated developer tests. Run these tests with your automated build and run them often with CI.
All tests and inspections must pass	Not 90% or 95% of tests, but *all* tests must pass prior to committing code to the version control repository.
Run private builds	To prevent integration failures, get changes from other developers by getting the latest changes from the repository and run a full integration build locally, known as a private system build.
Avoid getting broken code	If the build has failed, you will lose time if you get code from the repository. Wait for the change or help the developer(s) fix the build failure and then get the latest code.

Questions

Practicing CI is more than installing and configuring some tools. How many of the following items are you consistently performing on your project? How many of the other CI practices can improve your development capabilities?

- On average, is everyone on your team committing code at least once a day? Are you employing techniques to make it easier to commit code often?
- What percentage of each day's integration builds is successful (that is, the most recent build run has passed)?
- Is everyone on your team running a private build before committing to the repository so that integration errors are reduced?
- Have you scripted your builds to fail if any of your tests or inspections fail?
- Is a broken integration build a priority to fix on your projects?
- Do you avoid getting the latest code from the version control system when there is a broken build?
- How often do you consider adding automated processes to your build and CI system—on a continuous or even periodic basis?

Chapter 3

Reducing Risks Using CI

Quality means doing it right when no one is looking.

—Henry Ford

Things will always go wrong on a project. By effectively practicing CI, you find out what at every step along the way—rather than late into the development cycle. CI helps you identify and mitigate risks when they occur, making it easier to evaluate and report on the health of the project based on concrete evidence. How much of the software have we implemented? Answer: Check the latest build. How much test coverage do we have? Answer: Check the latest build. Who checked in the latest code? Answer: Check the latest build.

In this chapter, we cover risks that CI can mitigate, such as late discovery of defects, lack of project visibility, low-quality software, and the inability to create deployable software.

Most teams begin with good intentions, yet some are overwhelmed with problems on their projects. *These problems are a result of not managing risks.* As I mentioned earlier in the book, we don't often hear development groups say, "We think testing and code reviews (paired or otherwise) are bad practices." Yet, when affected by schedule pressure, these are usually the first practices a team will skip. This chapter focuses on the software risks you can reduce using different aspects of CI. By using CI, you can build a "quality safety net" and deliver software faster. When you press the "Integrate button" at every change, you build a foundation for reducing risks early and often, as indicated in Figure 3-1.

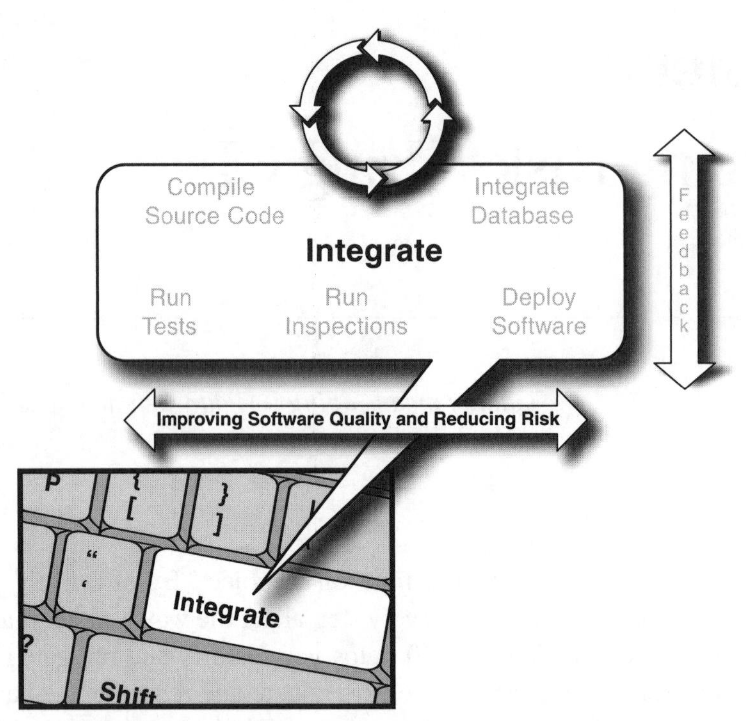

FIGURE 3-1 CI can help improve software quality and reduce risk

If you can reduce certain software risks, you can improve software quality. In describing the risks in this chapter, we use this template:

- An introduction and description of the *software risk*
- A *scenario* based on our experiences
- A *solution* to mitigate the risk using an aspect of CI

On any project, there are many risks to manage. We focus on the key risks that you can reduce by using CI. Of course, CI cannot *directly* assist with the business challenges of eliciting requirements from your customer, understanding the customer's industry, funding, or resource management, but by using CI you can discover problems with the software faster—while it's under development.

By building software with every change, CI can put time on your side. With CI, you can focus sooner on the larger, more interesting issues on your project. Because CI is an aggregate practice, the risks covered in this chapter span many software development practices.

- Lack of deployable software
- Late discovery of defects
- Lack of project visibility
- Low-quality software

You may say, "Oh, I've heard of all of these risks before. This is nothing new to me." However, you can be *aware* of a risk but not necessarily mitigating it. There are more efficient and productive ways to identify and address risks so that they are no longer a focus on your projects. Like most practices, it comes down to effective implementation. In later chapters, using the model of the Integrate button, we show you effective ways to recognize and reduce these risks.

Risk: Lack of Deployable Software

I was on a project in which we built the software on a separate machine every month or so. When we finally built the software, too close to the delivery deadline, most team members would stay until the late hours of the night to pull off another miracle. During this "integration hell," we found that we had interfaces that did not work, were missing configuration files, had multiple components providing similar functionality, and had difficulty in merging many changes that were part of the latest build. This sometimes caused us to miss critical milestones on the project.

On another project, the software integration build was a manual process initiated by the IDE. On average, we were manually integrating software on a weekly basis. In some cases, there were certain scripts used by the Configuration Management (CM) analyst to build the software that did not reside in the version control repository. The lack of automation increased the overhead of running the build. Because we were not performing the build in a clean environment on a separate machine, we had no confidence we were building the software correctly. The effects of all these were threefold:

- Little or no confidence in whether we could even *build* the software

- Lengthy integration phases before delivering the software internally (i.e., test team) or externally (i.e., customer), during which time nothing else got done
- Inability to produce and reproduce testable builds

Scenario: "It Works on My Machine"

There can be many reasons why a project team is unable to create working, deployable software: Anything from failing tests to the wrong files applied to the version control repository can contribute to a failed build. Here's one such scenario.

> *John (Technical Lead):* We're having a problem with the latest build on the test server.
>
> *Adam (Developer):* That's funny; it was working when I built it on my machine. Let me see… Yeah, it's still working.
>
> *John:* Oh, I see the problem. You didn't commit your new files into the Subversion repository.

Solution

We cannot overemphasize the importance of eliminating tight coupling between your IDE and your build processes. Use a separate machine solely for integrating the software. Ensure that everything you need to build the software is contained in the version control repository. Finally, create a CI system. Use a CI server such as CruiseControl along with an automated build using tools such as Ant, NAnt, or Rake. CruiseControl watches for changes in the version control repository and runs the project build script when it detects a change to the repository. You can increase the capabilities of this CI system to include having the build run through tests, perform inspections, and deploy the software in the development and test environments; this way you always have working software.

Scenario: Synching with the Database

If you are unable to recreate your database quickly during development, you will find it difficult to make changes. Often this is due to a separation between the database team and the development team—each team is focused on their own responsibilities with little collaboration between the two. How can the product be integrated if the teams aren't integrated? In a scenario like this, the database administrator, for instance, may not be committing most of the database scripts to the version control repository. These types of risks can then arise.

- Fear of making changes or refactoring the database or source code
- Difficulty in populating the database with different sets of test data
- Difficulty in maintaining development and testing environments (e.g., Development, Integration, QA, and Test)

This negatively affects development, because the database is not keeping up with the development team or vice versa. The software and database developers may all be running different versions of the database. Project members are unable to go to a single source point (version control repository) to get the latest database. The following dialog illustrates this problem.

Lauren (Developer): I'm having a lot of problems testing on v1.2.1.b1 of the database using build 1345.

Pauline (Database Designer): Oh no, with build 1345, you should use v1.2.1.b2, but I also need to make a few changes to it first.

Lauren: I just spent four hours for nothing.

Pauline: Well, you should have checked with me first.

Solution

This solution would necessitate fundamental change for some projects; it outlines an approach where the database is not a separate entity from development.

- Place all database artifacts in your *version control repository*. This means everything you need to recreate the database schema and data: database creation scripts, data manipulation scripts, stored procedures, triggers, and any other database assets.

- Rebuild the database and data from your *build script,* by dropping and recreating your database and tables. Next, apply the stored procedures and triggers, and finally, insert the test data.
- *Test (and inspect) your database*. Typically, you will use the component tests to test the database and data. In some cases, you'll need to write database-specific tests.

We go much deeper into this topic and discuss scenarios and solutions in Chapter 5.

Scenario: The Missing Click

Deploying your software manually wastes time and effort. On one project, we manually deployed the software as needed using the application server's Web administration utility. This was supposed to occur once a day, but because the team was typically sidetracked with other issues, this created bottlenecks when we needed the latest integrated build. This repetitive, mundane process took 10–15 minutes to complete every day—if all went well. The problem was that we were spending time on something that should have been automatic: deployment to the test machine. In addition, it was easy to cause problems if we didn't click the right buttons on the administration tool.

Here is an example of a typical problem resulting from a manual deployment approach.

Rachel (Developer): Is the latest build updated to the development server? Where is John?

Kelly (Developer): Oh, John is at lunch. He's supposed to have posted the update to the server.

Rachel: Well, I'll just wait for John to get back.

Later, John arrives...

Rachel: John, what happened with the latest build? It looks like the JSPs weren't precompiled, so we're receiving runtime errors now.

John (Technical Lead): Oops, sorry about that. I must have forgotten to select that option when I deployed with the Web tool yesterday.

Solution

On our projects, we automated the deployment process by adding it to the Ant build scripts that use the application server command-line options. This reduced the bottleneck of waiting for someone else to deploy the software and eliminated mistakes. We always had a testable version of the latest software available. We ran this Ant build script continuously from the CruiseControl CI server whenever we applied a change to the version control repository. For more information, see Chapter 8.

Risk: Late Discovery of Defects

On some projects, we performed testing manually. We didn't know if the latest changes to the software caused other problems—for example, the infamous cycle of fixing one defect only to cause other unrelated defects to surface. We had no confidence to make changes since we didn't know the downstream effects of a change. There was no way to ensure that developers were running the tests on the software since these tests were being performed manually.

Scenario: Regression Testing

Let's look at a regression-testing scenario.

> *Sally (Technical Lead):* I noticed that the latest version deployed to the test environment has the same bug that we had two months ago. Why is that?
>
> *Kyle (Developer):* I'm not sure. I tested all of my latest changes.
>
> *Sally:* Did you run all of the other tests for the other parts of the system?
>
> *Kyle:* No, I didn't have time to manually run through *those* tests. That's probably why I didn't find the bug before we went to test.

Solution

On new projects, we began writing unit and component tests in JUnit at the business, data, and common layers. For existing projects, we wrote unit tests for the code that was changed, based on defects. We configured the Ant build scripts to run all the unit tests and publish a report for every build.

The following steps demonstrate how you can use the CI system to enable automated regression testing on your project.

1. Write test code for all of your source code (an xUnit framework is a good place to start).
2. Run tests from your build script (Ant or NAnt are the most common).
3. Run tests continuously as a part of your CI system so that they are executed at every checkin to the version control repository (using CruiseControl or a similar CI server).

And as simple as that, you have automated regression testing on your project! We discuss more about making your tests an integral part of builds, at all levels, in Chapter 6.

Scenario: Test Coverage

If you write and run tests, you view the results but you also want to know how much of your code is actually being tested. Since most of the unit testing on our project was manual before our CI system, there was no way to independently verify that the tests were executed. How does the manager determine how much was actually tested? Consider the following interaction.

> *Evelyn (Manager):* Did you run unit tests before you committed your changes to the repository?
>
> *Noah (Developer):* Yes.
>
> *Evelyn:* Great. How's it going on the other feature you are implementing?
>
> What *didn't* Evelyn ask? Let's try it again.
>
> *Evelyn:* Did you write new tests or update existing tests for your new code?
>
> *Noah:* Yes.

Evelyn: Did all the tests pass?

Noah: Yes.

Evelyn: How did you determine whether enough of the code was tested adequately?

That line of questioning is a bit better, but it's still an unnecessarily qualitative analysis of something that can be described more concretely through some quantitative analysis. Let's go to the solution.

Solution

Once developers or teams believe they have written the corresponding tests for their source code, you can run a code coverage tool to assess the amount of source code that is actually executed by the tests. Many of the tools will display the percentage of coverage by package and class.

Using CI can ensure this test coverage is always up to date. For instance, you can run a test coverage tool as a part of your CI system's build script whenever there is a change to your version control repository. We discuss code coverage in Chapter 7.

Risk: Lack of Project Visibility

Manual communication mechanisms require a lot of coordination to ensure the dissemination of project information to the right people in a timely manner. Leaning over to the developer next to you and letting her know that the latest build is on the shared drive is rather effective, yet it doesn't scale very well. What if there are other developers who need this information and they are on a break or otherwise unavailable? If a server goes down, how are you notified? Some believe they can mitigate this risk by manually sending an e-mail. However, this cannot ensure the information is communicated to the right people at the right time because you may accidentally leave out interested parties, and some may not have access to their e-mail at the time.

Scenario: "Did You Get the Memo?"

There are many different scenarios for this risk; here's just one.

Evelyn (Manager): What are you working on, Noah?

Noah (Tester): I'm waiting for the latest build to be deployed to QA in order to start testing.

Evelyn: The latest build was deployed to the test server two days ago. Didn't you hear?

Noah: No, I've been out of the office the past few days.

Solution

To mitigate this risk, we installed and configured a CruiseControl CI server on our projects with the automated mechanism that sends e-mails to affected parties when a build fails. In addition, we added SMS notifications so that we received text messages on our mobile phones, in case we didn't have access to e-mail. We installed automated agents that checked the availability of the servers on a regular basis. For examples and more information, see Chapter 9.

Scenario: Inability to Visualize Software

On one project, we were making enhancements and modifying existing software. However, we had no reverse-engineering tool that was showing us the big picture: a model of the classes and relationships. If there was an up-to-date class diagram we could reference, we would have been better able to determine repetition of behavior or incorrect structure, and thereby reduce ineffective decisions.

Maile (Developer): Hi. I'm new to the project and I'd like to review the design. Are there any UML or other diagrams I can see?

Allie (Developer): Grr. We don't do the UML here. All you have to do is read the code. If you can't read the code, then maybe you don't belong here.

Maile: That's okay; I was just hoping I could see the big picture and determine the overall architecture rather than slowly interrogating the code. I'm more of a visual person.

Solution

In seeking to reduce the time between the introduction of a design defect and its resolution, we began generating diagrams of the design using the CI system. We ran an automated code documentation tool, called Doxygen, as part of the CI system. Doxygen documents the source code and creates UML diagrams that model the software. Because it was running as a part of the CI system, it was always up to date, based on the software that was most recently checked into the version control repository.

Although we could have created this with the CI system, we also chose to create a simple one- or two-page architecture document that described the software architecture, identifying the key components and interface for new developers.

Risk: Low-Quality Software

There are defects and then there are *potential* defects. You can have potential defects when your software is not well designed, is not following the project standards, or is complex to maintain. Sometimes people refer to this as code or design smells—"a symptom that something may be wrong."[1] Some believe that lower-quality software is solely a deferred project cost (after delivery). It can be a deferred project cost, but it also leads to many other problems before you deliver the software to users. Overly complex code, code that does not follow the architecture, and duplicated code all usually lead to defects in the software. Finding these code and design smells before they manifest into defects can save much time and money and can lead to higher-quality software. We examine a few such scenarios in this section.

On one project, we had no idea how maintainable our software was unless we manually reviewed all of the source code every day. We were unable to identify quality trends in the software under development. Many project members were feeling like they "didn't have time" to fix the internal qualities of the software and didn't know where to

1. From http://en.wikipedia.org/wiki/Code_smell.

start. Some projects had a coding standards document that was rarely consulted or followed. Other projects had no standard at all. On some of the projects, the entropy of the software was apparent, as we were afraid that making changes would break the software.

Scenario: Coding Standard Adherence

Here is a typical interaction concerning adherence to a coding standard.

> *Brian (Developer):* I'm finding it difficult to read your code. Did you read the 30-page coding standards document when you started last month?
>
> *Lindsay (Developer):* I am using the style I used in my previous job. The code I write is kind of complex so it may be difficult for you to grasp it.
>
> *Brian:* Writing code that others can't work with doesn't make you smarter; it makes you a less valuable resource. It's taking me longer to review and update the code. Please review the coding standards document as soon as you can. First, you can retrofit your existing code, and then get back to new code using the guidelines.

Solution

Instead of writing a 30-page standards document, we created a one-page annotated class that contained all of the coding standards.[2] We enforced the coding standard by using automated inspection tools as a part of the build scripts initiated by CruiseControl. While working primarily on Java projects, we used Checkstyle[3] and PMD[4] to report any lines of code that were not meeting the established standards. We pre-

---

2. See Java Coding Conventions on One Page, by William C. Wake, at www.xp123.com/xplor/xp0002f/codingstd.gif.

3. Checkstyle is a static analysis tool that assesses your source code and reports any deviations from the established coding standard. It is available at http://checkstyle.sourceforge.net/.

4. PMD is a metrics tool that reports any anomalies in your source code, such as unused variables, unused imports, or overly complex code. It is available at http://pmd.sourceforge.net/.

sented this information in the form of HTML reports, which we integrated into the CruiseControl CI server. On newer projects, we did not allow the build to pass if there were any violations of the coding standard.

Scenario: Architectural Adherence

Source code that does not follow the intended design is more difficult to maintain. Have you been on a project that had established a very elegant software architecture at the beginning of the project only to have it morph into a "Big Ball of Mud"[5] by the end of the project? Perhaps the architect designed the whole system using a UML modeling tool and said something like, "Follow this reference architecture." This may be the extreme and, as always, there are shades of gray in between.

A discrepancy between the intended and the actual architecture can be problematic. For example, let's say you have an architectural guideline like: "The data layer should never 'talk' to the business layer." Perhaps the architect used a UML modeling tool to forward-engineer the model based on this architecture into the source code. However, over time, the code changed and the architecture got out of sync with its intended design. For instance, let's say a new developer starts on the project and finds some useful methods in the business layer and calls them from the data layer. This is a violation of the project's architecture. How can you ensure that this doesn't happen?

Jenn (Architect): Are you guys following the architecture? I found some problems in one of the controllers in which one of you is calling a component in the data layer directly.

Mark and Charlie (Developers): (Perplexed expressions)

Jenn: The reason I created all of those UML diagrams is so that everyone will follow the established software architecture. You're not using the protocol that has been in place for months.

Charlie: I looked at those at the beginning of the project, but the architecture has changed a few times since then and it's difficult to keep up.

5. "A system…that has no real distinguishable architecture." From http://en.wikipedia.org/wiki/Big_ball_of_mud.

Solution

Add automated inspection tools to assess adherence to the project's architectural standards. For instance, you could add a rule that controller classes should never make direct calls to the data access objects. You can use dependency analysis tools such as JDepend[6] or NDepend to create reports for architectural adherence. You can run a tool such as this with every integration build.

Scenario: Duplicate Code

Duplicate code, which makes code more difficult to maintain, increases costs. Code that has been copied and pasted has been a risk on virtually every project we have seen. In fact, there are many well-known software development kits and tools where over 25% of the code has been duplicated. We analyzed all the software development projects at one company and found an average 45% of duplicated code. This can present problems when you have multiple copies of similar code that you need to maintain. For example, one system had five copies of similar code in different subsystems. Now, let's say you have some code that checks the authorization of a user who is currently logged in. Instead of writing a single method, the developer chooses to copy and paste the code everywhere he needs to authorize this user. You'll find another variation of code duplication when developers create their own logic rather than using a common utility. The code is not literally copied and pasted, but it still produces the same effect as explicit code duplication.

> *Mary (Developer):* Do you know how I can iterate over a collection of `User` objects?
>
> *Adam (Developer):* Yes, I wrote some code for that last week. You can find it in the `User` package.
>
> *Mary:* Great! I will copy it out of there and use it. Thanks.

---

6. JDepend is a tool to determine the architecture and design of your source code. It is available at www.clarkware.com/software/JDepend.html.

And so it goes, the code duplication continues. Unless you know whether the duplication is going up or down and where the duplication is occurring, it's difficult to determine what problems you're heading toward and where to refactor.

Solution

To create a solution, you first need to assess the problem. You can add automated inspection tools such as PMD's CPD[7] or the Simian[8] static analysis tools to report duplicate source code. We executed these inspection tools as part of the build process so that we could run them at any time. Using these tools, we determined the areas of code that had the most duplication and then we generalized the code into components. Using this approach, we were able to continually monitor our code duplication and reduce the amount of duplicated code in the system.

In a typical scenario, you might discover that multiple classes have the same or similar code. Follow these steps to reduce duplicate code.

1. Analyze the code using a code duplication analyzer such as Simian or PMD's CPD. Incorporate this into your build script.
2. Reduce the duplicated code by refactoring[9] the code into a single method or component that is called by the classes where it used to appear.
3. Run code duplication inspections *continuously* by incorporating a code duplication inspector into your CI system. This gives you the capability to determine code duplication over time.

Chapter 7 details the inspections you can run, how often, and when to apply them.

---

7. CPD, a utility of the PMD metrics tool, reports instances of copied and pasted source code. It is available at http://pmd.sourceforge.net/.

8. Simian (Similarity Analyser) provides support for C#, Java, Ruby, and a number of other languages. It is available for download at www.redhillconsulting.com.au/products/simian/.

9. "Refactoring is making changes to a body of code in order to improve its internal structure, without changing its external behavior." From "Refactoring with Martin Fowler: A Conversation with Martin Fowler, Part I," by Bill Venners, at www.artima.com/intv/refactor.html.

Summary

This chapter outlined the key risk areas that CI will help to mitigate, such as database integration, testing, inspection, deployment, feedback, and documentation. Table 3-1 provides an overview of the material covered in this chapter. You will find that by mitigating these risks using CI practices, you will improve software quality.

TABLE 3-1 Summary of Risks and Mitigations

Risk	*Mitigation*
Lack of deployable software	Use a CI system to build deployable software at any time. Create a repeatable build process that uses all software assets from the version control repository.
Late discovery of defects	Run builds that include developer tests with every change, so you can discover defects earlier in the software lifecycle.
Lack of project visibility	Know the health of your software at all times by running builds regularly. When effectively applying the practice of CI, the project status is no longer in question.
Low-quality software	Run tests and inspections at every change so you can discover potential defects that may be introduced into the code base by learning the complexity, duplication, design, code coverage, and other factors.

Questions

How many risks do you have on your project that CI can help mitigate? These questions should help you determine the risks on your project.

- When do you find the most defects on your project, in the beginning or in later parts of the lifecycle?
- How do you determine the quality on your software projects? Are you able to measure it?
- Which processes on your projects are manual? Have you determined which processes you can or should automate?

- Do you have all of the scripts to rebuild your database and data in your version control repository? Are you able to rebuild your database and test data during the build process?
- Are you able to perform regression testing whenever a change is made to the software? Are you able to run various types of regression tests, including functional, integration, load, and performance tests?
- Do you have the capability to determine which source code does not have a corresponding test? Are you using test coverage tools?
- What percentage of your software has duplicate code? Are you seeking to reduce this amount?
- At any point in time, how do you verify that the current source code adheres to the software architecture?
- How do you notify that the build or deployment is ready to test? Which communication mechanisms on your project are manual, and which should be automated?
- Are you able to view a current visual diagram of your software? How do you communicate the software architecture to a new developer on the project?

Chapter 4
Building Software at Every Change

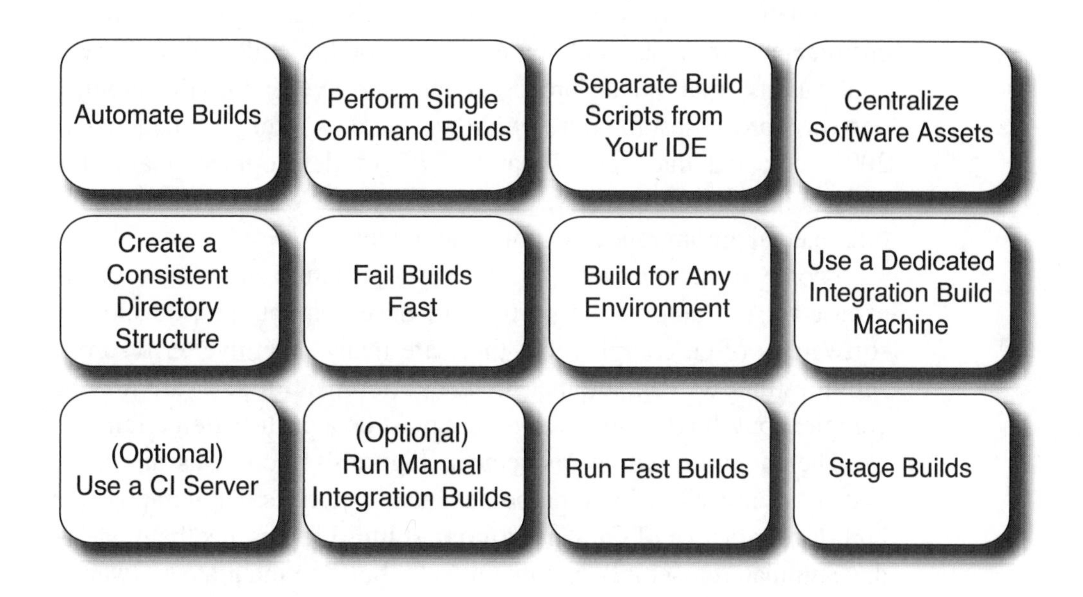

The whole damn universe has to be taken apart, brick by brick, and reconstructed.

—HENRY MILLER, AMERICAN WRITER AND PAINTER *(1891–1980)*

In the early 1900s, workers on the Ford assembly line manufactured cars by hand. A Model T took several days to create. Today, cars are infinitely more complex than the Model T, yet they now take a fraction of the time to assemble. Why is this? The answer is simple: *automation.* The automobile manufacturing industry has removed humans from repetitive tasks and replaced them with robots. So, too, can time-consuming tasks within a software process be mechanized using automated builds. In fact, in both industries, the volume of demand has necessitated this advancement. If a worker's effort in her eight-hour day is tied up in eight hours of manual tasks, there is absolutely no time left for monitoring the process and the product, planning improvements, and so on.

Sometimes developers are like the cobbler who provides all his customers with shoes, but forgets shoes for his children: We create applications to automate processes for users, yet we don't automate our own processes for *developing* software. A study[1] conducted in 2003 indicated that approximately 27% of development teams run daily builds. As an industry, you could say that we are still using the old, manual automobile assembly line model.

People sometimes refer to the complex nature of software as an excuse for not automating portions of development. Yes, developing software *is* often complex, but there are many repetitive, error-prone activities that we can automate. The development of software may be complex, but the *delivery* of software must be a push-button affair.

The Integrate button (as seen in Figure 4-1) contains an "automated assembly line" that embodies many practices that compose the high-level practice of CI. An **automated build** represents the modern-day automated assembly line that uses "robots" to integrate software.

In this chapter, we discuss the benefits of using a CI server to perform an integration build whenever a change occurs. Not all builds are built the same, so we cover the types of builds you will typically execute and how to stage your builds. We also cover the aspects of choosing and using a separate integration build machine for CI. Automated CI is not the only viable approach to running an integration build; we also cover a technique to run manual integrations using a queued approach. Since obtaining build feedback quickly is so important, we finish the chapter with the bane of CI, long-running builds, along with common questions about CI we've heard over the years.

---

1. Cited in "Software Development Worldwide: The State of the Practice" (with Alan MacCormack, Chris Kemerer, and Bill Crandall), *IEEE Software,* November–December 2003, vol. 20, no. 6, pp. 28–34 (Invited). www.pitt.edu/~ckemerer/CK%20research%20papers/SwDevelopmentWorldwide_CusumanoMacCormackKemerer03.pdf.

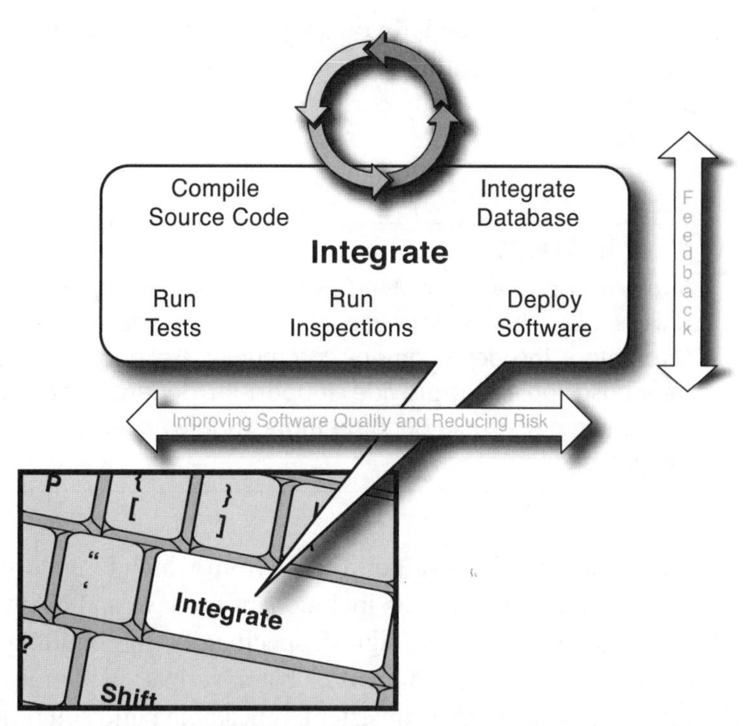

FIGURE 4-1 Building your software to improve software quality and reduce risk

Automate Builds

By writing automated build scripts, you reduce the number of manual, repetitive, and error-prone processes performed on a software project.

What is a **software build?** Is a build just compiling software components? Is a build compiling components *and* running automated tests? Is it a build only if inspections are included? A build can be any of these, yet the processes that you include in a build can more effectively reduce risks; however, the more processes added to a build, the slower the feedback. Therefore, you must determine which processes to include in an automated build. For example, in Chapter 2 we described the practice of running a *private build,* which consists of integrating changes from the team, and running a *full* build (which may include compile, test, inspections, etc.) on your workstation prior to committing code to the version control repository to prevent broken builds. On the other hand, if you are just trying out a couple of changes and do not intend to commit anything, you may choose to run a lighter-weight build that may only perform a compile and then execute a few unit tests.

"Ant It Great?"

Many of the examples used in this book use the Ant and NAnt build tools. This is because of their wide use and recognition throughout the development community. I expect (or hope) that new build tools that provide support for dependencies *and* programming constructs become more widely accepted in the coming years.

There are a variety of build tools from which to choose. Some of the most popular build tools include Ant for Java and NAnt for .NET. Using a scripting tool designed specifically for building software, instead of a custom set of shell or batch scripts, is the most effective manner for developing a consistent, repeatable build solution.

Remember, builds should be a push-button proposition. When you press the Integrate button, as shown in Figure 4-1, the assembly line process runs and produces *working* software. At times, organizations are unable to adopt CI because they are unable to *truly* automate their builds. In some cases, this inability is correlated to tightly coupled dependencies, such as third-party libraries and hard-coded references. I once saw a project with some examples of this, where:

- There were dependencies on shared drives, and parts of the build script were hard-coded for the K:\ drive (which was a problem since there wasn't a "K" drive on the developer's machine)
- And there were hard-coded references to the locations (C:\ drive) of certain tools that weren't residing on the developer's machine

Both of these examples not only make the script inoperable on a non-Windows machine, but they also make it inoperable on the developer's machine because the developer may not have mapped the drives or those directories on the C:\ drive. Attempting to run a script like this will only lead to frustration, as dependency after dependency is unable to be resolved, resulting in a failed build.

Would you consider software that hasn't been tested to be working software? How about software that was tested but hasn't been inspected? Suppose someone said, "Everything works except for the database"—is this working software? Some developers consider their software to be working if it compiles. There are different types of builds (covered later in this chapter), and you will be balancing between a need for a heavyweight build that verifies and produces working, deployable software (usually via many types of tests and inspections) versus the need for getting rapid feedback.

Perform Single Command Builds

Martin Fowler states, "Get everything you need into source control and get it so that you can build the whole system with a single command."[2] The Integrate button concept is realized only if you can run your build via a single command. For instance, typing `nant integrate` from the command line, as shown in Listing 4-1, is an example of a single command initiating an integration build.

LISTING 4-1 Build Script Run via a Single Command

```
> nant integrate
Buildfile: file:///C:/dev/projects/acme/project.build
clean:
svn-update:
all:
compile-src:
compile-tests:
integrate-database:
run-tests:
run-inspections:
package:
deploy:
BUILD SUCCEEDED
Total time: 3 minutes 13 seconds
```

A CI server needs a headless process, such as a single command script, to execute in an automated manner. When running an integration

2. "Continuous Integration" at www.martinfowler.com/articles/continuousIntegration.html.

build on a separate machine, it's not feasible or appropriate to rely on an IDE. Also, to run an integration build via a single command, you need to access all software assets (from a version control system) in order to build the software.

An automated build is just like having an Integrate button: "Press the button" and your software is built (and deployed). This means all software assets are cohesive and functionally testable. Figure 4-2 illustrates the activities that a build script will typically perform.

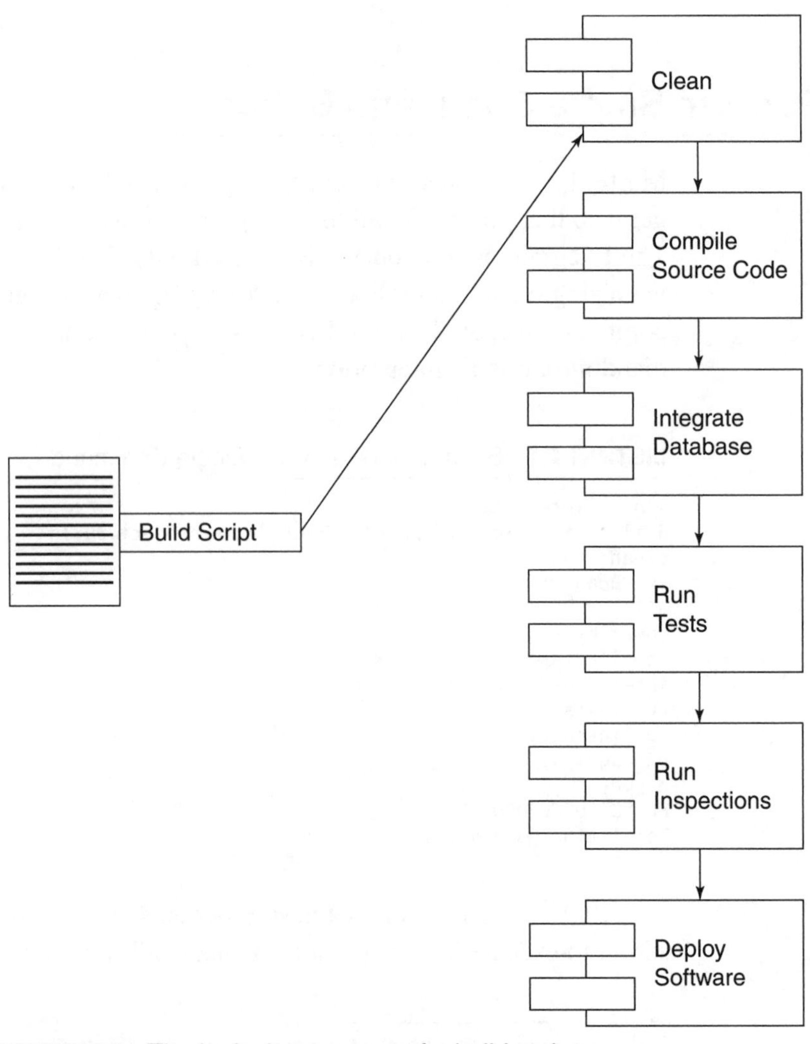

FIGURE 4-2 The logical processes of a build script

The high-level steps for building your software go something like this.

1. Create your build using a build scripting tool like NAnt, Rake, Ant, or Maven. Keep it simple at first; you can add more processes as you go.
2. Add each process (clean, compile, etc.) of the Integrate button within the build script.
3. Run the script from an IDE or the command line to build software.

Listings 4-2 through 4-6 demonstrate examples using the NAnt build tool for the .NET platform; however, you can achieve the same effect with other build scripting tools, such as Ant or Maven for Java, MSBuild for .NET, and Rake for Ruby, to name a few. The issue is not so much which tool you choose to use, but you should ideally use an existing build tool rather than creating a custom solution.

Listing 4-2 shows a NAnt script that uses the `delete` task to remove any directories and files before a new build. This reduces any chance that files from a previous build will adversely affect the new build.

LISTING 4-2 Clean Generated Directories Using NAnt

```
<target name="clean">
  <delete dir="${build.dir}" verbose="true" failonerror="false"/>
  <delete dir="${dist.dir}" verbose="true" failonerror="false"/>
  <delete dir="${reports.dir}" verbose="true" failonerror="false"/>
</target>
```

Listing 4-3 demonstrates C# compilation using the `csc` task. This task will compile all of the files in a certain directory and move the generated .dll file to a different directory. The second part of this example demonstrates the execution of a SQL script that runs a data definition script to create the tables in a database.

LISTING 4-3 Compile and Rebuild Database Using NAnt

```
<target name="build">
  <csc target="library" debug="${build.debug}"
    output="${build.dir}\bin\${config}\${nant.project.name}.dll">
      <sources failonempty="true">
        <include name="${project.localpath}/**/*.cs" />
      </sources>
  </csc>
</target>
```

```
<target name="integrate-database">
  <sql connstring="${project.db.conn}"
    delimiter=";"
    delimstyle="Normal"
    print="true"
    source="${data-definitions}"/>
</target>
```

Listing 4-4 is an example of running the `nunit2` task in NAnt to execute a suite of NUnit tests. Notice that if any of the tests fail, the build fails (as demonstrated by setting the `failonerror` attribute of the `nunit2` task to `true`). As the CI practice stated in Chapter 2, *all tests and inspections must pass* in order for a build to pass.

LISTING 4-4 Testing Using NUnit and NAnt

```
<target name="run-tests" depends="compile-src">
  <nunit2 failonerror="true">
    <formatter type="Xml"
      usefile="true"
      extension=".xml"
      outputdir="${build.dir}/results"/>
      <test
         assemblyname="${build.dir}\bin\${config}\${project}.Test.dll"
          appconfig="mydefaulttest.config"/>
  </nunit2>
</target>
```

Listing 4-5 demonstrates the execution of the `fxcop` task, which runs FxCop, a free tool for the .NET platform that inspects and reports on predefined code violations relating to performance, security concerns, naming conventions, and so on.

LISTING 4-5 Inspection Using FxCop and NAnt

```
<target name="fxcop">
  <fxcop>
    <targets>
      <include
        name="${build.dir}\bin\${config}\${project}.dll"/>
    </targets>
    <arg value="/out:${build.dir}\bin\${config}\fxcop.xml"/>
  </fxcop>
</target>
```

The last build activity shown in Figure 4-2 is for deployment. Listing 4-6 illustrates the use of a NAnt task for a simple deployment to an FTP server.

LISTING 4-6 Deployment Using FTP and NAnt

```
<target name="deploy">
  <connection id="staging"
    server="devqa.ib.com"
    username="helloworld"
    password="myftppwd" />
    <ftp connection="staging"
      remotedir="incoming"
      localdir="c:\dev\project\acme">
      <put type="bin">
        <include name="${build.dir}\bin\${config}\${project}.dll" />
      </put>
    </ftp>
</target>
```

If a build script is executed by a developer without any feedback, she will not know whether the build succeeded or failed. A very simple example of a failure notification is included in Listing 4-4. If any test run by the `nunit2` task fails, then the *entire* build is considered a failure. In fact, NAnt will end the build with a glaring `BUILD FAILED` message so there won't be any doubts.

This is by no means an exhaustive example of a build script. The benefits of a build script that fully enables the Integrate button would need to incorporate many more processes and paths.[3]

Separate Build Scripts from Your IDE

You should avoid coupling your build scripts with an IDE. An IDE may be dependent on a build script, but *a build script shouldn't be dependent on your IDE.* Figure 4-3 illustrates the proper dependency. This dependency is sometimes more subtle than you may think. For

3. For more on this topic, see the book's companion Web site: www.integratebutton.com/.

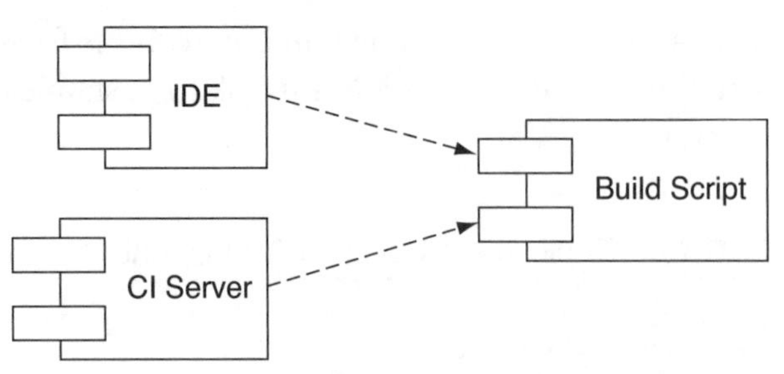

FIGURE 4-3 Decoupling your build script from the IDE

example, IDEs can make it easy to create build scripts, but they place the build files and dependencies within the directory structure of the installed IDE. To test the reusability of an IDE-generated build script, take the build script and run it on a new machine with only the operating system installed (and the associated build tool).

Creating a separate build script is important for two reasons.

1. Each developer may be using a different IDE, and it can be difficult to account for configuration differences in each IDE.
2. A CI server must execute an automated build without human intervention. Therefore, the same automated build script used by developers can and should be used by the CI server.

Centralize Software Assets

To build software effectively, all software assets must be centralized. By centralizing software assets into a version control system, you are able to better achieve the single command build described earlier in this chapter. Moreover, centralizing software helps prevent the "but it works on my machine" problem, where a developer is unable to recreate a defect that occurred in some other environment, such as the testing area or the user's machine. We cover different techniques in centralizing software assets in this section.

One approach to centralization of software assets is to use the version control repository to host all files. In the book *Software Configuration Management Patterns*, Stephen Berczuk and Brad Appleton call this the "Repository pattern." The pattern indicates that "a workspace consists of more than just code," including all of the following:

- Components, as either source or library files
- Third-party components, such as JAR files, libraries, DLLs, and so on, depending on the language and platform
- Configuration files
- Data files to initialize an application
- Build scripts and build environment settings
- Installation scripts for some components[4]

When using a version control repository to centralize *all* software assets, you still make the judgment call as to what constitutes "all." Use the level or risk to decide the minimum types of software assets that go into the version control repository. For example, one of the risks for a product with a long lifespan is that subsequent versions of compilers and tools may cause problems, sometimes subtle and undetectable, with your software. This is a risk because you may need to go back and compile the earlier version.

Moreover, certain versions of tools don't work well with others. It's easy for developers to pull down whatever version of a tool they think is appropriate, possibly running into problems and chasing false positives or negatives. Similarly, going back and producing an old build (e.g., to reproduce a customer problem or fix a bug) may require a specific set of tools that were used *at that point* in development. As such, you'll probably conclude that there's almost no part of your project that could not benefit in the future, for some reason, from the version tracking and centralization of assets in a project repository.

Create a Consistent Directory Structure

Using a version control repository to manage all software assets does all of the important things just discussed; in addition, it makes it possi-

4. From *Software Configuration Management Patterns* by Stephen Berczuk and Brad Appleton.

ble to perform scripted retrievals from a CI server. To do so effectively, to be able to draw on the repository for all the myriad asset combinations you can use throughout the project, you must create a consistent, logical directory structure.

One approach is to base the directory structure on typical software development project activities such as requirements, design, implementation, and testing. Whether you use these or other named "buckets" for the structure, the salient point is to keep their distinctions and contents defined and consistent. In addition, it is important that each task in your build is retrieving from a directory that contains *only the source code and related scripts for that task,* not the entire project. For instance, your integration build script can get all source code and related scripts from the `implementation` directory. This can speed up builds significantly, whereas retrieving all files, such as documents and binary files, can make builds crawl. A simple directory structure such as the following can help separate source files from others so that it's easier to run builds.

- `implementation`
- `requirements`
- `design`
- `management`
- `deployment`
- `testing`
- `tools`

Of course, almost all of these top-level directories might have many subdirectories below them. The `implementation` directory should have only source files in it and can be the primary directory for running builds.

Fail Builds Fast

Good builds know how to fail fast. It is annoying to fail after so many other portions of the build have passed, and you are losing precious time identifying the failed targets. The high-level steps to create fast-failing builds are

1. Integrate components (get latest changes from repository and compile)
2. Run true unit tests (i.e., quick tests that don't have a database or any other dependency)
3. Run other automated processes (rebuild database, inspect, and deploy)

This is only one recommended order of build execution. It all depends on what is more likely to fail most often on a particular project. The more likely it is to fail, the sooner you should have it execute within the build script. Also, keep in mind that the order of execution is sometimes dictated by what must be built first. For example, source code needs to be compiled before running developer tests. Builds are most effective when they send a build failure as soon as possible. The Run Fast Builds section, later in this chapter, addresses ways to reduce your build duration and to stage builds so that they provide faster feedback.

Build for Any Environment

A software project often requires you to deploy to different environments. You may find it useful to maintain different configuration files in your repository to execute against different environment configurations (development, integration, test, QA, and production) by using .properties, .xml, or .ini files. Each platform, language, and scripting tool will have its own variation on configuration. A build's configurability relies on its build scripts to alter the predefined configurations available in the software without changing the core functionality of the build scripts. In many cases, you can provide these configuration "hooks" by altering configuration files used by the application. Frequently, you can also configure the frameworks and APIs on which an application relies. The technique will vary depending on the platform's convention. The following is a list of configurable values that you will likely find in most environments.

- Logging verbosity
- Application server configuration
- Database connection information
- Framework configuration

Although the environments that you test or deploy to may be different, the build scripts do not need to be different. Configuration files (such as .properties or .include files) let you account for variations rather than having to copy and paste values for each environment within the build scripts. Here is another area, just like source code, where duplicated code leads to greater complexity and lower reliability. To ensure that you can create working software in any environment, improve your build's configurability by parameterizing the build scripts. As demonstrated in Figure 4-4, you can run the same build script and provide an associated properties file to customize for each build environment. For instance, you can call this build script:

```
ant -f build.xml -Denvironment=qa
```

when deploying to the QA environment. `environment` is a property that was defined in the Ant script. `-D` indicates it's a system parameter passed to the Ant script.

Build Types and Mechanisms

There are different types of builds, and each type has different, but sometimes overlapping, parties who are interested in the build status or who also will use it. These builds can be triggered using different mechanisms, such as user-driven, scheduled, polling for changes, and event-driven mechanisms.

Build Types

Build types occur in a three-level hierarchy: for the individual, the team, and users (the customer). A developer (or pair) runs a private

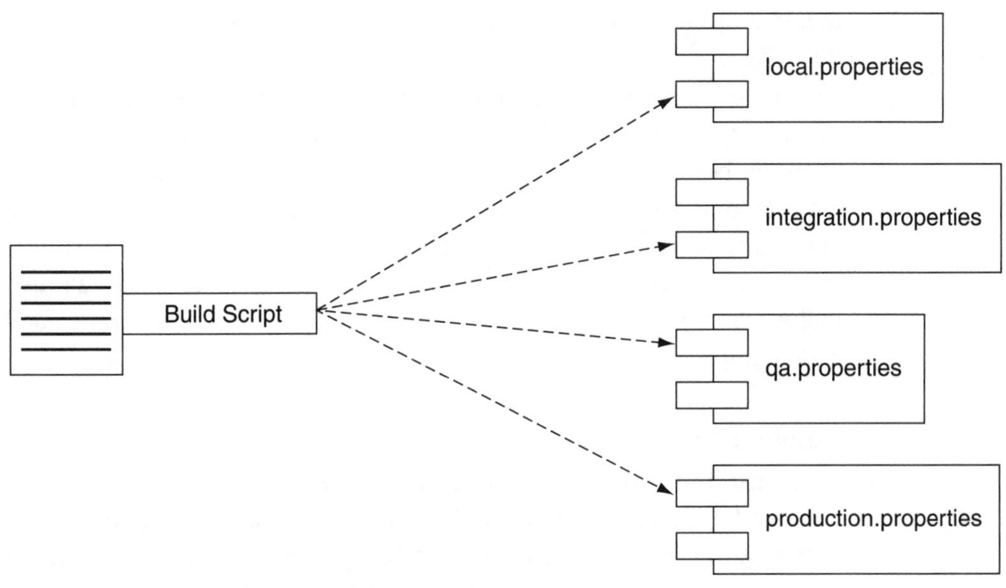

FIGURE 4-4 Configurable builds for different environments

build, an integration build integrates the results with the rest of the team, and a release build readies the software for the users.

Private Build

A developer will run a **private build** prior to committing code to the repository. By running a private build, you integrate your changes with the last changes available in the version control repository. This can prevent broken builds. The steps to running a private build are

1. Check out the code you will alter from the repository.
2. Make changes to that code.
3. Get the latest system changes from the repository.
4. Run a build that includes execution of all your unit tests.
5. Commit your code changes to the repository.

Integration Build

An **integration build** integrates changes committed to the repository by the team against the **mainline** (also known as the **head** or **trunk**).

Ideally, an integration build should run on a separate, dedicated machine.

Fowler[5] discusses different types of builds that can be run as part of an integration build. He calls these "staged builds," which include a "commit build" and "secondary build(s)." A commit build is your fastest integration build (< ten minutes) and includes a compile and the unit tests. A secondary build is an integration build that runs slower tests, such as component, system, and performance tests. It can also include automated inspections such as coding standard adherence and code complexity.

Release Build

A **release build** readies the software for release to users. One of the goals of CI is to create deployable software. A release build may occur at the end of an iteration or some other milestone, may include more extensive performance and load tests, and must include any acceptance tests. Moreover, many release builds also create the installation media to run it in the user's environment. A release build may also be used to ready it for QA, if you are using a separate, staged process and team.

Build Mechanisms

Not all builds are triggered in the same manner. To trigger a certain build in the most appropriate manner, you must consider the build's purpose and frequency. In some situations, there may be scripts that are so large or have so many dependencies that it shouldn't be run automatically; instead, it should always be run on demand. In other cases, the automatic execution can be run under CI. The following list describes the types of build mechanisms.

- **On-demand**—This is a user-driven process in which someone manually initiates an integration build.
- **Scheduled**—Scheduled processes are driven by time, for instance, so that it runs on an hourly basis, whether or not a

---

5. See Continuous Integration at www.martinfowler.com/articles/continuousIntegration.html.

change has occurred. A scheduled activity may be appropriate for an off-hour process, such as running a set of exhaustive security or load tests on the software. You can use `cron` to schedule tasks, but many of the CI servers support a scheduling capability as well.

- **Poll for changes**—A process wakes up on a regular interval and checks for changes to the version control repository. If changes are detected, it runs the integration build. All CI servers support some type of "poll for changes" mechanism.
- **Event-driven**—Event-driven is like polling for changes, but instead of the CI tool, the version control repository triggers the build, based on a predefined change event. If the version control repository detects a change, it initiates the build script.

Triggering Builds

Table 4-1 links the build type with how the build might be triggered.

TABLE 4-1 Triggering Builds Using Different Mechanisms

Build Type	*Build Mechanism*
Private	On-demand
Integration	On-demand, poll for changes, scheduled, event-driven
Release	On-demand, scheduled

Use a Dedicated Integration Build Machine

When you dedicate a machine to integration builds, you drastically reduce assumptions about environment and configuration, and you help prevent the "but it works on my machine" problem from occurring too late in development. Any local workstation typically has slightly different configurations and dependencies, often undetectable, from the deployment environments. If a developer makes local changes and forgets to commit a few files to the version control repository, the CI system, which is running on a separate machine, runs an integration build and finds these omissions. Furthermore, you can put application and database servers into known states each time an integration build occurs, which can reduce assumptions and enable much faster discovery and resolution of problems. When individuals know that the latest integration build failed, they can avoid getting the bad source code from the version control repository. The integration build machine acts as a safety net, ensuring that the software is working as expected.

Often someone asks how much it costs to have a dedicated integration build machine. This is an important question and has an even more important answer. The following scenario demonstrates how this question plays out.

Peter (Technical Lead): I'd like for us to purchase a dedicated integration build machine for our Logistics project.

Bill (Project Manager): Why do you need a separate machine?

Peter: So that we are able to build our software directly from our Subversion repository every time a change occurs. We will also have the capability to clean and reapply the environment, including the test data. All of this will allow us to find and fix problems sooner.

Bill: That sounds good, Peter, but we really don't have the funds for that. I am guessing it will cost at least $1,000 for this—is that right?

Peter: The reason we had to come in last Saturday was because of integration problems. By getting an integration build machine, we can save considerable time and money. The time saved will easily pay for the cost of the machine many times over. We had to manually integrate and test before Monday's demo. We really need this machine to integrate our software automatically with every change.

Bill: Okay, what we can do is go ahead and use one of the extra machines in the server room. You can remove everything on that machine and make it your integration build machine.

As demonstrated in Bill and Peter's conversation, you don't need to spend money to purchase a new machine. An extra machine that's not being utilized can become the CI machine. If a dedicated integration build machine isn't available, start by using your own development machine. This is better than not integrating at all, but this isn't a long-term solution. Be sure to use a separate location (i.e., directory or partition) on your machine.

There are a few items to consider when creating an integration build machine. By focusing on these issues you'll receive the maximum benefits from it.

- **Recommended system resources**—A lot can be gained by using the right tools. By increasing hardware resources, a build's duration can be reduced (discussed later in this chapter). In general, it is worth the money to increase hardware resources for an integration build machine rather than wasting time waiting for slow builds.
- **All software assets in the version control repository**—Anything that has to do with developing the software needs to be committed to the version control repository. This includes source code, build scripts, configuration files, tools (such as application server, database server, and static analysis tools), test code, and database scripts/files (see the Centralize Software Assets section, earlier in this chapter).
- **Clean environment**—Before performing an integration build, the CI script needs to remove any code dependencies on the integration environment. Ensure that it is removing all of the source code and binaries from the previous integration build in order to baseline the environment. Also make sure that the CI system sets test data and any other configuration elements to a known state. This approach reduces assumptions by removing dependencies and building the software as if it were on a new machine.

By using a dedicated build machine that is capable of running builds efficiently, the build process can be run often; moreover, the build environment becomes truly repeatable by reducing environmental assumptions.

The Magic Machine

Many developers have had this machine at one point or another. The situation occurs when you have written and thoroughly tested your software, but when it is deployed on another machine (like one of the testing machines), something doesn't work. There are many possible reasons: Perhaps you forgot to commit a file to the version control repository, maybe the testing machine's configuration is different, or an application server's pooling mechanism is set for fewer connections. But in all cases, it means that something is *different* between your machine and the other machine(s). This is when you exclaim, "But it works on my machine!" because you can't even get it to fail there. Could it be a "magic" machine?

"Magic machines are those one-of-a-kind magical pieces of hardware that happen to be the only machines capable of building a company's software application. This scenario isn't as far-fetched as it may seem. I've run across these wizardly beasts a number of times in my career. These machines turn demonic, though, when dependencies are lost or when the inevitable bit rot strikes. It's easy to see how a normal machine in a company's infrastructure can turn enchanted: over time, developers inadvertently added hard dependencies into the machine's script, made references to fully qualified directory paths, or even installed tools that only exist on a select machine, which slowly prevented the build from being able to run on any other machine."[6]

Magic machines occur because of the "hard-wired" dependencies to the machine on which you are building. This can also occur on the integration build machine. Sometimes people will add an environment variable or apply a configuration change to the build machine to solve a problem, but forget to script it so that it can be used on another machine. If your build machine were to fail to work, what would be the impact? How long would it take you to get up and running again?

There can be many solutions to this problem. You can script most dependencies into your build and include the dependency in your repository. Another option is to create an image of certain dependencies, such as your database or application server. Furthermore, you can refactor your build scripts to remove many of the hard-coded dependencies (for instance, environment variables) and make a relative reference instead.

6. From http://www-128.ibm.com/developerworks/java/library/j-ap10106/index.html.

Use a CI Server

It makes sense to use a CI server when performing CI. Of course, you can create your own tool or perform integrations manually; however, these days there are many excellent tools on the market that provide valuable features and the capability to extend those features. Therefore, it's unnecessary to create your own CI server. However, if you were to write your own server, you would probably want to incorporate many of these features.

- Poll for changes in the version control repository on a specified time interval.
- Perform certain actions on a scheduled basis, such as hourly or daily.
- Identify a "quiet period" during which no integration builds are performed for the project.
- Support for different build scripting tools including command-line tools such as Rake, make, Ant, or NAnt.
- Send e-mails to the concerned parties.
- Display a history of previous builds.
- Display a dashboard that is Web accessible so that everyone can review integration build information.
- Support multiple version control systems for your different projects.

And the list goes on. Most CI servers have already implemented these features. There is sure to be a tool that fits your needs and development environment. CruiseControl, Luntbuild, Continuum, Pulse, and Hudson are a few of the tools that you can use to perform CI. Appendix B explores and evaluates the various CI servers on the market at the time this book was published.

So, should you use a CI server, manual integrations, or a combination? We will leave it up to you. We obviously favor using a CI server. However, there are good reasons for manually performing integrations, especially given the minimal tool support for preventing broken code from entering the repository.

Run Manual Integration Builds

An alternative or complementary technique to using a CI server is to perform a manual integration. A **manual integration build** is a practice where only one person at a time can commit changes to the repository. It utilizes a queue in which developers manually run an integration build on a separate integration machine to ensure the build always stays in the green.

By running a CI server, your team is performing an *automated* (nonsequential) integration build that can be run at any time. As discussed earlier in the book, a CI server can poll for changes to the repository every few minutes or so. Once it finds a change, it kicks off an automated build. The problem with automated integrations is that they can lead to broken builds. In its current practice, CI is very reactionary. Often you don't discover the problem until it has been committed to the repository—which means that other developers will get broken code when they check out from the repository. Moreover, a broken build can disrupt the flow of developers' work.

To prevent broken code from ever entering the repository, some teams utilize these manual, sequential integrations. Some teams will use a physical token (I observed one team that used the Staples Easy button) or a simple file lock to signify who is integrating—since only one person (or pair) is integrating at a time.

Manual integration can be effective in preventing broken builds, but it doesn't scale particularly well for larger teams. Furthermore, a side effect of this form of integration is that team members may stack up many changes they make for a larger and less frequent integration, rather than smaller and more frequent ones that maximize quality. In addition, if you are exclusively manually integrating your build, there is no guarantee the practice will be followed. Using a CI server provides a safety net to know the integration will occur. Some groups will use a combination of sequential and automated integrations. For instance, a team that exclusively uses automated CI can combine the approach of separate private builds by each developer to prevent broken integration builds. Much of this is personal preference. We clearly lean toward automated integrations, but there definitely are unique benefits of a manual, sequential integration to keep the build in the green.

Run Fast Builds

Stopping your development activities to wait for feedback slows the rhythm of development for everyone on the project. Consequently, builds that take a long time to complete often cast an unfavorable shadow over the practice of CI. Rapid feedback in CI is crucial. The shorter the duration of the integration build, the faster you will receive feedback.

Integration Build Scalability and Performance

Your **build scalability** indicates how capable your build system is of handling an increase in the amount of code that it integrates and analyzes. Your **build performance** refers to the duration of your build. Ideally, as your code base gets larger, your CI system should be capable of handling this increase without much degradation in performance.

If developers are not committing code to a version control repository frequently, the reason may be a slow integration build. To begin to reduce build duration, perform a high-level analysis of the integration build environment to determine the bottlenecks. Next, analyze the findings and determine the most appropriate improvement, then attempt to make changes in the build process to reduce the build's duration. Lastly, reevaluate the build duration to determine if further improvements are warranted.

At a high level, here is an approach you can use to diagnose and reduce a build's duration.

1. Gather build metrics.
2. Analyze build metrics.
3. Choose and perform improvements.
4. Reevaluate; repeat if necessary.

Ten-Minute Builds

In *Extreme Programming Explained*, Second Edition, Kent Beck suggests that a good rule of thumb is to keep your (integration) builds to no more than ten minutes. Many developers who use CI follow the practice of not moving on to the next task until their most recent checkin integrates successfully. Therefore, builds taking longer than ten minutes can interrupt their flow. This suggestion can work for most projects. Your ten-minute commit build doesn't need to run every type of test or inspection. You can offload the time it takes to run a build by running multiple build types in succession (as mentioned earlier, what Fowler calls "staged builds").

Gather Build Metrics

The first step in improving a build's duration is to capture build metrics. Table 4-2 lists some common metrics that can produce a more qualitative analysis of your integration build process. You probably won't need to gather all of these build metrics every time, but it is a useful exercise if you are unsure about a problem or would rather not waste time attempting to fix problems that don't exist.

TABLE 4-2 Integration Build Metrics

Integration Build Metric	*Description*
Compilation time	The time it takes to compile the software, and how it compares to your past compile times.
Number of source lines of code (SLOC)	This indicates the system's size or at least what needs to be compiled.
Number and types of inspections	The number of different types of inspections you are performing. Consider eliminating any redundancy.
Average assembly generation time	The time it takes to generate the assembly, archive, or however you are packaging the software.
Test execution time (based on category)	The time it takes to perform testing at each level: unit, component, and system (these are described in Chapter 6).

Integration Build Metric	*Description*
Ratio between successful and unsuccessful builds	Divide the number of failed builds into the number of total builds to determine the ratio between successful and unsuccessful builds.
Inspection time	The time it takes to perform all of the automated inspections.
Deployment time	The time it takes to deploy the software into the target environment from the integration build.
Database rebuild time	The time it takes to rebuild your database.
Integration build machine system resources and usage	Improving the memory, disk speed, and/or processor can improve the performance of your integration builds. This helps determine whether an integration build machine has an application server or database server or some other process that is using up memory or processor speed.
Version control system load	Helps determine the version control system's peak-time load, how long it takes to check out/update your project from the integration build machine, and if the network bandwidth, processor, memory, or disk drives are adequate.

Analyze Build Metrics

Next, analyze the metrics gathered using Figure 4-5 as a general guide for determining which improvement will best reduce build duration. These improvement tactics are prioritized using the following criteria: scalability, performance, and difficulty in implementation. Many solutions can depend on the code base size and certain automated build processes that take a while to run (such as automated developer tests). You may want to document the approach and rationale to refer to the next time you seek to reduce build duration.

Choose and Implement Improvements

With metrics in hand and an improvement strategy in mind, you can begin to target specific improvements to implement.

Improvement Tactic	Priority	Scalability	Performance	Difficulty
Use a dedicated integration build machine	1	↑	↑	↓
Increase integration build machine(s) hardware capacity	2	↑	—	↓
Improve test performance	3	↓	↑	—
Streamline integration builds	4	↓	—	↓
Optimize infrastructure	5	—	—	↑
Optimize build process	6	↓	—	↓
Build system components separately	7	↓	—	—
Improve software inspection performance	8	↓	↑	↓
Perform distributed integration builds	9	↑	↑	↑

Legend (Impact on scalability, performance, and difficulty):

High ↑ Medium — Low ↓

FIGURE 4-5 Integration build duration improvements

Use a Dedicated Integration Build Machine

We covered the merits of using a dedicated integration build machine in an earlier section. Using a dedicated integration build machine has a number of performance-enhancing benefits, such as reducing false positive or negative builds and enabling faster builds.

Increase Integration Build Machine(s) Hardware Capacity

Often, improving the hardware capacity of a machine is a quicker, low-cost approach to reducing integration build duration. You've probably heard that "CPU cycles are cheaper than people cycles"; however, the machine must be upgradeable, and this method only works until you've maximized the machine's upgrade capability. The following

> **Buying an Integration Build Machine**
>
> When I was working on a large project in the 1990s, we had used the same integration build machine for a while. Our integration builds were taking about two hours to complete (for more than 1 million lines of code)—if there were no failures. Rather than accepting the fact that the build took this long, another developer and I asked management if we could purchase the "fastest machine on the market." We researched and submitted a request to purchase a machine with the top specifications in disk speed, memory, and processor speed. It was our belief that hardware is cheap when compared to the cost of person-hours waiting on a build, and thankfully the project manager agreed. With the new machine, we reduced the build time to 30 minutes.

list of questions can help you determine if integration build machine hardware is at maximum capacity.

- What is the current CPU speed? Are there options to improve speed on the machine? Is it expandable to a faster processor or to a Symmetric Multiprocessing (SMP) configuration?
- How much of available memory does the machine utilize?
- Is the system using all of its available network bandwidth?

Depending on the answers to these questions, there are several options for improving build performance and scalability.

- Perform available upgrades to CPU, disk, or memory.
- Offload processes to other systems.
- Eliminate unnecessary system processes.

Improve Test Performance

Even in a well-functioning CI system, a bulk of the integration build time will be taken up by the execution of automated tests. Evaluating and improving the performance of these tests can dramatically reduce build duration. Capture the following metrics to help you improve test performance.

- Time automated tests. Examine the test execution timings provided by your testing framework.
- Use a performance-testing tool to analyze certain areas of your test code. In addition, many xUnit testing frameworks provide a reporting utility that displays the time taken to execute each test.
- Use inspection tools to analyze your test code and test complexity.
- Verify that your unit tests are actually unit tests, not component or system tests. A quick way to determine this is to remove your network cable, shut down your database, and run your tests. Which tests still run? The tests that still run are (or should be) your unit tests.

After performing a high-level evaluation of the test environment, you'll have a better idea of how to improve test performance. Several strategies will suggest themselves, including the following.

- Separate automated tests by category—unit, component, and system—and run these tests at different times (e.g., unit tests at every commit, component/system tests in a secondary build). See Chapter 6 for details on test categorization.
- Refactor your tests based on the results of the inspection tools.
- Use mocks/stubs for components that may otherwise be too difficult or complex to use in the unit-testing environment. For example, a common implementation of a mock object is mocking the interface for data access.
- Separate long-running integration tests into separate specialized test suites.
- Execute your tests in parallel.
- Run different types of tests based on build type: A commit build is followed by secondary builds, a full integration build, or release build.

Stage Builds

As mentioned earlier, another approach to reducing build duration is to run a lightweight build followed by a "heavyweight" build (which

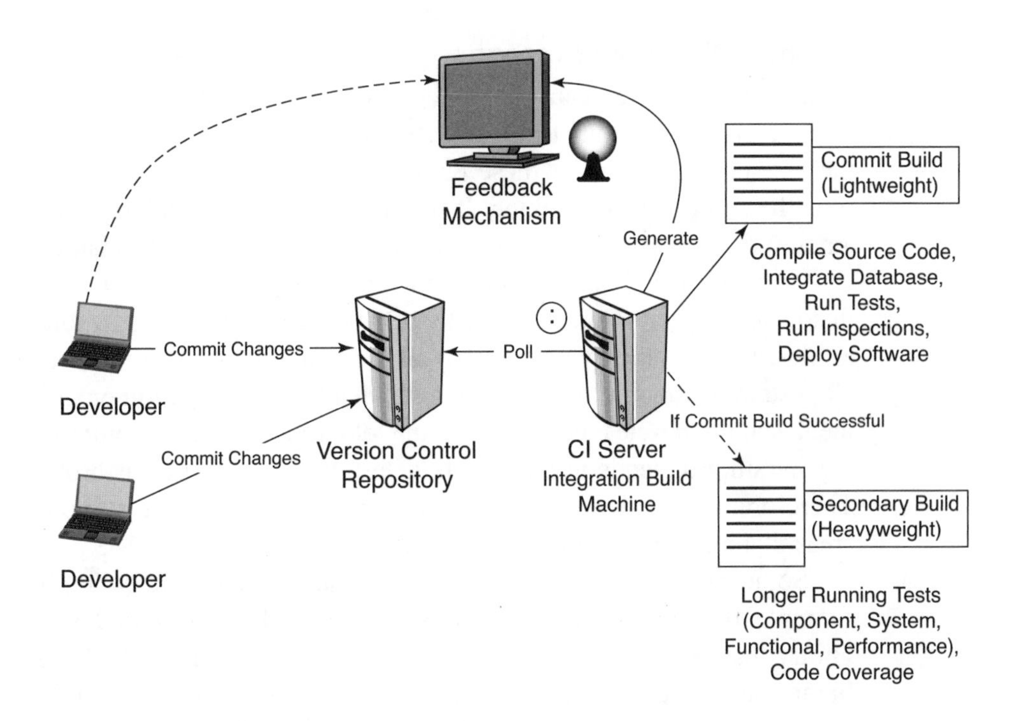

FIGURE 4-6 A staged build process

Fowler refers to as *staged builds:* a commit build followed by a secondary build). Figure 4-6 illustrates this approach. In running staged builds, you first run an initial integration "commit" or lightweight build that integrates the software components and runs unit tests to root out any obvious problems. After this lightweight build is successful, a more exhaustive integration build is run to include component tests or system tests, inspections, and deployment. This supports the practice of "fail builds fast," described earlier in this chapter.

Examine Infrastructure

You may discover that integration builds are slow because of the system infrastructure. Perhaps network performance is slow or there is a slow-performing virtual private network connection. Geographically dispersed systems and unreliable hardware or software can also induce performance issues. Investigate and improve any infrastructure resources to reduce the build duration.

Optimize the Build Process

Large code bases can cause the integration of software components to take a considerably long time. To determine if the problem is related to the size or integration of these components, ascertain the amount of time the compile step is taking. If it turns out this step is taking a large amount of time, perform an incremental build instead of a full build.

An incremental build will compile and/or regenerate only the files that have changed. This can be risky because, depending on how this is implemented, you may not receive all the benefits of CI. An effective CI system is about reducing risks and, ideally, an integration environment should be cleaned by removing old files and then compiling/regenerating the code to effectively determine if anything has broken. Therefore, use incremental builds judiciously as you investigate other areas that lead to slow-performing builds.

Some areas may lend themselves to an incremental build. For example, if you have a Java system with a native DLL or shared object library that rarely changes, it might be reasonable to only rebuild that library once a day. In fact, some may argue that this infrequent DLL or shared object be treated as a separate CI project and referenced as part of your project using project dependencies.

Build System Components Separately

Sometimes integration builds take a long time to execute because of the time it takes to integrate the source code and other associated files. In this case, you can break apart the software into smaller subsystems (modules) and build each of the subsystems separately.

To build the system components individually, create separate projects for each subsystem that can be isolated. This can be done from within a CI system—just make one of the subsystems the master project. If there are any changes to one project based on the dependencies, the other projects are rebuilt as well. Figure 4-7 demonstrates a sample project layout based on separating the project into discrete components to achieve faster builds.

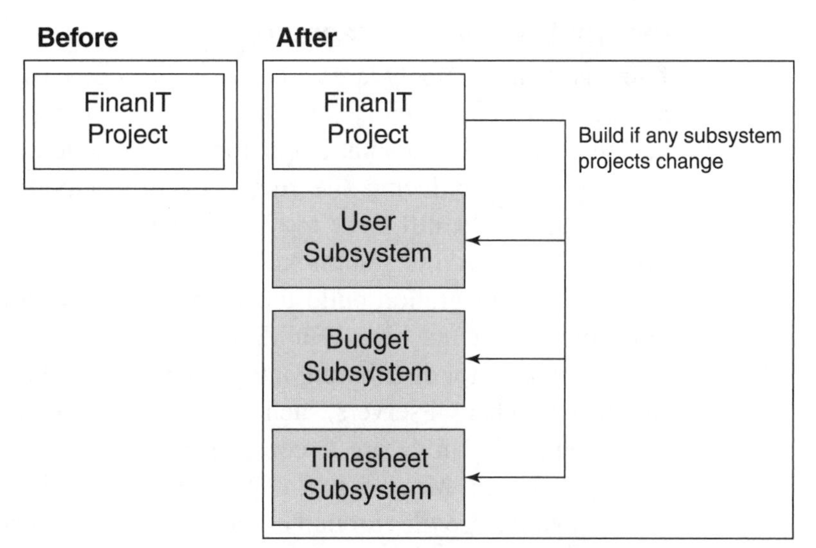

FIGURE 4-7 Building system components separately

Improve Software Inspection Performance

Just like testing performance, inspection performance may be slowing down your CI system. Use the following list of questions to determine if inspections are slowing down integration builds.

- Which metrics are used? Does each metric provide tangible value?
- Are there two or more tools providing the same metrics, which may decrease your build performance?
- Are you running automated inspections with every build? Are there certain analyses that can run as part of a secondary or periodic build?
- Are there inspections that you can run on specific subsystems rather than the entire code base?

This next list identifies possible solutions to improve software inspection performance.

- Remove unused and unnecessary inspections.
- Reduce duplicate inspections.
- Reduce the frequency of certain inspections.

Perform Distributed Integration Builds

If you have an extremely large code base and you've tried adding more processing speed, memory, and disk speed to the integration build machine, and you've also attempted to reduce build duration in other ways, including reducing the frequency of component and system tests, but the build still takes too long, then you should consider performing distributed integration builds.

There are integration build tools that specialize in leveraging the power of multiple machines. BuildForge[7] and ParaBuild[8] are tools that provide features for distributing integration builds. There are also contributions to other CI servers, such as CruiseControl; however, distributed integration builds are a complex problem with an even more complex solution. Moving part of the build to another machine may mean copying large files around as part of the build process, which has the potential to slow things down even more. Try to exercise all other options for reducing your build duration *before* attempting this solution.

Reevaluate

We have discussed several approaches, including improvements to test performance, the build process, hardware capacity, and design. Which improvements did you try and what is the build's duration now? It's time now to try the improvement with the rest of the team and gauge whether an additional improvement cycle is necessary. If you have already gone through this process once, repeating the improvement cycle should be less time-consuming and less painful.

How Will This Work for You?

At this point, you may agree that by executing an integration build with every change to the software you can reduce many risks on a project. However, you may be thinking, "This works fine on *your*

7. See www.buildforge.com for more information.

8. See www.viewtier.com/products/parabuild/index.htm for details.

project, but it won't work on mine because we don't have the time, resources, and money" or "We're a *different* type of project—not like the ones you've described." The following questions and answers deal with some of these concerns.

"My project has seven billion lines of code. How is this going to work for me?"

Okay, so your project probably doesn't have "seven billion" lines of code, but let's just say you're on a large project and feel like CI causes too many interruptions. The larger the project, the more you need CI because of the constancy of change. It's like saying, "I'd rather not know about problems that exist in our code base; I'd rather wait until later when I don't remember what I was working on." This is not to say, however, that incorporating CI into a large project won't take more time than on a smaller project. It simply equates to more pain that can be reduced, more success you can gain more often, and more flexibility with your project assets to create more artifacts.

The primary concern with a large project is keeping the build fast. You may want to run longer-running processes periodically (or staged, as described earlier) rather than continuously. Examples include component tests, system tests, functional tests, and inspections. Splitting the code base into separate projects can also help improve the integration build duration.

"I have a legacy application, so how will this work for me?"

If you are not running a CI system, it may take some time to create a build script to support your source code, since build scripts must be written so that they can be executed by an automated process. However, even if you don't have automated tests, you can start adding automated tests for every change request (i.e., if there is a defect, the first thing you can do is write an automated test). Then, include the execution of this test into the build script and run it as a part of the CI system.

"What if our source code is in multiple version control repositories?"

This question is often related to the next question about distributed development. Let's suppose you have one project in Subversion called

Project Management System and another in CVS called Financial Management System. If there is a change to the Financial Management System, the Project Management System must be built because it uses an API in the Financial Management System. Your CI server should provide the capability for build dependencies. This forces a build to occur on one project based on the initiation of a build on another project.

"Our project is separated geographically, so how can we practice CI?"

Do you have development teams working at remote locations finding it difficult to practice CI? This may occur because of slow network connectivity or high security to protect intellectual property. Most CI servers include the capability to use project dependencies. Imagine a project in Virginia that is developing a software product that has "special sauce" algorithms, and a development group in California responsible for developing other components for the product. The company uses a CVS version control repository in Virginia, which contains the special algorithms. In addition, it establishes a new subversion repository in California. The technical lead in Virginia configures the CruiseControl CI server to support two projects: one project in Virginia and the other in California. Before an integration build is successfully executed for the team in California, the CI server kicks off the project in Virginia. This will only work, however, if components are decoupled well.

"My integration builds are taking too long!"

See the Run Fast Builds section, earlier in this chapter.

"We frequently get build failures. Are we doing something wrong?"

Yes, you're committing code that doesn't work! It could be that your code is not compiling, your tests or inspections are failing, or your database scripts are generating errors. One way to solve this problem is to run a private build (see Chapter 2) to emulate the integration environment as much as possible on development machines before committing changes to the version control repository. This means that each developer puts the latest changes from the version control repository onto her development machine, ensures all tests and inspections run successfully, and that the database is successfully rebuilt with test data. This also means each developer should have a "sandbox" in her environment that runs the same processes that the integration build runs. The most important principle to understand is that you should *prevent the larger builds from failing,* and this means following a process to integrate and verify all changes with your own build capabilities *before* committing changes to the version control repository. Figure 4-8 demonstrates the steps involved in running a private build before committing changes to the repository.

"We can't afford a separate build machine."

Hardware is cheap when compared to the amount of time that can be lost when an integration problem occurs. It doesn't have to cost you a lot of money. As indicated earlier in this chapter in Bill and Peter's conversation, you can find an unused computer as your build machine at first. Then, after the team experiences the benefits of fully integrated builds, you can invest money in a more capable machine. Without a separate build machine, you'll also spend time attempting to diagnose a problem only to discover that a file had not been committed to the version control repository. That took time, and time is money. Do your best to put your "sales hat" on and convince management that it will

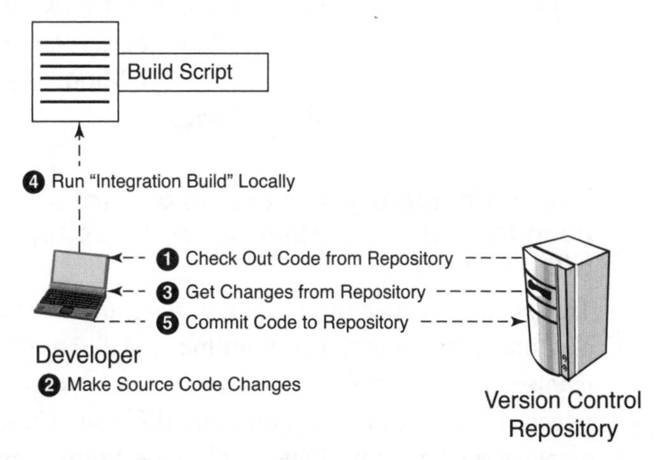

FIGURE 4-8 Running a private build to reduce integration build errors

save money in the end to purchase a build machine. In using the phrase "the long run," we're talking about recouping the money within a few weeks (depending on the size of your team), not months or years. In addition, you'll receive the quality benefit of a repeatable build process that provides the capability to release working software *at any point in time* (based on your business needs).

"Our software is too complex; we have to do things manually" or "No—we have all sorts of stuff going on."

This is the perfect reason to create a CI system, because you are probably spending too much time performing redundant processes. If your software is complex and has many dependencies, there is even more incentive to create a system that puts all the pieces together and runs a suite of tests and inspections to ensure everything is working correctly and *continuously*. This is not to say that it will be easy for you to create a repeatable build process. In fact, the larger the development infrastructure, the more time it'll probably take to create this build system.

But creating a build system is easy if you think of the process as a series of small steps. First, clean up the directory structure for the version control repository so that source code, test code, configuration files, and anything else needed is easily available. Next, use your build scripting tool to create a simple build script that just compiles the source code. Then add tests and inspections. Try to evolve the build over time rather than throwing everything in at one time. As a matter of fact, that is how we've brought about most of our CI systems. As you get the rewards of the first few steps, you are definitely motivated to carry on more. Work seems to go more smoothly following the "write a little, test a little" scenario.

"Our software uses a version control repository, but we need to support multiple versions using branching. How will this work?"

This is an important point. *CI is run against the mainline* (head/trunk). You must ensure that this mainline is stable at *all* times. Development teams can become distributed or disjointed supporting various efforts, which makes communication more difficult. There are good reasons to create branches, but changes must be brought back to the mainline.

Although many build management systems can run builds for more than one development line, a "CI integration build" runs against the mainline.

Summary

This chapter identified some of the practices for building software. The build consists of the activities that create working software: compilation of source code, database integration, testing, inspection, deployment, and feedback. This list isn't exhaustive; consider other activities that can be made a part of the Integrate button.

Table 4-3 summarizes the practices covered in this chapter.

TABLE 4-3 CI Practices Discussed in This Chapter

Practice	*Description*
Automate builds	Create build scripts that are decoupled from IDEs. Later, these build scripts will be executed by a CI system so that software is built at every repository change.
Perform single command builds	Assuming certain tools have been downloaded, you should be able to type one command to execute a build from your build script to get the latest code and run an entire build.
Separate build scripts from your IDE	You should be able to run your automated build without needing an IDE.
Centralize software assets	To decrease the number of broken dependencies, centralize all software assets. This lessens the chance of broken builds when moving to a different machine.
Create a consistent directory structure	Create a consistent, logical directory structure, which makes it easy to build the software.
Fail builds fast	The faster the feedback occurs, the faster the problem can be fixed. Execute build activities in the order of what is most likely to fail *first.*

(Continued)

TABLE 4-3 CI Practices Discussed in This Chapter *(Continued)*

Practice	*Description*
Build for any environment	Run the same automated build on your workstation, on the integration build machine, and for any other platform environment as necessary.
Use a dedicated integration build machine	Use one machine dedicated to running your builds. Ensure that the integration location is free of old build artifacts.
Use a CI server	In addition to or as an alternative to running manual integration builds, use a CI server, such as CruiseControl, to automatically poll for version control changes and run an integration build on a separate machine.
Run manual integration builds	Run a sequential integration build manually using an automated build as an approach to reduce integration build errors. Some use this approach as an alternative to a CI server.
Run fast builds	Try to get your integration builds down to ten minutes by increasing computing resources, offloading slower tests, offloading or reducing inspections, and running staged builds.
Stage builds	Run lightweight "commit" builds that perform compile, unit test execution, and deployment followed by heavyweight "secondary" builds that include component, system, and other slower-running tests and inspections.

Questions

- Is your build automated? Are you able to run your build without your IDE?
- Have you centralized all of your software assets into your version control repository? Are you able to perform a complete build by getting all necessary files from the version control repository?
- Do you ensure that the build tasks that are more likely to fail are at the beginning of your build scripts so that you receive notification of a build failure quickly?

- Do you have an "Integrate button" for your software build processes? Is your database integration automated? Testing? Inspection? Deployment? Are you receiving and using feedback from the process?
- Does your integration build process occur on a separate machine?
- What is the duration of your integration builds? Are you seeking to shorten your build duration to improve feedback?
- Are you using a CI server to integrate your software? Or do you have a disciplined process for manually integrating builds?
- How often does your project perform integration builds: weekly, nightly, or hourly? Or is it at every change (continuously)?

Part II

Creating a Full-Featured CI System

Chapter 5
Continuous Database Integration

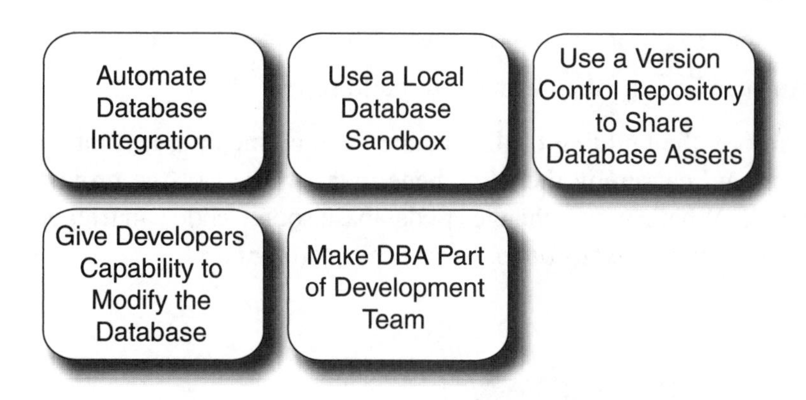

Things do not change; we change.
—HENRY DAVID THOREAU

Continuous Database Integration (CDBI) is the process of rebuilding your database and test data any time a change is applied to a project's version control repository.

Do you ever feel like your source code and database are operating in different "galaxies" throughout the development lifecycle on projects? As a developer, you may wait several days for a change to the database. You may even be restricted from making minor test data changes, or are afraid to make data changes for fear of ruining the one *shared* database for fellow developers. Situations like these are not unusual, and effectively utilizing CDBI can help alleviate some of these challenges and many others as well.

Revisiting the theme of the book, database integration is one of the parts of the Integrate button (see Figure 5-1), because it is based on the principle that database code (DDL, DML, configuration files, etc.) is, in essence, no different from the rest of the source code in a system. In fact, the artifacts related to database integration:

- Should reside in a version control system
- Can be tested for rigor and inspected for policy compliance
- And can be generated using your build scripts

Therefore, the building of the database can be incorporated into a CI system and can enjoy the same benefits as the rest of the project source code. What's more, changes to database source code can trigger an integration build *just as other source code changes do.*

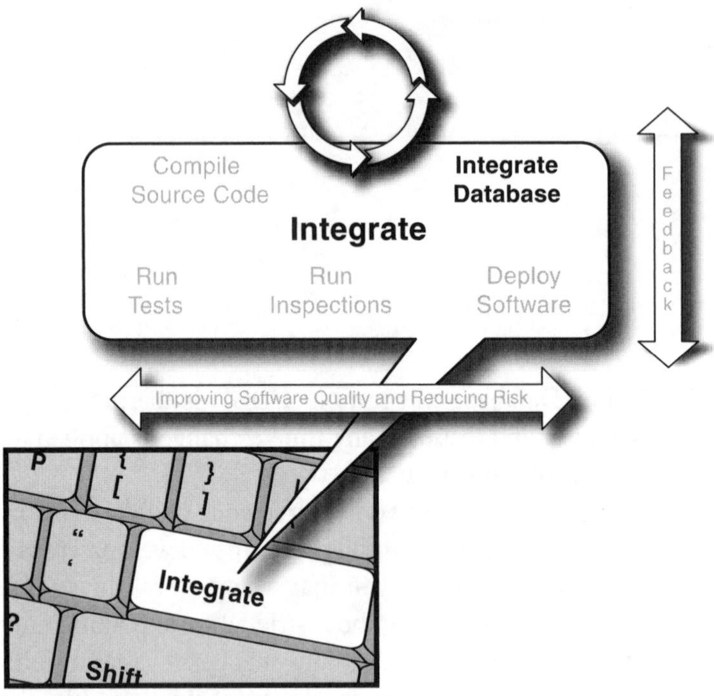

FIGURE 5-1 Database integration in the Integrate button

Not All Data Sources Are Alike

Some projects, or portions of projects, don't use a database exactly the way that we define it in this chapter. However, most projects need to persist data, be it in a flat file, an XML file, a binary file, or an RDBMS. Regardless of your chosen persistent store, the principles of CDBI apply.

As a first step in describing how to automate database integration with CI, we start by describing how to incorporate database integration into a build process. The scripts used to build, configure, and populate a database need to be shared with the rest of the project team, so we discuss which database files are committed to a version control repository. Automating a database integration build process solves only part of the problem, so we go one step further by rebuilding the database and data at *every* software change—making the verification process continuous. If a team is adopting CDBI for the first time, most people on a project will probably need to modify their development practices, so we finish the chapter looking at effective CDBI practices.

Refactoring Databases

The topics covered in this chapter could even be the subject of a separate book.[1] Other materials already make the case for treating your database as just another type of source code that is managed through the version control repository. This chapter gives you the essentials to automate and run database integration processes continuously.

1. In fact, Scott Ambler and Pramod Sadalage have much more in a book called *Refactoring Databases*. Martin Fowler and Pramod Sadalage wrote about similar topics in "Evolutionary Database Design," at www.martinfowler.com/articles/evodb.html.

Automate Database Integration

On many projects, a database administrator (DBA) can often feel like a short-order cook. DBAs typically have analytical skills that took many years to cultivate, but they often spend most of their time performing low-level command tasks. What's more, this job role can also be stressful, because the DBA often becomes a development bottleneck as the team members wait for the DBA to apply one small change to the database after another. Here's a familiar scenario.

Nona (Developer): Hi Julie, will you set up a development database for me on the shared development machine?

Julie (DBA): I am in the middle of something. I should be able to set it up later this afternoon. Would you like the data from last week or an export of today's data?

Nona: Today's data.

Julie: Okay, I can have that for you by tomorrow morning.

10 minutes later...

Scott (Technical Lead): I am unable to perform testing on the test server because there are no assigned records for the Reviewer role.

Julie: Oh, let me create some test records that are assigned this role. I think Nona may have used up all of those records.

Scott: Thanks. While you're at it, would you remove the Y/N constraint on the APPROVED columns on the PERSON table? We'd like to use different flags on this column.

It's more of the same on a typical day for the DBA. Not only is this a poor use of the DBA's talents, it causes a significant bottleneck, especially in the continuous approach promoted by CI. If you asked any DBA what they'd rather do on a day-to-day basis, they would probably tell you that they'd rather spend time on data normalization, improving performance, or developing and enforcing standards, not giving people database access or recreating databases and refreshing test data. In this section, you'll see how you can automate these repetitive tasks so both the DBA's and the team's time is spent on improving the efficacy and

TABLE 5-1 Repeatable Database Integration Activities

Activity	*Description*
Drop database	Drop the database and remove the associated data so that you can create a new database with the same name.
Create database	Create a new database using Data Definition Language (DDL).
Insert system data	Insert any initial data (e.g., lookup tables) that your system is expected to contain when delivered.
Insert test data	Insert test data into multiple testing instances.
Migrate database and data	Migrate the database schema and data on a periodic basis (if you are creating a system based on an existing database).
Set up database instances in multiple environments	Establish separate databases to support different versions and environments.
Modify column attributes and constraints	Modify table column attributes and constraints based on requirements and refactoring.
Modify test data	Alter test data as needed for multiple environments.
Modify stored procedures (along with functions and triggers)	Modify and test your stored procedures many times during development (you typically need to do this if you are using stored procedures to provide behavior for your software).
Obtain access to different environments	Log in to different database environments using an ID, password, and database identifier(s).
Back up/restore large data sets	Create specialized functions for especially large data sets or entire databases.

efficiency of the database—not on simple administration. Table 5-1 identifies database integration activities typically performed by a project member that can be automated.

Once you have automated these database-related tasks, you'll find yourself solving problems just by dropping and creating a database followed by inserting test data. This chapter's examples utilize Ant, but the principles apply to any build platform that supports communicating with a database. If your build platform is NAnt, Rake, or Maven, you can do the same things this chapter demonstrates. Listing 5-1 executes a series of SQL statements to create a database including its related tables, comments, constraints, and stored procedures. The script also applies test data for the given environment, such as development or

QA. Using this process, you can simply type `ant db:prepare`[2] from the command line and the build process will perform the tasks outlined in Table 5-1. If you'd like to see this same process using other tools, like NAnt or Maven, we've provided additional examples at the book's associated Web site.[3]

LISTING 5-1 build-database.xml: Automating Database Integration Using Ant

```
> ant -f build-database.xml db:prepare
Buildfile: build-database.xml

db:create:
      [sql] Executing file: data-definition.sql
      [sql] 8 of 8 SQL statements executed successfully

db:insert:
      [sql] Executing file: data-manipulation.sql
      [sql] 60 of 60 SQL statements executed successfully

BUILD SUCCESSFUL
Total time: 20 seconds
```

As you can see, using a single instruction from the command line enables the execution of SQL scripts that define (`db:create`) and manipulate a database (`db:insert`). We describe each of these tasks in more detail in subsequent sections.

Figure 5-2 shows the steps to automate your database integration.

The following sections present a discussion of each component in Figure 5-2.

Creating Your Database

To automate database integration, you must first create a database. In this script, you typically drop and recreate the database, enforce data integrity through constraints and triggers, and define database behav-

2. To manage other environments from the command line, incorporate a feature into your build script to override the default configuration. For instance, in Ant this would be `ant -Denvironment=devqa <targetname>`.

3. At www.integratebutton.com/.

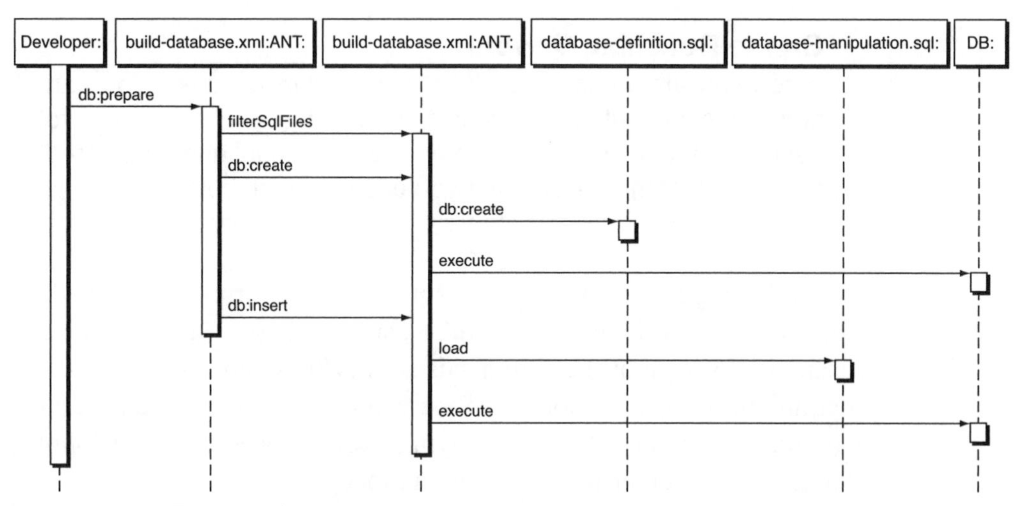

FIGURE 5-2 The sequence of automated database integration

ior through stored procedures or functions. We are using Ant to automate the *execution* of this process in Listing 5-2; however, as mentioned earlier, you can also use make, shell, batch, Rake, Ruby, or any number of tools. Notice that Ant provides a task to execute a SQL script via the `sql` task. Using a build platform like Ant allows you to perform the database integration activities using a sequential approach and enforce dependencies on other targets (a set of tasks) in the script. The example in Listing 5-2 demonstrates the use of Ant's `sql` attributes, such as `driver`, `userid`, and `password`, to connect to the database.

LISTING 5-2 build-database.xml: Defining Your Database Using an Ant Script

```
<target name="db:create" depends="filterSqlFiles" description="Create
  the database definition">
   <sql
      driver="com.mysql.jdbc.Driver"
      url="jdbc:mysql://localhost:3306/"
      userid="root"
      password="root"
      classpathref="db.lib.path"
      src="${filtered.sql.dir}/database-definition.sql"
      delimiter="//"/>
</target>
```

Create Reusable Scripts

When you are writing a script that you plan to reuse, you can define the attributes in a single file so that you only need to define them one time for use in all of your manual and automated scripts, rather than every time you use these attributes.

In Listing 5-3, data-definition.sql is the SQL script that's called by the Ant script in Listing 5-2. We're using a MySQL database in this example, so some of the commands are MySQL-dependent. The data-definition.sql file is responsible for creating the database and its tables, enforcing data integrity, and applying stored procedures. The following is a typical order for this creation process.

1. Database and permissions
2. Tables
3. Sequences
4. Views
5. Stored procedures and functions
6. Triggers

The order of creation within your DDL statements may vary based on database object dependencies. For example, you may have a function that depends on a view, or vice versa, so you may need to list the view first, for example.

LISTING 5-3 data-definition.sql: Sample Database Definition Script for MySQL

```
DROP DATABASE IF EXISTS brewery//
...
CREATE DATABASE IF NOT EXISTS brewery//

GRANT ALL PRIVILEGES ON *.* TO 'brewery'@'localhost' IDENTIFIED BY
'brewery' WITH GRANT OPTION//
GRANT ALL PRIVILEGES ON *.* TO 'brewery'@'%' IDENTIFIED BY 'brewery'
WITH GRANT OPTION//

USE brewery//
...
CREATE TABLE beer(id BIGINT(20) PRIMARY KEY, beer_name VARCHAR(50),
brewer VARCHAR(50), date_received DATE);
CREATE TABLE state(state CHAR(2), description VARCHAR(50));//
```

```
...
CREATE PROCEDURE beerCount(OUT count INT)
BEGIN
    SELECT count(0) INTO count FROM beer;
END
//
```

Technically Speaking...

You may find it easier to organize your targets and scripts by database definition type (such as a table, view, and function) or by subsystem (e.g., Property and Application).

Manipulating Your Database

Once you've created a database from a build script, you'll need to provide initial data (e.g., lookup tables) and test data for testing code that relies on the database. This is where you supply the test data for your particular environment or testing context. What's more, you may also find yourself needing to use different SQL data files to support different environments, like development, test, QA, and production environments.

The example in Listing 5-4 shows an Ant script pointing to a SQL file, whose contents are inserted as test data into a database.

LISTING 5-4 build-database.xml: Manipulating Your Database Using an Ant Script

```
<target name="db:insert" depends="filterSqlFiles" description="Insert
  data">
   <sql
      driver="com.mysql.jdbc.Driver"
      url="jdbc:mysql://localhost:3306/brewery"
      userid="brewery"
      password="brewery"
      classpathref="db.lib.path"
      src="${filtered.sql.dir}/database-manipulation.sql"
      delimiter=";"/>
</target>
```

The SQL script in Listing 5-5 represents test data. This is the script that is referenced in Listing 5-4. In a typical script, you'll have many more records than the three shown in Listing 5-5. Our intent is to give you an idea of what the SQL scripts often execute. Tools like DbUnit and NDbUnit[4] can help seed the data that is inserted into and deleted from a database as well.

LISTING 5-5 data-manipulation.sql: Sample Database Manipulation Script for MySQL

```
INSERT INTO beer(id, beer_name, brewer, date_received) VALUES (1,
'Liberty Ale','Anchor Brewing Company','2006-12-09');
INSERT INTO beer(id, beer_name, brewer, date_received) VALUES (2,
'Guinness Stout','St. James Gate Brewery','2006-10-23');
INSERT INTO state (state, description) VALUES('VT','Vermont');
INSERT INTO state (state, description) VALUES('VA','Virginia');
INSERT INTO state (state, description) VALUES('VI','Virgin Islands');
```

To achieve the benefits of automated database integration, you'll need to provide scripts for inserting, updating, and deleting data. These data manipulation scripts execute as part of an overall build process. Next, we discuss how to tie these scripts together with the orchestration script.

Creating a Build Database Orchestration Script

A database integration orchestration script executes the DDL and Data Manipulation Language (DML) statements. Listing 5-6 shows an Ant script that uses the `sql` task to call the data-definition.sql and data-manipulation.sql files we created in Listing 5-3 and Listing 5-5. You'll incorporate this orchestration into your higher-level build and integration processes.

LISTING 5-6 build-database.xml: Database Integration Orchestration Script Using Ant

```
<target name="db:prepare" depends="db:create, db:insert"/>
<target name="db:create">
...
<target name="db:insert" depends="filterSqlFiles">
...
```

4. DbUnit is available at www.dbunit.org/ and NDbUnit is available at www.ndbunit.org/.

Are You on Autopilot?

As you are automating your database integration, a few things may trip you up. It's easy for manual activities to unintentionally accumulate in your database integration process. Try to resist this. As Andrew Hunt and David Thomas mention in *The Pragmatic Programmer*: Don't Repeat Yourself (or DRY, for short), keep your build scripts "DRY." An easy form of "duplication" to miss is when we get acclimated to clicking through the database vendor's GUI application wizard rather than interfacing through the command line where it can run scripted. Another potential problem is the tendency to wait until there are many DDL/DML changes before committing back to the version control repository. Database changes can be pervasive, so try to make and check in small, incremental changes to your database; this will make it easier to test and debug.

Use a Local Database Sandbox

A significant challenge on many software development projects is making changes to the database structure. Many projects I've observed typically use one shared database, so when developers make changes to this shared development database they can adversely affect others on the team—causing each developer's private build to break (if their tests are part of the build). If developers have their own local code "sandbox" to isolate their coding changes from other developers, wouldn't it be great if they had a "database sandbox" too?

Multiple Database Instances

You may not have the resources to get a database for each developer. In this situation, you could assign each developer a separate schema on a central database server or use one of the freely available, lightweight, open source equivalent databases. Furthermore, many of the more widely used RDBMSs provide free developer versions.

Another important capability you gain by automating your database integration is that everyone on the team will be able to create a local instance of the database on their workstations. Every team member can then create a database "sandbox" to make and test database changes without affecting others. If your database integration is scripted, creating a new database instance is a push-button affair; conversely, if you don't automate your database integration, it is more difficult to recreate your database and run tests on your workstation. Figure 5-3 provides an illustration of each developer using a local database instance.

Using automated database integration, you are able to get the latest version of your database scripts along with your application source code. Each developer is able to create a local instance of the database, modify the version of the database on his workstation, test the changes, and commit the changes back to the repository. These changes will be integrated and tested with the rest of the software as part of the CI system. When another developer refreshes her private workspace with changes from the repository, the database changes are

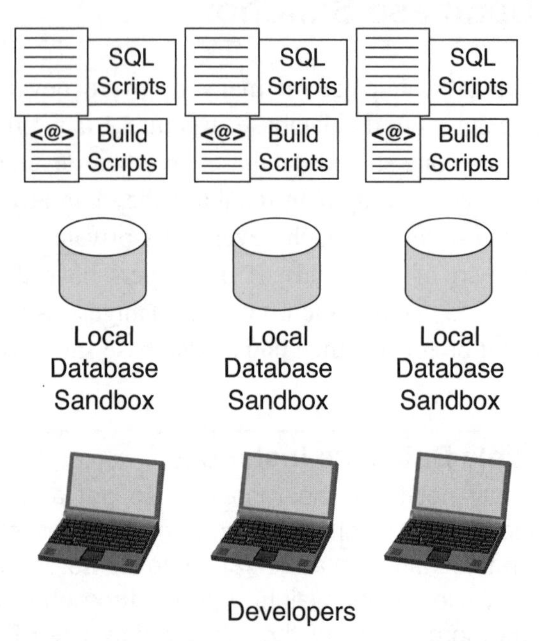

FIGURE 5-3 Each developer uses a local database sandbox

Supporting Multiple Database Environments

The next logical step after creating a local database sandbox is creating different database instances to support multiple database environments. For example, you may need to create a database that contains all of your migrated production data. Assuming there are many records in this database, you probably don't want to include it in your local development database. Usually, this will only be the DML (data changes), *not* the DDL (create, alter, and drop statements to the database). By automating your database integration, you can modify build script parameters to include the data to support these environments. This way, you can execute one command to provide data for different database environments. The same goes for versions. You may want to test new code against a prior version of the database. Use automated database integration to provide this capability with a "push of the Integrate button."

copied down to her workstation along with the other source code changes, and her next private build will incorporate the changes in her local database instance.

The next section identifies the reasons and approach for using a version control repository for database integration.

Use a Version Control Repository to Share Database Assets

Sharing your database integration scripts is a best practice, plain and simple. All software assets need to be in a version control repository, and this includes all database assets. Such assets might include the following:

- DDL to drop and create tables and views, including constraints and triggers
- Stored procedures and functions

- Entity relationship diagrams
- Test data for different environments
- Specific database configurations

For numerous project scenarios, you should be able to recreate your entire database from "scratch" using the scripts in your version control repository (for large data sets, you may store data export scripts rather than row-by-row DML scripts). Once you've applied all your database assets to the version control repository, you'll have a history of all of the database changes, so you can run prior versions of the database with the latest code (or with prior versions of the code as well). This also reduces the gridlock on projects when all the developers need to go to the DBA for everything. Once database assets are in one place, you can make a change to a database column, perform a private build on your machine, commit it to the version control system, and know you will receive feedback after the integration build is run.

Sometimes during development the database will need to undergo large-scale changes. In most cases, these changes will require the expertise of several people on the team and a longer duration to complete. When such situations arise, it is best to create a task branch[5] to commit the changes back into the version control repository rather than break the mainline and slow the activity of the rest of the team. Without CDBI, often the DBA will be making these large-scale database alterations, and he may be less suited to make all the changes at once to the database, dependent application source code, associated test code, and shared scripts because he may lack the knowledge of the source code that developers are writing.

Just as you have a consistent directory structure for your source code, you'll want to do the same for your database. Define the location of database assets—probably somewhere in the implementation/construction directory where your source code is located. In your database directory, define subdirectories for each of the database entity types and environments. Listing 5-7 shows a directory structure for an implementation directory (using a MySQL database).

5. In *Software Configuration Management Patterns,* Stephen P. Berczuk and Brad Appleton describe a *task branch* as having "part of your team perform a disruptive task without forcing the rest of the team to work around them. . . ."

LISTING 5-7 Sample Implementation Directory

```
implementation
    bin
    build
        filtered-sql
    config
        properties
        xml
    database
        migration
    lib
        mysql
    src
    tests
tools
    mysql
```

Just as with your source code, choose a directory structure that works well for you, one that clearly defines the entities while making it adaptable to changes.

Directory Structure and Script Maintenance

In the beginning, you may find that the directory structure is less important, but beware of making frequent directory structure changes, as you'll spend additional time updating your scripts to account for these changes.

Now that you've automated your database integration activities and are checking them into the version control repository to share with others on the team, let's make the process continuous so that it is run with every change to the software.

Continuous Database Integration

This is where the "rubber meets the road." The reason to automate, share, and build the database integration processes is so you can make these processes continuous. Using CDBI, your database and your source code are synchronized many times a day. Once you commit your database changes to your version control repository, the CI system proceeds like this: It gets a complete copy of the system source code, including your database data definition and manipulation scripts; recreates your database from the source; integrates your other source code; and then runs through your automated tests and inspections to ensure that the change(s) didn't introduce defects into your system's code base. Figure 5-4 demonstrates how the changes made by each developer are synchronized with the integration build based on the mainline in the version control repository.

Figure 5-4 shows that the changes that were made at 10 AM (by Mike) *and* the changes that were made at 10:15 AM (by Sandy) are

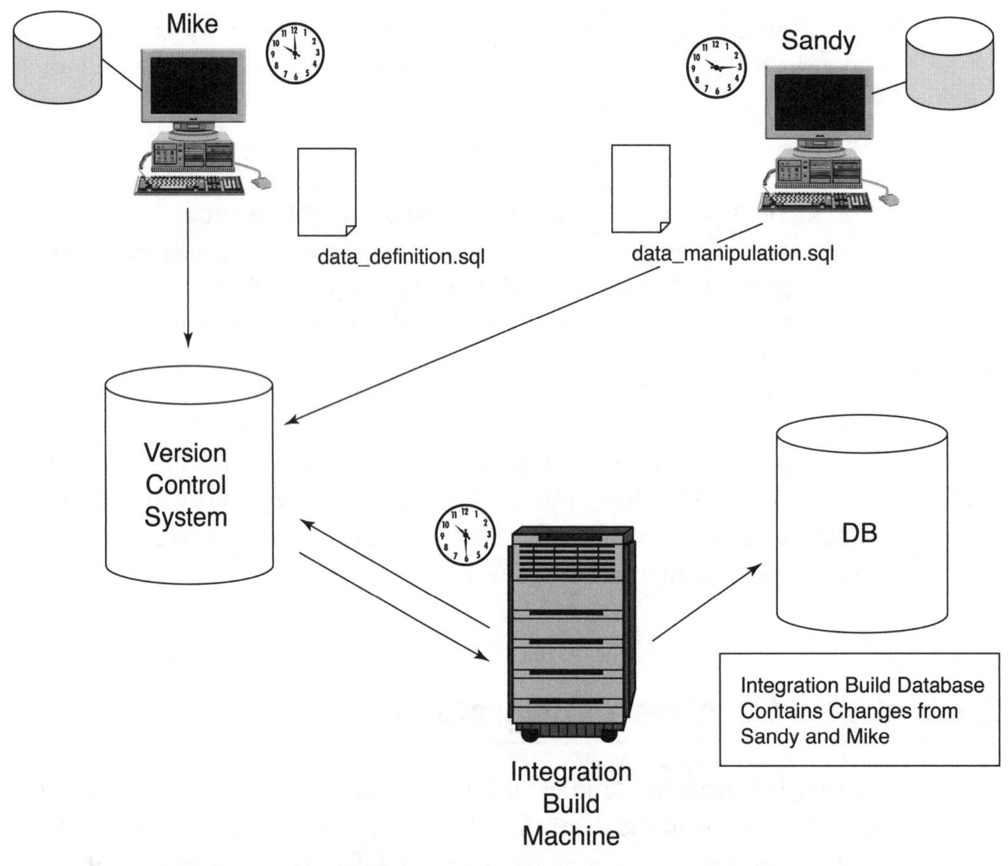

FIGURE 5-4 Single source for database changes

included in the integration build that occurred at 10:30 AM. The integration build machine uses a single source point, provided by the version control repository, to synchronize and test changes as a part of the integration build.

Once you have automated your database integration and incorporated it into your build scripts, making it run *continuously* is simple. Your database integration tasks, along with the rest of your build, should be executed using one command (such as an Ant/NAnt `target`). To run your database integration tasks continuously, you only need to make sure these database integration build task commands are executed as a part of the automated build.

Give Developers the Capability to Modify the Database

Each developer should have the capability to modify any of the database scripts. This doesn't mean that every developer *will* modify these database scripts, because not every developer will have the necessary database expertise. Because each developer will have his own database sandbox, each can modify the local database and then commit the changes to the version control repository. This will reduce the DBA bottleneck and empower developers to make necessary changes. The DBA can evaluate the new changes to the repository by reviewing the integration builds or working with the developers if the build breaks.

As the adage goes, with this additional authority comes additional responsibility. Changes to the underlying database structure can have far-reaching impacts on the system. The developer who makes changes to the database structure must assume the responsibility for thorough testing before committing these changes. We feel it is far more likely in today's industry for a developer to have a knowledge of databases and database scripting—and the DBA is still there to "oversee" what changes, if any, move into the system.

The Team Focuses Together on Fixing Broken Builds

Since you treat the database the same as the other source code, you may experience broken builds because of a database error. Of course, errors may occur in any part of your build: source code, deployment, tests, inspections, as well as the database. When using CDBI, database integration is just another part of the build, so the playing field is leveled: Whatever breaks the build, the priority is to fix it. The payoff comes after this; the fix is now integrated, and that particular issue is prevented from recurring.

Make the DBA Part of the Development Team

Break down barriers and make members of your database team a part of the development team. You may already be doing this, but all too often there is a "wall" between the DBA and the software developers. As mentioned earlier, treat your database code and your other source code in the same manner. The same goes for the people on your team. This is probably the most controversial of the CDBI practices. We've worked on teams that have used CDBI with the DBA on the development team, and we've also seen the more traditional approach with the DBA on another team, the database team. CDBI worked in both environments, but it worked significantly better when the DBA was a part of the team.

Some people ask, "If the DBA is no longer dropping and recreating tables, creating test environments, and granting access, then what is she doing?" The simple answer is, "Now she can do her job!"—spending more time on higher-level tasks such as improving database performance, improving SQL performance, data normalization, and other value-added improvements.

Database Integration and the Integrate Button

The rest of this book covers topics concerning the additional parts of the Integrate button: continuous testing, inspection, deployment, and feedback. This section covers some specific issues concerning these practices when it comes to database integration.

Testing

Just as with source code, you'll want to test your database. We cover testing in detail in Chapter 6. There are tools you can use for database-specific testing such as PL/Unit, OUnit for Oracle, and SQLUnit. Your database may contain behavior in stored procedures or functions that needs to be tested and executed as a part of the build script, just like the behavior of your other source code. You may also want to test the interactions of constraints, triggers, and transactional boundaries by performing application security data tests.

Inspection

As with your other source code, you should be running inspections on your data source. This includes not just your DDL, but reference and testing data as well. There are tools you can incorporate and run in your automated build process so that you do not need to run these inspections manually. Here are a few ideas for inspections on your database.

- Ensure efficient data performance by running `set explain` against your project's rules to target optimizations for your SQL queries.
- Analyze data to ensure data integrity.
- Use a SQL recorder tool to determine which queries are being run the most. These queries might be candidates for stored procedures.
- Ensure adherence to data naming conventions and standards.

Deployment

As we have indicated, the goal of CDBI is to treat your database source code and other source code in the same manner. The Continuous Deployment process will deploy your database to your development and test database instances just as it deploys your other code to its different environments (e.g., application servers). If you need to migrate from one database to another, you will be able to better test the migration process by running through the process on a continuous or scheduled basis.

Feedback and Documentation

When you incorporate continuous feedback and CDBI into your CI system, you will find out if your build failed because of the latest database changes. By default, most CI systems send the build status to the people who last applied changes to the version control repository. Just like with the source code, the CI system notifies those who made database changes quickly so that they can make the necessary fixes to the database.

Documentation is about communication, and there is much about the database you'll want to communicate to other project members or your customer. Your Entity Relationship Diagram (ERD) and data dictionary are excellent candidates for generating as a part of your continuous build process, perhaps as a secondary build (described in Chapter 4).

Summary

This chapter demonstrated that database assets are the same as other source code. Therefore, the same principles apply.

- Automate your database integration using orchestrated build scripts that are run continuously, after any change to your database or its source code.
- Ensure a single source for database assets by placing them in a version control repository.

- Test and inspect your database scripts and code.
- Change database development practices by ensuring that all database integration is managed through the build scripts, that all database assets are checked into version control, and that all developers (who interact with the database) have a database sandbox.

Table 5-2 summarizes the practices covered in this chapter.

TABLE 5-2 CI Practices Discussed in This Chapter

Practice	*Description*
Automate database integration	Rebuild your database and insert test data as part of your automated build.
Use a local database sandbox	All developers should have their own copy of the database that can be generated via SQL scripts. This can be on their workstations or even shared on a development server—as long as all developers have their own copy on this shared server.
Use a version control repository to share database assets	Commit your DDL and DML scripts to your version control system so that other developers can run the same scripts to rebuild the database and test data.
Give developers the capability to modify the database	Avoid the DBA bottleneck that occurs when database changes are restricted to just one or two people. Give developers the capability to modify the DDL and DML scripts and commit them to the version control repository.
Make the DBA part of the development team	Be sure the DBA can run the same automated build—which includes a database rebuild that other developers run—to ensure consistency. By making the DBA a part of the development team, the shared experiences can benefit both the database and the development teams.

Let's see how Julie, Scott, and Nona are doing now that they're using CDBI.

Nona (Developer): I need to refresh my test data. What do I need to do?

Scott (Technical Lead): Just run `ant db:refresh` from the command line. Before you do that, get the latest changes out of Subversion by typing `ant scm:update`, because I made a few changes to the USER database table and the source code that uses this change.

Julie (DBA): Do you guys need any help?

Scott: Yeah, we are having a performance problem on one of the queries. Do you have time to look at it? Also, I think we need to denormalize the PRODUCT table. Can you model the table changes, prototype the DDL changes, and set up a code branch so Nona can modify her code for your changes? When you two are satisfied with the changes, merge the branch and commit it to Subversion so that they run as part of the integration build. Thanks, Julie.

Nona: . . . Sure, Scott. Should we use the test database rather than the development database?

Scott: Yeah, just run `ant -Denvironment=test db:refresh`.

The developers and DBAs, who often perform roles that seem opposing or distant, are now continually working toward the same goal, and both are accomplishing more of their tasks that require analysis or design.

Questions

These questions can help you determine your level of automation and continuous database integration.

- Are you capable of recreating your database from your automated build process? Can you rebuild your database at the "push of a button?"
- Are the scripts (build and SQL) to your database integration automation committed to your version control repository?
- Is *everyone* on your project capable of recreating the database using the automated build process?
- During development, are you able to go back to prior versions of the database using your version control repository?
- Is your database integration process continuous? Are your software code changes integrated and tested with the latest database whenever you apply those changes to the version control repository?
- Are you running tests to verify the behavior of your database stored procedures and triggers?
- Is your automated database integration process configurable? Are you able to modify the userid, password, unique database identifier, tablespace size, and so on using a single configuration file?

Chapter 6
Continuous Testing

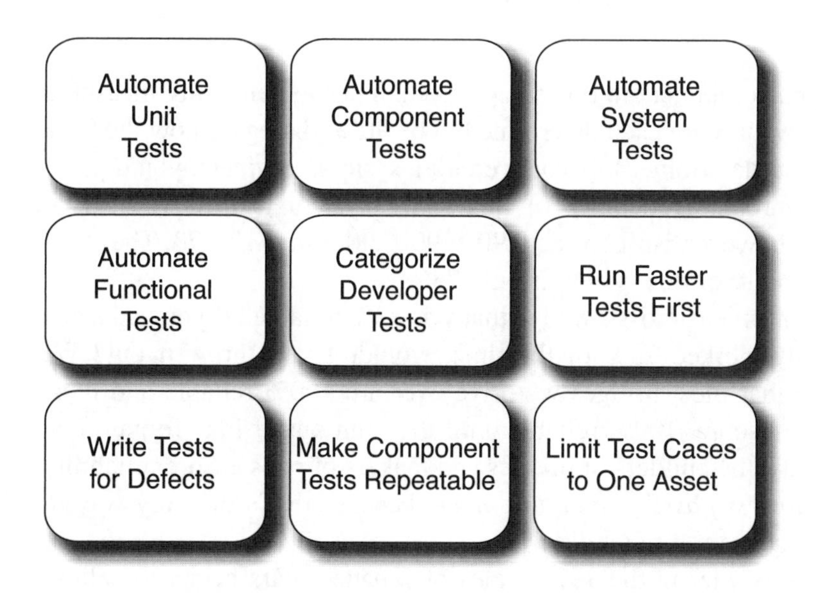

Practice makes perfect.
—ENGLISH PROVERB

re·li·a·ble—adjective—Giving the same result in successive trials.[1]

A tenet of systems engineering says that the reliability of a linear system is the *product* of the reliability of each of the system's components. For example, imagine a system with three components like that shown in Figure 6-1.

1. From www.m-w.com/cgi-bin/dictionary?va=reliable.

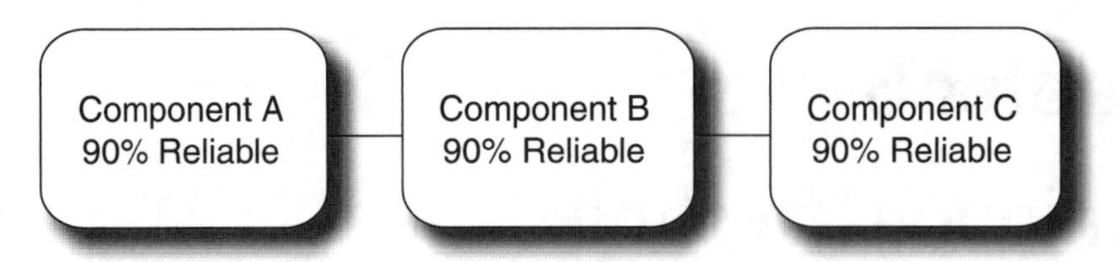

FIGURE 6-1 A system with three components

Each component in this sample system has its reliability measured and the values are each determined to be 90% (disregard how the 90% value was determined). If you weren't a systems engineer, you'd probably figure the reliability of this *entire* system is then 90%. That answer, however, isn't correct: .90 * .90 * .90 is *actually* .73. The overall reliability of this system is only 73%.

Ever driven across a bridge that was 73% reliable? If you had a pen that only worked 73% of the time, wouldn't you throw it out? We assume that most bridges we drive over are 100% reliable and most pens we use are 100% reliable until they run out of ink. To gain that reliability, the builders of bridges and makers of pens ensure reliability at the *lowest possible building block,* because that's the only way to ensure the overall reliability.

This is why in the 1970s sales of Japanese cars began to eclipse sales of U.S.-made cars. The Japanese manufacturers identified and applied this principle, and the reliability of Japanese-made cars was simply much better than their U.S. counterparts. The Japanese manufacturers realized they had to ensure reliability at the lowest possible level.

Now imagine a software system (which, by the way, is nonlinear—this essentially means you have to also consider the reliability of the interface or connector between each object). Probably none of us has ever worked on a software system with three components (i.e., objects) like in Figure 6-1. Most software systems have hundreds if not thousands of objects! A linear system composed of 100 components each having 99% reliability would yield a system that is only 37% reliable.

If you wanted to build a software application that had a Service Level Agreement of 100% (or close), you'd absolutely have to ensure reliability at the individual object level. If you can't ensure and measure reliability at the lowest level, you can't possibly do that at the system level. Yet this is how we, as an industry, have largely been constructing and delivering software. Design it, build it, then throw it over the wall to the Quality Assurance (QA) team, who tests at the system level and inevitably finds some number of defects. At some point, we then unleash the system on our customers, who unsurprisingly also find defects, sometimes to the detriment of corporate profits, your reputation, or both.

So as a bottom line, if we are to build software systems that are truly reliable, we have to ensure reliability at the object level, which can only be achieved through successful unit testing. Otherwise, we can't possibly hope to build highly reliable applications. Of course, just writing the unit test for an object doesn't necessarily guarantee reliability. The test must *effectively* exercise the use of the object; moreover, the test must be run *often.*

Because objects in a software system communicate with each other, tests must be run *any time* and *every time* something in the system changes. Building continuous testing into your CI system gives you this capability. Figure 6-2 shows you where we are in creating a

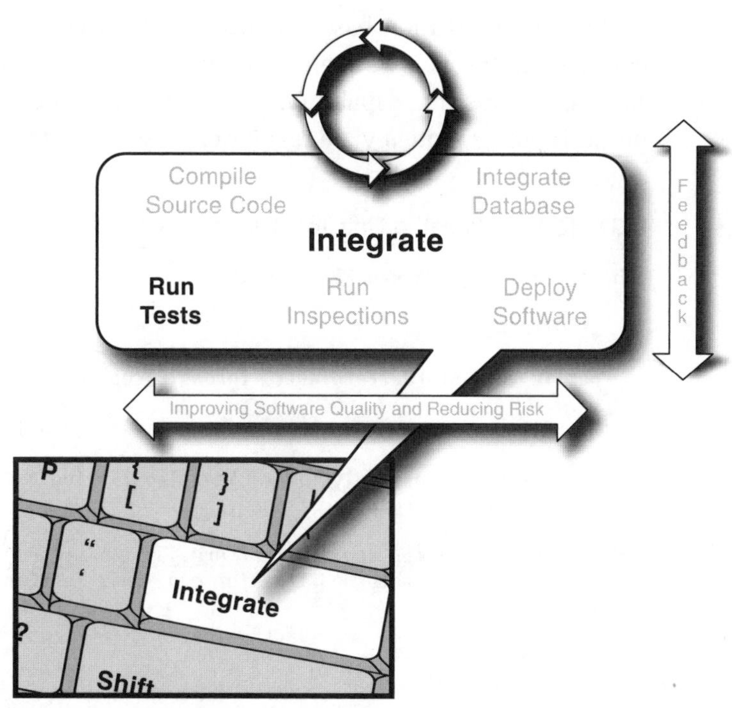

FIGURE 6-2 Integrate button—running automated developer tests

fully implemented, automated build and CI system using the Integrate button illustration.

Automate Unit Tests

People often use the term “unit test” rather broadly. This can cause confusion, especially when people start claiming their unit tests “take too long to run.” Defining a common vocabulary for developer tests can assist in categorizing them into efficient groups, which can make all the difference in creating an effective CI system capable of running fast builds.

Unit tests verify the behavior of small elements in a software system, which are most often a single class. Occasionally, though, the one-to-one relationship between a unit test and a class is slightly augmented with additional classes because the classes under test are tightly coupled.

Listing 6-1 shows a unit test written with the TestNG framework. TestNG is annotation-based, hence the `@testng.test` Javadoc-like comment in the `starPatternTest` method. This test case verifies, via Java 1.4’s `assert` capability, that the class `RegexPackageFilter` properly filters strings via a regular expression pattern.

LISTING 6-1 Isolated Unit Test Using TestNG

```
public class RegexPackageFilterTestNG {
    /**
     * @testng.test
     */
    public void starPatternTest() throws Exception{

        Filter filter = new RegexPackageFilter("java.lang.*");

        assert filter.applyFilter("java.lang.String"):
            "filter returned false";

        assert !filter.applyFilter("org.junit.TestCase"):
            "filter returned true for org.junit.TestCase";
    }
}
```

Some unit tests require minimal outside dependencies, which are *only* other classes. Those dependent classes are themselves simple and don't have deep object graphs. Occasionally, unit tests even employ **mocks,** which are simple objects that substitute for real, more complicated objects. If a dependent object itself does depend on an outside entity like a file system or database and isn't mocked, the test becomes a component test (defined next).

Listing 6-2 shows an example of a unit test written in Ruby that verifies the behavior of a filtering type. This test would still be considered a unit test even though it uses two classes, `RegexFilter` and `SimpleFilter`, because it only uses one *type* to verify behavior.

LISTING 6-2 Isolated Unit Test Using Ruby

```
require "test/unit"
require "filters"

class FiltersTest < Test::Unit::TestCase

  def test_regex
    fltr = RegexFilter.new(/Google|Amazon/)
    assert(fltr.apply_filter("Google"))
  end

  def test_simple
    fltr = SimpleFilter.new("oo")
    assert(fltr.apply_filter("google"))
  end

  def test_filters
    fltrs = [SimpleFilter.new("oo"), RegexFilter.new(/Go+gle/)]
    fltrs.each{ | fltr |
      assert(fltr.apply_filter("I love to Gooogle on the Internet"))
    }
  end
end
```

The key aspect for unit tests is having no reliance on outside dependencies such as databases, which have the tendency to increase the amount of time it takes to set up and run tests. Unit tests can be created and run early in the development cycle (i.e., day one). Because of the rapid time between coding and testing the results, unit tests are an efficient way of debugging.

Automate Component Tests

Component or **subsystem tests** verify portions of a system and may require a fully installed system or some external dependencies, such as databases, file systems, or network endpoints, to name a few. These tests verify that components interact to produce the expected aggregate behavior. A typical component test requires the underlying database to be running and may even cross architectural boundaries. Because larger amounts of code are exercised by each test case, more code coverage is obtained per test, and therefore, these tests tend to run longer than unit tests.

Listing 6-3 presents a sample component test that utilizes the DbUnit framework to seed a database, and then attempts to find data based on the contents of the database. DbUnit uses XML files, which it reads and then inserts the corresponding data into matching database tables.

LISTING 6-3 Component Test Using DbUnit

```
public class DefaultWordDAOImplTest extends DatabaseTestCase {
    protected IDataSet getDataSet() throws Exception {
        return new FlatXmlDataSet(new File("test/conf/wseed.xml"));
    }

    protected IDatabaseConnection getConnection() throws Exception {
        final Class driverClass =
              Class.forName("org.gjt.mm.mysql.Driver");
        final Connection jdbcConnection =
        DriverManager.getConnection(
           "jdbc:mysql://localhost/words",
          "words", "words");
         return new DatabaseConnection(jdbcConnection);
    }

    public void testFindVerifyDefinition() throws Exception{
        final WordDAOImpl dao = new WordDAOImpl();
        final IWord wrd = dao.findWord("pugnacious");
        for(Iterator iter =
              wrd.getDefinitions().iterator();
                                  iter.hasNext();){
            IDefinition def = (IDefinition)iter.next();
            TestCase.assertEquals(
                 "def is not Combative in nature; belligerent.",
                 "Combative in nature; belligerent.",
                 def.getDefinition());
        }
    }
```

```
    public DefaultWordDAOImplTest(String name) {
        super(name);
    }
}
```

Component-level tests use more dependencies than unit tests, but still not necessarily as many as higher-level system tests (defined shortly). Component-level tests exercise code via an API, but these *may or may not* be exposed to clients. In Listing 6-3, an object in a Data Access Object (DAO) layer is essentially tested via an exposed interface. Another example of a component test is exercising an action class in a Struts architecture via the StrutsTestCase framework, as shown in Listing 6-4. This test obviously requires a database to be running; however, the Web container is mocked out and the API exercised isn't necessarily exposed to clients.

In Listing 6-4, the StrutsTestCase framework has been combined with DbUnit to provide both a database seeding functionality and a mock container. The `DeftMeinMockStrutsTestCase` class is a template, which requires that the `getDBUnitDataSetFileForSetUp` method be implemented.

LISTING 6-4 Component Test Using StrutsTest

```
public class ProjectViewActionTest extends DeftMeinMockStrutsTestCase {
   public void testProjectViewAction() throws Exception {
      this.addRequestParameter("projectId", "100");
      this.setRequestPathInfo("/viewProjectHistory");
      this.actionPerform();
      this.verifyForward("success");

        Project project = (Project)this.getRequest()
          .getAttribute("project");
           assertNotNull(project);
           assertEquals(project.getName(), "DS");
  }

  protected String getDBUnitDataSetFileForSetUp() {
      return "dbunit-seed.xml";
  }

  public ProjectViewActionTest(String name) {
      super(name);
  }
}
```

This type of test is also commonly referred to as an **integration test.** The difference between this type of test and a system test is that integration tests (or component tests or subsystem tests) don't always exercise a publicly *preferable* API. For example, a system test would exercise a Web application through its Web pages, but a component test would exercise the business layer *under* the application Web pages.

Automate System Tests

System tests exercise a complete software system and therefore require a fully installed system, such as a servlet container and associated database. These tests verify that external interfaces like Web pages, Web service end points, and GUIs work end to end as designed. System tests have the tendency for lengthy runtimes in addition to prolonged set-up times. But when you are successfully running your automated unit and component tests, you are identifying a number of lower-level issues beforehand and you simply plan intervals for running this longer test, perhaps as part of a secondary integration build or even during off-hours, like overnight.

System tests are fundamentally different than **functional tests,** which test a system much like a client would use the system. For example, in Listing 6-5 the test mimics a browser by manipulating the site via HTTP; however, this test doesn't *use* a browser. A framework like Selenium,[2] which drives a browser, can be used to create functional tests. You still perform automated and manual functional testing at another interval after completing automated systems tests—one does not preclude the other.

Listing 6-5 contains a sample JWebUnit test case, which attempts a Web site login and then verifies whether the attempt was successful. While it may not be obvious in this code, the entire system (a servlet container and a database) has to be installed and running for this test case to work. Note that the setup here isn't in the test case but is part of a larger aspect of the build.

2. Selenium is a Web-based, cross-browser functional testing tool available at www.openqa.org/selenium/.

LISTING 6-5 System Test Using JWebUnit

```
public class LoginTest extends WebTestCase {

  protected void setUp() throws Exception {
     getTestContext().
         setBaseUrl("http://pone.acme.com/meinst/");
  }

  public void testLogIn() {
    beginAt("/");
    setFormElement("j_username", "aader");
    setFormElement("j_password", "a1445");
    submit();
    assertTextPresent("Logged in as aader");
  }
}
```

Automate Functional Tests

Functional tests, as the name implies, test the functionality of an application from the viewpoint of a client, which means the tests themselves mimic clients. These tests are also known as **acceptance tests.**

As mentioned earlier, frameworks like Selenium actually control a browser and enable it to interact with a Web site. Selenium tests are written in tabular forms, which represent a work flow, complete with commands and assertions. The code in Listing 6-6 is a Selenium test case that attempts a Web site login and then verifies if the attempt was successful.

LISTING 6-6 Functional Test Using Selenium

TestLoginSuccess		
open	/ib/app	
verifyTitle	Integrate Button - Welcome	
verifyTextPresent	Welcome to The IntegrateButton.com. Please log in to access exclusive material for the book.	
clickAndWait	link=Log In	
type	inputUserId	admin
type	inputPassword	admin
clickAndWait	loginSubmit	
assertTextPresent	Logout	

clickAndWait	Link=Logout	
assertTextPresent	Log In	
verifyTitle	Integrate Button - Welcome	
assertTextPresent	Welcome to The IntegrateButton.com. Please log in to access exclusive material for the book.	

As demonstrated in Listing 6-6, Selenium utilizes table models for testing, which are highly effective communication mechanisms that someone can author without needing to be a developer. As you can see, this test does a number of things: It verifies aspects of a page as well as fills in forms and verifies data.

We need a common understanding that tests are differentiated specifically by the setup they require (seeding databases, etc.), which correlates directly to how long they take to run. Test categorization is especially important in the context of CI—when builds run long in too many contexts, it can drastically affect you and your team's perception of CI.

Categorize Developer Tests

Writing and running tests is obviously a good thing, but unless we treat them as an architectural component that requires proper categorization and structure, they can start looking like a hurdle, instead of the key, to success. As the code base increases during your project, we're talking about *a lot* of tests—and if you run all written tests at all times in your CI system, builds take longer and longer to complete.

Categorizing developer tests into respective buckets (unit tests, component tests, system tests, and even functional tests) helps you to run slower running tests after the faster running tests. For example, running system tests every time the repository changes is a time- and resource-consuming task and delays notifying interested parties if there happens to be an issue with the build. If this delay is too long and developers have moved on to other activities, one of the primary benefits of Continuous Integration is not realized. Why not run unit tests every time someone checks code in, as they don't take much time to execute, and then schedule periodic intervals to run component tests (or after commit builds) and then another interval scheme for system tests? Those intervals can be increased as iterations come to a close, and you probably want to run them more often in the initial project stages too.

Frameworks like NUnit for .NET and versions of JUnit and TestNG for Java have annotations that make categorizing tests quite easy; in other frameworks, segregating tests is a bit more challenging. For example, with older versions of JUnit, there is no mechanism within the framework itself or within Ant to easily divide tests into three groups. This still can be achieved, however, with a simple *naming scheme* or, even easier, with an appropriate *directory strategy*.

One practice for developer testing is to place unit tests in a separate directory from the source code. For example, a project directory structure would have a `src` folder for the source code and a `test` folder for associated tests. A sample project could have a `root` directory like that shown in Listing 6-7.

LISTING 6-7 Sample Project Directory

```
root
      build.xml
      build.properties
      src/
      test/
```

The `src` directory contains directories that hold source code, while the `test` directory is further divided into more specific directories such `unit`, `component`, and `system`. For example, the directory listing would appear as shown in Listing 6-8.

LISTING 6-8 Directory Listing of test

```
test/
      unit/
      component/
      system/
```

The `unit`, `component`, and `system` directories in Listing 6-8 hold associated tests for each category. The `system` directory, for example, would have a directory structure which maps to the system tests' package names (which usually map to the corresponding class under the tests' packages), as shown in Listing 6-9.

LISTING 6-9 Sample Directory Structure of the system Folder

```
test/
      system/
       test/
        com/
         acme/
          stock/
            LogInTest.java
            AccountTest.java
```

Now that the tests are segregated into separate directories, your chosen build system needs an update. In the case of Ant, running categorized tests becomes a matter of defining targets that use the `batchtest` element found in Ant's JUnit task, which is displayed in Listing 6-10.

LISTING 6-10 The JUnit Task's batchtest Element

```
<batchtest todir="${testreportdir}">
   <fileset dir="test/unit">
     <include name="**/*Test.*"/>
         </fileset>
</batchtest>
```

The naming pattern referenced in the `include` element is generic—it's the directory referenced in the `dir` attribute of `fileset` that specifies what tests to run, which in this case are the unit tests.

Don't forget that you can also automate functional tests, such as those defined with Selenium; however, these tests will follow a different execution paradigm with additional test runners that can be easily segregated, for example, into unique Ant tasks. By defining a common manner for categorizing tests, such as through annotations or naming patterns, you are all set to instruct your CI system to run each category when appropriate, and your build times are completely manageable. This means that tests can be run at regular intervals instead of being abandoned when they take too long to execute.

Run Faster Tests First

Typically, the majority of a build's runtime is spent on tests, and the longest tests are those with dependencies on outside objects such as databases, file systems, and Web containers. Unit tests require the least setup (by definition, none), and system tests need the most (everything). By defining and grouping tests by type—unit, component, and system—development teams can fashion a build process that runs *test categories* rather than a gigantic test task that runs everything at once. Unit tests run most often (with every commit); component tests, system tests, and functional tests can be run with secondary builds or on periodic intervals.

Unit Tests

A true unit test should run to completion (successfully) in a fraction of a second. If a unit test takes longer, take a close look at it—it's either broken, or instead of being a unit test, it is really a component-level test. The XP mantra of "test a little, code a little, test a little..." is predicated on the notion of rapid testing. If unit testing takes enough time that the developer can focus on something else, it's taking too long. It will become a burden, and will soon become something to avoid instead of depend on.

In a CI environment, builds are run any time someone applies a change to the version control repository; therefore, unit tests should be run each time someone checks in code (called the **commit build**). There is little configuration cost, and the resource cost to run them is negligible.

Component Tests

Component tests, which usually have multiple dependencies, take a bit longer to run. As such, they should be run as part of secondary builds or periodically; regardless, they should be run before committing code into a repository (in your private build). As we covered in Chapter 4, component tests can be run as part of a secondary, and more "heavyweight," integration build that follows the commit build. Component tests have a specific cost to them: Dependencies have to be put in place and configured. These tests alone may only take a few seconds; however, in the aggregate, this time adds up. Some projects with lightweight component tests can get away with running them with every commit build.

For example, the component test shown in Listing 6-11 takes, on average, four seconds to run.

LISTING 6-11 Sample Component Test

```
using System;
using System.Collections;
using NUnit.Framework;
using NHibernate.Cfg;
using NDbUnit.Core.OleDb;
using NDbUnit.Core;

namespace NHibernate.words
{
   [TestFixture]
   public class WordTest
   {
      private const string CONN = @"Provider=SQLOLEDB..";
      private const string SCHEMA = @"Dataset2.xsd";
      private const string XML = @"XMLFile2.xml";

      private OleDbUnitTest fixture;
      private ISessionFactory sessFact;

      [SetUp]
      public void SetUp()
      {
         this.fixture = new OleDbUnitTest(CONN);
         this.fixture.ReadXmlSchema(SCHEMA);
         this.fixture.ReadXml(XML);
         this.sessFact =
             new Configuration().Configure().BuildSessionFactory();
      }

      [Test]
      public void verifyFinder()
      {

        this.fixture.PerformDbOperation(DbOperationFlag.CleanInsert);
        ISession session = this.sessFact.OpenSession();

        IQuery qry = session.GetNamedQuery("word.finder.bySpelling");
            qry.SetAnsiString("spelling", "pugnacious");
         IList list = qry.List();
```

```
        Assert.AreEqual(((Word)(list[0])).PartOfSpeech, "adj");
           session.Close();
        }
    }
}
```

This test does a couple of things that cause the total test time to increase, and it is also more complex to configure. First, the test seeds a database via NDbUnit,[3] which is a database seeding framework. In this case, NDbUnit does an insert of the data found in the XML file XMLFile2.xml, which also means an XML parsing step. This test case then configures `NHibernate`, and then a test is run and a word is retrieved from the database.

Any wonder why this test takes four seconds to run? Each additional test case in this class may not add too much time; however, execute this ten more times and the total time is now approaching a minute.

System Tests

System and functional tests, which require a fully installed system, take the longest to run. Additionally, the complexity of configuring a fully functional system occasionally limits the full automation of these tests. Running system tests with every commit build could be a recipe for disaster, but sometimes these types of tests are run with secondary or periodic builds. Otherwise, nightly (off-hour) runs are good for these tests.

The next time you add a test case to your build, consider the long-term implications of running all of your tests, and then start optimizing your build to categorize your tests so you can stage their execution.

Write Tests for Defects

Developer testing and CI may *decrease* the frequency of software defects, but the fact of the matter is that defects will *still* occur. That's

3. NDbUnit is an open source project for .NET, available at www.ndbunit.org/.

okay, though—mistakes happen and mistakes can be fixed and, ideally, learned from. Making the same mistake twice, though, is quite unforgivable.

Some use the term **defect-driven development** when referring to writing tests for defects; however, that term has always sounded rather negative. Defects don't *drive* development—*preventing* those nasty aberrations drives development! If anything, defects halt development—it's the act of addressing them and then ensuring they don't come back that keeps the wheels moving. Here is a proven strategy for guaranteeing that once a defect is found, it doesn't come back.

When a defect is discovered, find and isolate the offending code. If the project has a healthy number of test cases, it's probably a good bet that the defect has occurred in some portion of untested code (maybe an unconsidered path)—and most likely in the interaction of components. For example, Listing 6-12 presents a `find` method in a `Hibernate` DAO class, which attempts to retrieve a word from a database.

LISTING 6-12 DAO with a Defect

```
public IWord findWord(String word) throws FindException{
  Session sess = null;
  try{
    sess = WordDAOImpl.sessFactory.getHibernateSession();

    final Query qry = sess.getNamedQuery("word.finder.bySpelling");
    qry.setString("spelling", word);

    final List lst = qry.list();
    final IWord wrd = (IWord)lst.get(0);
    sess.close();
    return wrd;
  }catch(Throwable thr){
    try{sess.close();}catch(Exception e){}
    throw new FindException("Exception while finding word: "
        + word + " "+ thr.getMessage(), thr);
  }
}
```

This class has been reasonably tested in a series of component-level tests that utilize DbUnit. These tests verify the basic CRUD (create, read, update, and delete) operations. For example, Listing 6-13 shows a test for the `find` method.

LISTING 6-13 Sample Sunny Day Test Case

```
public void testFindVerifyDefinition() throws Exception{
  final WordDAOImpl dao = new WordDAOImpl();
  final IWord wrd = dao.findWord("pugnacious");

  for(Iterator iter = wrd.getDefinitions().iterator();
      iter.hasNext();){
        IDefinition def = (IDefinition)iter.next();
        TestCase.assertEquals(
          "def is Combative in nature; belligerent.",
          "Combative in nature; belligerent.",
          def.getDefinition());
  }
}
```

During functional testing of the larger application (in this case, a dictionary), it is discovered that if the user attempts to search for a word that isn't in the dictionary, the application heaves a nasty exception stack trace, which utterly confuses users. After some crafty detective work, someone discovers that the `findWord` method in `WordDAOImpl` throws an unexpected `IndexOutOfBoundsException` (which is masked by a `FindException`) if no word is returned via the `Hibernate` API.

This aberrant behavior wasn't accounted for! A defect has been discovered! All is not lost, though. Remember, we are forgiven for creating this defect, but only *once*. We have an opportunity to fix this nefarious glitch, but if it breaks *again* we should rethink our approach.

The first step in regaining your pride is to write a test case that exposes the defect. Read that sentence again slowly. Your first reaction may be to fix the offending code and move on to other, more exciting things (happy hour!); however, if you go that route, you lose an excellent chance to ensure that the same bug never comes back again. Start by writing a test case that triggers the same exact behavior that was reported in the defect summary. In this case, we need to cause the code to throw an `IndexOutOfBoundsException`, such as the one shown in Listing 6-14. Remember that we're writing a test to pass on the behavior, not to fail.

LISTING 6-14 Test Case Verifying the Defect

```
public void testFindInvalidWord() throws Exception{
  final WordDAOImpl dao = new WordDAOImpl();
  try{
     final IWord wrd = dao.findWord("fetit");
```

```
      TestCase.fail("This should throw an exception");
   }catch(FindException ex){
      Throwable thr = ex.getOriginalException();
      TestCase.assertTrue("Should be instance of " +
        IndexOutOfBoundsException",
         ex.getOriginalException() instanceof
            IndexOutOfBoundsException);
   }
}
```

If you run this test, it passes. Therefore, you've proven that there is a defect. Now you can fix it.

This methodology, by the way, is slightly different than the prevailing "defect-driven development" approach, which suggests writing a *failing* test case first and then to keep running that test (while fixing the defect) until the test stops failing. For example, the code in Listing 6-15 is a defect-driven test case.

LISTING 6-15 Sample Defect-Driven Style Test Case

```
public void testFindInvalidWordException() {
  final WordDAOImpl dao = new WordDAOImpl();
  try{
     final IWord wrd = dao.findWord("fetit");
  }catch (FindException e){
     TestCase.fail("Didn't find word fetit");
  }
}
```

This test case, of course, fails when first run (assuming the defect is still present). This practice does work; however, it presents some opportunities for refinement. Writing a test case that purposely fails at *first* present these challenges.

- It is difficult to write a failing test in this scenario that uses an assert properly.

  Because of this, asserts may not ever be added, even after the test case doesn't fail anymore. This means the test case isn't necessarily passing—it is merely not failing.

- At this point in the game, it is tricky to know how the fix will affect behavior, so in attempting to fail the test you end up guessing what the fix may be.

In Listing 6-15, the assumption is made that the fix will cause the code to no longer throw an exception. This is true, but it's only part of the whole story.

- Once a fix has been made in the code under test, the failing test works; however, it doesn't actually verify the change in behavior.

At this point, because the test case works, most people don't go back to update it. In our case, in order to fix the defect we in essence need to break the test, which is the opposite of what defect-driven development advocates.

Examining the code closely reveals that we need to check for an empty list before attempting to grab the first element. We're left with a design choice at this point—should the code return `null`, return an empty `Word`, or throw an exception? The decision is made to return `null` if the parameter value cannot be retrieved from the database via Hibernate (see Listing 6-16).

LISTING 6-16 Updated Code That Fixes the Defect

```
public IWord findWord(String word) throws FindException{
  Session sess = null;
  try{
     sess = WordDAOImpl.sessFactory.getHibernateSession();

     final Query qry = sess.getNamedQuery("word.finder.bySpelling");
     qry.setString("spelling", word);

     final List lst = qry.list();
     IWord wrd = null;
     if(lst.size() > 0){
       wrd = (IWord)lst.get(0);
     }
     sess.close();
     return wrd;
  }catch(Throwable thr){
     try{sess.close();}catch(Exception e){}
     throw new FindException("Exception while finding word: "
         + word + " "+ thr.getMessage(), thr);
  }
}
```

With the code under test conceivably fixed, the test is run again and this time it fails. This next decision is what differentiates this approach from others—in fixing our test case, we will assert the new behavior. The defect-driven example would work by now, and the chances are we'd leave the test case as so. But that test case doesn't provide too much value now. We need to assert that when an invalid word is passed into the `findWord` method, `null` is returned. We also need to assert than an `Exception` isn't thrown. The updated test case is shown in Listing 6-17.

LISTING 6-17 Updated Test Case Verifying the Fix

```
public void testFindInvalidWord() throws Exception{
  final WordDAOImpl dao = new WordDAOImpl();
  try{
     final IWord wrd = dao.findWord("fetit");
    TestCase.assertNull("Should have received back a null object", wrd);
  }catch(FindException ex){
     TestCase.fail("This should not throw an exception");
  }
}
```

Now we're done and we've accomplished two things. First, the defect has been corrected. Congratulations! Second, a regression test is now in place that truly asserts the correct behavior of the fix.

Which practice should we follow: defect-driven development, or should we call it **continuous-prevention development**? They both drive you to:

- Fix the defect
- And prevent the defect from recurring

Continuous-prevention development, however, has the tendency to drive you to carry out a third step, which is asserting any new behavior triggered by the defect's fix.

Make Component Tests Repeatable

Many Web applications work against databases. Databases, however, present quite a large dependency for testing, leaving you with two choices: Either mock out as much as possible and avoid the database altogether for as long as possible, or pay the price and utilize the database. The latter choice presents a new series of challenges—how do you control the database during testing? Even better, how do you make those tests repeatable?

By far, the easiest way to make your testing cake *and* eat it is to use a database-seeding framework like any of the xDbUnits (such as NDbUnit for .NET, DbUnit for Java, and PDbSeed for Python). These frameworks abstract a database's data set into XML files and then offer the developer fine-grained control as to how this data is seeded into a database during testing. For example, the snippet shown in Listing 6-18 is from a DbUnit XML seed file.

LISTING 6-18 Sample DbUnit Data File

```
<word WORD_ID="1" SPELLING="pugnacious" PART_OF_SPEECH="Adjective"/>
<definition DEFINITION_ID="10"
  DEFINITION="Combative in nature; belligerent."
  WORD_ID="1"
  EXAMPLE_SENTENCE="The pugnacious youth had no friends left to pick on."/>
<synonym SYNONYM_ID="20" WORD_ID="1" SPELLING="belligerent"/>
<synonym SYNONYM_ID="21" WORD_ID="1" SPELLING="aggressive"/>
```

Via DbUnit's `DatabaseTestCase`, the data in the XML file is manipulated via operations such as insert, update, and delete. The specific database is configured by implementing the abstract `getConnection` method, and the XML file is located via the `getDataSet` method (see Listing 6-19).

LISTING 6-19 Sample Database Test Case

```
public class DefaultWordDAOImplTest extends DatabaseTestCase {
    protected IDataSet getDataSet() throws Exception {
        return new FlatXmlDataSet(
          new File("test/conf/words-seed.xml"));
    }

     protected IDatabaseConnection getConnection() throws Exception {
        final Class driverClass =
              Class.forName("org.gjt.mm.mysql.Driver");

        final Connection jdbcConnection =
        DriverManager.getConnection(
              "jdbc:mysql://localhost/words",
             "words", "words");
         return new DatabaseConnection(jdbcConnection);
    }
```

```
    public void testFindVerifyDefinition() throws Exception{
       final WordDAOImpl dao = new WordDAOImpl();
       final IWord wrd = dao.findWord("pugnacious");

       for(Iterator iter =
          wrd.getDefinitions().iterator(); iter.hasNext();){
         IDefinition def = (IDefinition)iter.next();
         assertEquals("Combative in nature; belligerent.",
              "Combative in nature; belligerent.",
               def.getDefinition());
       }
    }

    public DefaultWordDAOImplTest(String name) {
        super(name);
    }
}
```

Note, though, that this class makes the assumption that the database is located on the same machine on which the test is run. This may be a safe assumption on the developer's workstation, but obviously this configuration can present a challenge in CI environments.

One solution is to pull out the hard-coded connection strings and place them into properties files. There is, however, a more effective mechanism. If DbUnit is utilized to seed a database, you can infer that the application itself then uses a database. If this is the case, it is a common practice to avoid hard-coding connection information within a code base; therefore, why not configure DbUnit to read the same file that the application under test reads?

For example, in Hibernate applications, database connection information is usually defined in the hibernate.cfg.xml file. You can easily write a utility class that parses this file and obtains the proper connection information. Even better, as shown in Listing 6-20, you can rely on Hibernate to provide the desired information.

LISTING 6-20 Hibernate Configuration Utility

```
public class DBUnitHibernateConfigurator {
 static Configuration configuration = null;

 private DBUnitHibernateConfigurator() {
  super();
 }

 private static Configuration getConfiguration()
    throws HibernateException {
```

```
    if (configuration == null) {
     configuration = new Configuration().configure();
    }
    return configuration;
  }

  public static IDataSet getDataSet(final String fileName)
      throws ResourceNotFoundException,
       DBUnitHibernateConfigurationException {
   try{
    return DBUnitConfigurator.getDataSet(fileName);
   }catch(DBUnitConfigurationException e2){
     throw new DBUnitHibernateConfigurationException(
        "DBUnitConfigurationException in getDataSet", e2);
   }
  }

   private static String getProperty(final String name)
      throws HibernateException {
    return getConfiguration().getProperty(name);
   }

  public static Properties getHibernateProperties()
      throws ResourceNotFoundException,
        DBUnitHibernateConfigurationException{
   try{
    final Properties hProp = new Properties();
    hProp.put("hibernate.connection.driver_class",
      DBUnitHibernateConfigurator.getProperty(
        "hibernate.connection.driver_class"));
    hProp.put("hibernate.connection.url",
      DBUnitHibernateConfigurator.getProperty(
        "hibernate.connection.url"));
    hProp.put("hibernate.connection.username",
      DBUnitHibernateConfigurator.getProperty(
        "hibernate.connection.username"));
    hProp.put("hibernate.connection.password",
      DBUnitHibernateConfigurator.getProperty(
        "hibernate.connection.password"));
    return hProp;
   }catch(HibernateException e){
     throw new DBUnitHibernateConfigurationException(
       "HibernateException in getHibernatePropertiesFile", e);
   }
  }

   public static IDatabaseConnection getDBUnitConnection()
      throws DBUnitHibernateConfigurationException{
    try{
     final Properties props =
       DBUnitHibernateConfigurator.getHibernateProperties();
     return DBUnitConfigurator.getDBUnitConnection(props);
    }catch(DBUnitConfigurationException e1){
     throw new DBUnitHibernateConfigurationException(
       "DBUnitConfigurationException in getDBUnitConnection", e1);
```

```
   }catch (ResourceNotFoundException e2) {
    throw new DBUnitHibernateConfigurationException(
      "ResourceNotFoundException in getDBUnitConnection", e2);
   }
  }
}
```

Note how the class in Listing 6-20 puts the Hibernate connection information in a `Properties` object, which is then converted into DbUnit's `IDatabaseConnection` type in a `DBUnitConfigurator` class. The DbUnit connection type is then returned via the `getDBUnitConnection` method. DbUnit's `IDataSet` type, which represents those XML files containing all the data, is returned via the `getDataSet` method. This method frees developers from having to provide a path to a file—something especially tricky in different environments.

In Listing 6-21, a custom abstract test case class can be created which requests that implementers feed the desired data set information for a particular test case.

LISTING 6-21 Convenient Test Case

```
public abstract class DefaultDBUnitHibernateTestCase extends
DatabaseTestCase {
 public DefaultDBUnitHibernateTestCase(String name) {
  super(name);
 }

  protected void setUp() throws Exception {
   super.setUp();
   DefaultHibernateSessionFactory.
      closeSessionAndEvictCache();
   DefaultHibernateSessionFactory.
      getInstance().getHibernateSession();
  }

  protected void tearDown() throws Exception {
   DefaultHibernateSessionFactory.
      closeSessionAndEvictCache();
   super.tearDown();
 }

  protected IDatabaseConnection getConnection() throws Exception {
   return DBUnitHibernateConfigurator.
      getDBUnitConnection();
  }

  protected IDataSet getDataSet() throws Exception {
   final String fileName = this.getDBUnitDataSetFileForSetUp();
```

```
    DatabaseTestCase.assertNotNull("data set file was null", fileName);
    return DBUnitHibernateConfigurator.getDataSet(fileName);
  }

  protected abstract String getDBUnitDataSetFileForSetUp();
}
```

A sample resulting test case that implements `DefaultDBUnitHibernateTestCase` is shown in Listing 6-22.

LISTING 6-22 The New Test Case in Action

```
public class WordDAOImplTest extends DefaultDBUnitHibernateTestCase {

 public void testUpdateWordSpelling() throws Exception{
  WordDAOImpl dao = new WordDAOImpl();
  IWord wrd = dao.findWord("pugnacious");

  wrd.setSpelling("pugnacious-ness");
  dao.updateWord(wrd);

  IWord wrd2 = dao.findWord("pugnacious-ness");
  assertEquals("should be id of 1", 1, wrd2.getId());
 }

 public void testFindVerifyDefinitionsSize() throws Exception{
  WordDAOImpl dao = new WordDAOImpl();
  IWord wrd = dao.findWord("pugnacious");

  Set defs = wrd.getDefinitions();
  assertEquals("size should be one", 1, defs.size());
 }

 protected String getDBUnitDataSetFileForSetUp() {
  return "words-seed.xml";
 }

 public WordDAOImplTest(String name) {
  super(name);
 }
}
```

DbUnit offers an API (as shown earlier) that can be utilized effectively via composition, which creates enormous opportunities for powerful combination frameworks, too. With this added flexibility, testing various architectures at different layers becomes quite easy. For example, developer testing of Struts applications can be challenging. A common tactic is to utilize a framework like HttpUnit, which simulates

HTTP requests; however, this can be tedious work and doesn't offer the desired precision for Struts architecture that heavily utilizes `Action` classes and a configuration for mapping requests.

The StrutsTestCase project was created to address this issue. With this framework you can easily isolate and test Struts' `Action` classes. This project, however, requires a developer to extend a base class which handles mocking of a servlet container. If a Struts application requires the use of a database, you may be left in a quandary.

Via DbUnit's API, a combination framework can be created that utilizes the seeding capabilities of DbUnit with the mocking capabilities of the StrutsTestCase project (see Listing 6-23).

LISTING 6-23 Combination Struts and Hibernate Test Case

```
public abstract class DefaultDBUnitMockStrutsTestCase
   extends MockStrutsTestCase {

 public DefaultDBUnitMockStrutsTestCase(String testName) {
  super(testName);
 }

 public void setUp() throws Exception {
  super.setUp();
  this.executeOperation(this.getSetUpOperation());
 }

 public void tearDown() throws Exception{
  super.tearDown();
  this.executeOperation(this.getTearDownOperation());
 }

 private void executeOperation(DatabaseOperation operation)
    throws Exception{
  if (operation != DatabaseOperation.NONE){
   final IDatabaseConnection connection =
     this.getConnection();
  try{
   operation.execute(connection, this.getDataSet());
  }finally{
   closeConnection(connection);
  }
 }
}

 protected void closeConnection(IDatabaseConnection connection)
   throws Exception{
  connection.close();
 }
```

```
 protected abstract Properties getConnectionProperties();

 protected abstract String getDBUnitDataSetFileForSetUp();

 protected IDatabaseConnection getConnection() throws Exception {
  final Properties dbPrps = this.getConnectionProperties();
  DatabaseTestCase.
    assertNotNull("database properties were null", dbPrps);
  return DBUnitConfigurator.getDBUnitConnection(dbPrps);
 }

 protected DatabaseOperation getSetUpOperation() throws Exception {
  return DatabaseOperation.CLEAN_INSERT;
 }

 protected DatabaseOperation getTearDownOperation() throws Exception {
  return DatabaseOperation.NONE;
 }

 protected IDataSet getDataSet() throws Exception {
  final String fileName = this.getDBUnitDataSetFileForSetUp();
  DatabaseTestCase.assertNotNull("data set file was null", fileName);
  return DBUnitConfigurator.getDataSet(fileName);
 }
}
```

Once again, you may be left with the option of hard-coding connection information or reusing existing files for this purpose. Testing a Struts application that uses Hibernate? Not a problem—just combine the new `DefaultDBUnitMockStrutsTestCase` with its handy utility for reading Hibernate files.

For example, Listing 6-24 is a class that implements a `DefaultMerlinMockStrutsTestCase` class, which combines the DbUnit capability of `DefaultDBUnitMockStrutsTestCase` with the handy Hibernate reader utility defined previously in Listing 6-20.

LISTING 6-24 The Combo Framework in Action

```
public class ProjectListActionTest
  extends DefaultMerlinMockStrutsTestCase {

 public void testProjectListAction() throws Exception{
  this.setRequestPathInfo("/viewProjects");
  this.actionPerform();
  this.verifyForward("success");

  IProject[] projects = (IProject[])this.getRequest().
     getAttribute("projects");
  assertNotNull("object was null", projects);
 }
```

```
 public ProjectListActionTest(String name) {
  super(name);
 }

 protected String getDBUnitDataSetFileForSetUp() {
  return "dbunit-project-seed.xml";
 }
}
```

Now you have one excellent test case, making it difficult for anyone to complain that they can't test this application in a repeatable manner.

Limit Test Cases to One Assert

During the drive of development with tight schedules and impending happy hours, it's tempting to try and fit everything into a test case. This haphazardness tends to lead to an abundance of assert methods ending up in one test case. For example, the code in Listing 6-25 attempts to verify the behavior of `HierarchyBuilder`'s `buildHierarchy` method as well as the behavior of the `Hierarchy` object in one test case.

LISTING 6-25 A Test Case with Too Many Asserts

```
public void testBuildHierarchy() throws Exception{
    Hierarchy hier = HierarchyBuilder.buildHierarchy(
        "test.com.vanward.adana.hierarchy.HierarchyBuilderTest");
    assertEquals("should be 2", 2,
        hier.getHierarchyClassNames().length);
    assertEquals("should be junit.framework.TestCase",
        "junit.framework.TestCase",
        hier.getHierarchyClassNames()[0]);
    assertEquals("should be junit.framework.Assert",
        "junit.framework.Assert",
        hier.getHierarchyClassNames()[1]);
    }
```

Note that there are three assert methods in Listing 6-25. This is a valid JUnit test case; there is nothing prohibiting the inclusion of multiple asserts in a test case. The problem with this practice, however, is that JUnit is built to be *fast-failing*. If the first assert fails, the whole test case is abandoned from the point of failure. This means that the next two asserts aren't run during that test run.

Once a code fix is completed and the test is rerun, the second assert may fail, which causes a repeat of the whole fix-rerun test case cycle. If when running the second try, the third assert fails, yet again, the process repeats. Notice an inefficient pattern here?

A more effective practice is *to try and limit one assert to each test case.* That way, rather than repeating the three-step process just described any number of times, you can get all your failures without intervention in *one test run.* For example, the code from Listing 6-25 would be refactored into three separate test cases (see Listing 6-26).

LISTING 6-26 Test Case Refactoring

```
public final void testBuildHierarchyStrSize() throws Exception{
    Hierarchy hier = HierarchyBuilder.buildHierarchy(
     "test.com.vanward.adana.hierarchy.HierarchyBuilderTest");
     assertEquals("should be 2", 2,
        hier.getHierarchyClassNames().length);
}

public final void testBuildHierarchyStrNameAgain() throws Exception{
    Hierarchy hier = HierarchyBuilder.buildHierarchy(
      "test.com.vanward.adana.hierarchy.HierarchyBuilderTest");
    assertEquals("should be junit.framework.TestCase",
       "junit.framework.TestCase",
       hier.getHierarchyClassNames()[0]);
}

public final void testBuildHierarchyStrName() throws Exception{
    Hierarchy hier = HierarchyBuilder.buildHierarchy(
      "test.com.vanward.adana.hierarchy.HierarchyBuilderTest");
    assertEquals("should be junit.framework.Assert",
       "junit.framework.Assert",
       hier.getHierarchyClassNames()[1]);
}
```

With three separate test cases, in the first test run, three failures are reported. This way, you can limit yourself to one fix-rerun cycle. This practice, of course, leads to a proliferation of test cases. This is why we have the separate directory structure introduced at the beginning of this chapter. And the number of test cases is growing at the rate of your code, so you must be making progress!

Summary

How reliable do you want your software to be? Source code is only as reliable as the test coverage, and tests are only as valuable as their execution frequency. By segregating tests into four *automatable* categories mapping to unit, component, system, and functional, a CI system can be configured to execute tests in an efficient manner. Unit tests can be run during checkins; component, system, and functional tests on some regular interval—such as with a secondary build.

Table 6-1 summarizes the practices covered in this chapter.

TABLE 6-1 CI Practices Discussed in This Chapter

Practice	*Description*
Automate unit tests	Automate your unit tests, preferably with a unit testing framework such as NUnit or JUnit. These unit tests should have no external dependencies such as a file system or database.
Automate component tests	Automate your component tests with unit testing frameworks such as JUnit, NUnit, DbUnit, and NDbUnit if you are using a database. These tests involve more objects and typically take much longer to run than unit tests.
Automate system tests	System tests are longer to run than component tests and usually involve multiple components.
Automate functional tests	Functional tests can be automated using tools like Selenium (for Web applications) and Abbot for GUI applications. Functional tests operate from a user's perspective and are typically the longest running tests in your automated test suite.
Categorize developer tests	By categorizing your tests into distinct "buckets," you can run slower running tests (e.g., component) at different intervals than faster running tests (e.g., unit).
Run faster tests first	Run your unit tests prior to running component, system, and functional tests. You can achieve this by categorizing your tests.
Write tests for defects	Increase your code coverage by writing tests based on new defects and ensuring that the defect does not surface again.
Make component tests repeatable	Use database testing frameworks to make certain that the data is a "known state," which helps make component tests repeatable.

Practice	*Description*
Limit test cases to one assert	Spend less time tracking down the cause of a test failure by limiting your automated tests to one assertion per test.

Questions

Use this list of questions to evaluate your test process in light of the CI environment and what it can provide for you.

- Are you categorizing your automated tests, such as unit tests, component tests, system tests, and functional tests?
- Are you configuring your CI system to run each test category with different staged builds?
- Are you writing automated unit tests for each defect?
- How many asserts are in each of your test cases? Are you limiting each test case to one assert?
- Are these tests automatable? Has your project committed automated developer tests to the version control repository?

Chapter 7
Continuous Inspection

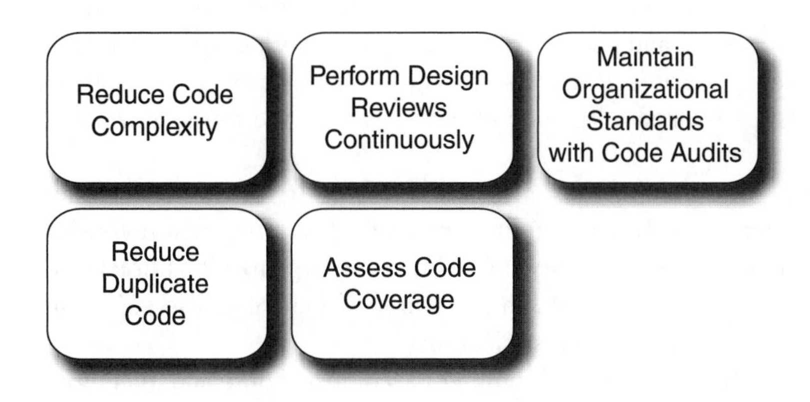

That man is great who can use the brains of others to carry out his work.
—DONN PIATT

Peer-based code reviews are generally considered beneficial to the overall quality of a code base because they present opportunities for an objective analysis by a second pair of eyes. For this same reason, XP's pair programming practice offers some of the same objective analysis benefits. Static source code analysis tools like Java's PMD and .NET's FxCop, which scan files for violations of predefined rules, offer some of the same analysis benefits.

All three of these techniques for code analysis (code reviews, pair programming, and static code analysis), however, are only marginally useful unless rigorously applied—their analysis benefits fade over time without proactive reinforcement. Moreover, code reviews and pair programming are performed by humans, who are error prone and have a limited capacity to quickly and successfully conduct endless, repetitive tasks.

Code reviews, when conducted efficiently, such as through the venerable Fagan inspection process,[1] *can* be impressively effective; however, they are run by humans, who tend to be emotional. This means that colleagues may not be able to tell other colleagues when their code stinks, and people collaborating in a work environment have the tendency to *subjectively* review one another's work. There is also a time cost associated with code reviews, even in the most informal of environments.

Pair programming has also been shown to be effective when applied correctly. Having another pair of eyes constantly reviewing code can yield higher quality code; however, organizations practicing this innovative technique are in the minority. Pairs can also suffer the same issues of emotion and subjectivity.

The difference between human-based inspection and that done with a static analysis tool is twofold.

- These tools are incredibly cheap to run often. They only require human intervention to configure and run once—after that, they are automated and provide a savings as compared to a person's hourly rate.
- These tools harness the unflinching and unrelenting objectiveness of a computer. A computer won't offer compromises like "Your code looks fine if you say mine looks fine," and it won't ask for bio-breaks and personal time if you run an automated inspection tool every time the version control repository changes.

These tools are also customizable—organizations can choose the most relevant rules for their code base and run these rules *every* time code is checked into the version control repository. These tools become, in essence, tireless watchers of source code, which is practically impossible to mimic with human activity.

1. For more information on the Fagan inspection process, see http://en.wikipedia.org/wiki/Fagan_inspection.

These tools also work very well in geographically distributed teams (i.e., some developers work from home, others at the office, and others in another state, country, continent, etc.). It helps mitigate any additional risks with people out of range for verbal collaboration.

Automated static code analysis scales more efficiently than humans for large code bases; some tools offer hundreds of different rules, which a human can't possibly remember while reviewing a series of files. Moreover, running a tool's myriad rules against your code base will take less time than having your partner review *one package.* Having a human manage the review of *all* code is a costly proposition!

Automating code inspections with analysis tools handles 80% of the big picture and allows humans to intervene in the 20% that matters. For instance, Java's PMD will run 180+ rules against a file *every time* it changes. If a particularly important rule is violated, such as a high cyclomatic complexity[2] value, someone can take a look. Can you imagine trying to accomplish this targeting process manually? Why would anyone want to? The key to remember with automated code reviews is that they are not a replacement for manual ones—they are merely an enhancement for applying human intelligence where it's most needed.

We are not advocating an "either/or" scenario in which you must decide which review technique to use, automated or manual. Automated inspection tools augment in-person reviews, and they have become necessary because code has become infinitely longer and denser. The beauty with automating code inspections is that when you do perform a manual review, the process is much more effective because the low-level details of code have already been scanned. The human reviews become more focused on aspects that automated tools cannot process, such as whether the code meets the requirements and if it will be easy to maintain in the long run.

Figure 7-1 demonstrates how inspection is another piece of the one-command build necessary for running a CI system.

2. Cyclomatic complexity is the number of paths through a section of code such as a method. It is discussed more later in this chapter.

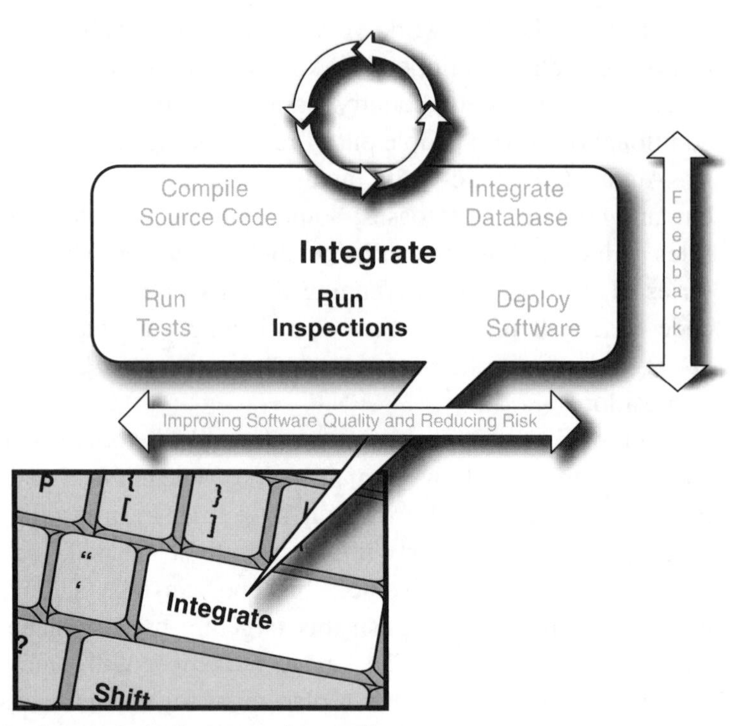

FIGURE 7-1 Integrate button—run inspections

What Is the Difference between Inspection and Testing?

There are subtle differences between inspecting and testing software. Testing is dynamic and executes the software in order to test the functionality. Inspection analyzes the code based on a set of predefined rules. Chapter 6 identified many types of testing, including unit, component, and system tests, which are executed against running software. Inspectors (or static and dynamic analysis tools) are directed by identified standards that teams should adhere to (usually coding or design metrics). Examples of inspection targets include coding "grammar" standards, architectural layering adherence, code duplication, and many others that we discuss in this chapter. Testing and inspection are similar concepts in the sense that both do not change the software code; they only show where problems may reside. You do not achieve higher quality software by inspecting and testing alone, of course; the value isn't manifested until you take action on the problems that are reported by the tests and inspections.

How Often Should You Run Inspectors?

Continuous inspection reduces the time between a discovery and a fix. You've also freed up more human time for actually devising the fix. Software inspection helps determine areas of the system that require greater attention. In reality, software development teams working manually can only conduct reviews of small, targeted areas of the system at a time. How do you determine which areas to examine, and how do you find this time? Then, not *if,* but *when* you find defects, you need the time after the review to correct the defects, and you must try to remember the logic and assumptions in place at the time. After this, the software components must be reviewed again.

On projects that perform manual reviews only, a problem may be introduced in the code several months before it is actually discovered. Time is lost, and the context of the problem may have been lost also. However, if your process of writing code is immediately followed by running automated inspectors (as well as tests, of course), you have built a secure future where defects will likely be discovered and fixed in a matter of minutes. Reducing the proximity between when a defect is introduced and when it is fixed improves code quality; of course, preventing defects from ever being introduced is even better, and inspections make this more likely, too.

Find Defects before They Are Introduced

Reduce the time between discovery of a defect and the subsequent fix by using continuous inspection.

Many IDEs have built-in inspection features to assist with automated code formatting, unused variables, and poor language usage—

to name a few. Using an IDE to run automated inspections locally is highly encouraged, but these inspections should also be run with an automated build and CI to prevent false positives and to ensure a repeatable and consistent approach.

Code Metrics: A History

Decades ago, a few smart people began studying code to see if there were measurements one could take that correlate to defects. This was an interesting proposition—by studying patterns in buggy code, the hope was that formal models could be created and used to detect problems *before they became defects*. When applied well, this has provided useful knowledge for code improvement.

Then some other smart people also decided to see if, by using code, they could measure developer productivity. On the surface, it seemed fair enough: "David produces more code than Bill; therefore, David is more productive and worth every penny we pay him. Plus, I noticed Bill hangs out at the water cooler a lot. I think we should fire Bill." It became evident, however, that this metric could become abused. Some lines of code measurements included the counting of comments; furthermore, this metric actually favors copy-and-paste style development. Later they said, "David wrote a lot of defects! Every other defect we find is assigned to him. It's too bad we fired Bill—his code is practically defect-free."

The classic metric of lines of code per developer as a means to indicate value was a spectacular disappointment.[3] Many managers may have been surprised, but most developers were not. Thankfully, that phase eventually led to a rebound phase where people came to view complexity as delivering less value, not the other way around.

3. From www.martinfowler.com/bliki/CannotMeasureProductivity.html.

Reduce Code Complexity

Have you ever noticed that long methods are sometimes hard to follow? Ever had trouble understanding the logic in an excessive, deeply nested conditional? Your instincts are correct. Long methods and methods with a high number of paths are hard to understand, and in fact they actually have been shown to be directly proportionate with defects.

A number of studies over time have shown a correlation between the number of paths through code and defects. One metric that arose from these studies is called the Cyclomatic Complexity Number (CCN). The CCN is a plain integer that measures complexity by counting the number of distinct paths through a method. Various studies with this metric over the years have determined that methods with a CCN greater than 10 have a higher risk of defects than other code of the same bulk.[4]

In Java, JavaNCSS[5] is an excellent tool that determines the lengths of methods and classes by examining source files, and it also counts the cyclomatic complexity of every method in a code base. By configuring JavaNCSS either through its Ant task or via a Maven plug-in, an XML report is generated, which lists these data:

- The number of classes, methods, noncommenting lines of code, and varying comment styles in each package
- The number of noncommenting lines of code, methods, inner classes, and Javadoc comments in each class
- The total number of noncommenting lines of code and the cyclomatic complexity

JavaNCSS ships with a few style sheets that can generate an HTML report summarizing the data. Figure 7-2 shows a sample HTML report generated by Maven.

4. From www.sei.cmu.edu/str/descriptions/cyclomatic_body.html.

5. JavaNCSS is available at www.kclee.de/clemens/java/javancss/. CCMetrics and Source Monitor provide CCN measurements for .NET.

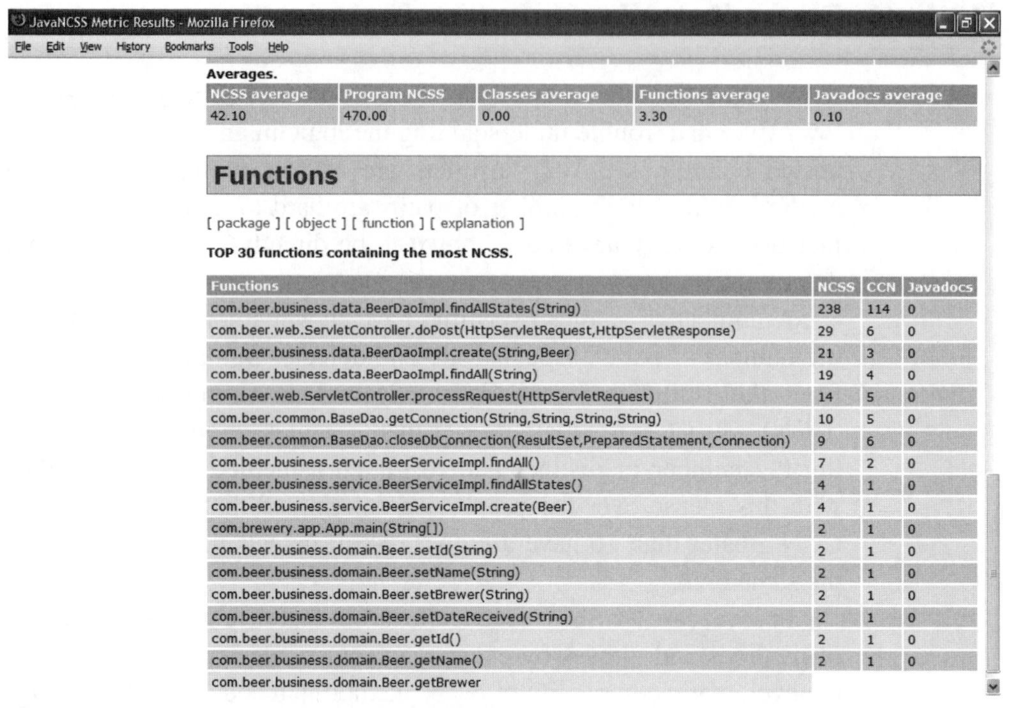

Averages.

NCSS average	Program NCSS	Classes average	Functions average	Javadocs average
42.10	470.00	0.00	3.30	0.10

Functions

[package] [object] [function] [explanation]

TOP 30 functions containing the most NCSS.

Functions	NCSS	CCN	Javadocs
com.beer.business.data.BeerDaoImpl.findAllStates(String)	238	114	0
com.beer.web.ServletController.doPost(HttpServletRequest,HttpServletResponse)	29	6	0
com.beer.business.data.BeerDaoImpl.create(String,Beer)	21	3	0
com.beer.business.data.BeerDaoImpl.findAll(String)	19	4	0
com.beer.web.ServletController.processRequest(HttpServletRequest)	14	5	0
com.beer.common.BaseDao.getConnection(String,String,String,String)	10	5	0
com.beer.common.BaseDao.closeDbConnection(ResultSet,PreparedStatement,Connection)	9	6	0
com.beer.business.service.BeerServiceImpl.findAll()	7	2	0
com.beer.business.service.BeerServiceImpl.findAllStates()	4	1	0
com.beer.business.service.BeerServiceImpl.create(Beer)	4	1	0
com.brewery.app.App.main(String[])	2	1	0
com.beer.business.domain.Beer.setId(String)	2	1	0
com.beer.business.domain.Beer.setName(String)	2	1	0
com.beer.business.domain.Beer.setBrewer(String)	2	1	0
com.beer.business.domain.Beer.setDateReceived(String)	2	1	0
com.beer.business.domain.Beer.getId()	2	1	0
com.beer.business.domain.Beer.getName()	2	1	0
com.beer.business.domain.Beer.getBrewer			

FIGURE 7-2 CCN report generated with Maven

This report section, labeled "Top 30 functions containing the most NCSS (Noncommenting Source Statements)," details the largest methods in the code base, which usually correlate to high cyclomatic complexity. For instance, the report lists the class `BeerDaoImpl`'s `findAllStates` method as having 238 lines of code and a cyclomatic complexity (labeled as CCN) of 114.

You may be wondering, "So what does that mean?"

Because high cyclomatic complexity values tend to correlate with defects, our next course of action is to verify the existence of any corresponding tests. If there are tests, how many are there? A rule of thumb for test coverage related to cyclomatic complexity is to have test cases equal in number to the cyclomatic complexity value (i.e., in the example of the `findAllStates` method, 114 test cases would be required). It would be unlikely to actually have 114 test cases for this method, but having a few is a great start in reducing the risk of defects in this method.

If there aren't any associated test cases, this method is wildly at risk and you should write some tests immediately. Some may think it's time to refactor; however, that would break the first rule of refactoring: Write a test case before you change anything.[6] Once test cases are in place, you can begin to lower your risk by refactoring. The most effective way to reduce cyclomatic complexity is to apply the **extract method technique**[7] and distribute the complexity into smaller, more manageable, and therefore more testable, methods. Of course, then the next step after creating each smaller method is to write inspectors and tests for it.

In a CI environment, evaluating a method's complexity *over time* becomes possible. The first time you run the inspection report, this method's complexity value can be monitored in subsequent inspections for any growth (or decline). If you see growth, you can then take appropriate action.

If a method's CCN value keeps growing, teams can

- Ensure a healthy number of related tests are present to reduce risk
- Evaluate the possibility of refactoring the method to reduce any long-term maintenance issues

Because JavaNCSS also reports on documentation trends, these values can be monitored for organizational standards. The tool reports single-line comments and multiline comments that occur in addition to Javadocs. In some software circles, the mere presence of a high count of inline code comments is an indication of complexity.

JavaNCSS isn't the only tool that can facilitate complexity reporting in the Java platform. PMD, another open source project that analyzes Java source files, has a series of rules that report on complexity, including cyclomatic complexity, long classes, and long methods. Checkstyle is another open source project with similar rules. Both PMD and Checkstyle have Ant tasks and Maven plug-ins like JavaNCSS.

6. See the section entitled The Value of Self-testing Code in Chapter 4 of Martin Fowler's book, *Refactoring*.

7. See www.refactoring.com/catalog/extractMethod.html.

Complexity has been shown to correlate with defects. Use your inspections to monitor a code base's complexity values, and take action to monitor trends or lower defect risks with test cases and refactoring.

Perform Design Reviews Continuously

There are other useful metrics that blossomed in the latter part of the twentieth century. Have you ever noticed that objects that have a lot of dependencies on other objects become somewhat *brittle?* If one of their dependencies changes, the object itself may break. From the other direction, when you change an object that every other object in a system depends on, it creates issues elsewhere. (This tendency is commonly referred to as the "collateral damage" effect.) It is important to be poised for unanticipated change (the one constant), and you don't want dependencies holding you back from creating changes that you wish to make.

Two metrics most helpful in determining over-coupling are known as **Afferent Coupling** and **Efferent Coupling** (sometimes called **Fan In** and **Fan Out,** respectively). These simple integer metrics count the relationships to or from objects. Both Afferent and Efferent Coupling signify an architectural maintenance issue: Either an object has responsibility to too many other objects (highly afferent) or the object isn't sufficiently independent of other objects (highly efferent).

These dependency metrics can be extremely helpful in determining the risk in maintaining a code base. Objects or namespaces/packages with too much responsibility present a risk when those objects need to be changed. If their behavior changes somehow, other objects in the software system may stop functioning as intended. Objects that are highly dependent on other objects present brittleness in the face of change—they too may stop functioning as intended if one of their imported objects changes, even in subtle ways.

What's more, both Afferent and Efferent Coupling can be combined to form an **Instability** value. For example, the following equation can represent an object's (or namespace's/package's) level of instability in the face of change. Note that a value of one is instable, while a value of zero is stable.

Instability = Efferent Coupling / (Efferent Coupling + Afferent Coupling)

NDepend for the .NET platform is an open source project that reports Efferent Coupling, Afferent Coupling, Instability, and a number of other interesting architectural metrics. These metrics are reported by assembly and by class. The tool is easily executed via NAnt and produces reports in both XML and HTML formats. The HTML report in Figure 7-3, for example, displays metrics for a .NET assembly, which in this case is the NUnit framework.

Note how the `nunit.framework` assembly has an Afferent Coupling of 204 and an Efferent Coupling of 43. This is the core code of the NUnit framework, which means this code can't change easily. Hence, the Instability value for this assembly is 0.17—because so many other objects depend on this core code, there is little chance that this code can change *without* something breaking quickly. For another assembly containing tests, `nunit.mocks.tests`, NDepend reported an

NDepend Report - Mozilla Firefox

File Edit View Go Bookmarks Tools Help

Assemblies Metrics

Assembly	# Types	# Abstract Types	# IL instruction	# lines of code	# lines of comment	% comment	Afferent Coupling	Efferent Coupling	Relational Cohesion	Instability	Abstractness	Distance
nunit.testutilities v2.2.8.0	42	1	973	121	108	47%	7	45	0.33	0.87	0.02	0.11
mock-assembly v2.2.8.0	6	0	65	8	165	95%	15	10	0.17	0.4	0	0.6
nonamespace-assembly v2.2.8.0	1	0	12	1	69	98%	5	5	1	0.5	0	0.5
timing-tests v2.2.8.0	2	0	91	17	65	79%	0	18	0.5	1	0	0
notestfixtures-assembly v2.2.8.0	1	0	10	1	49	98%	0	2	1	1	0	0
nunit.core v2.2.8.0	101	18	11722	1770	3620	67%	92	86	4.26	0.48	0.18	0.34
nunit-console-runner v2.2.8.0	3	0	1435	244	161	39%	4	59	1.33	0.94	0	0.06
nunit-gui-runner v2.2.8.0	14	0	24774	3411	1082	24%	7	275	1.86	0.98	0	0.02
nunit.mocks v2.2.8.0	11	5	850	138	161	53%	5	30	2.27	0.86	0.45	0.31
nunit.uikit v2.2.8.0	45	2	18830	2837	1644	36%	11	318	1.29	0.97	0.04	0.01
nunit.util v2.2.8.0	44	6	10972	1661	1906	53%	83	140	1.45	0.63	0.14	0.24
nunit.framework v2.2.8.0	49	6	4015	532	2428	82%	204	43	2.86	0.17	0.12	0.7
nunit.mocks.tests v2.2.8.0	6	1	1403	180	49	21%	0	26	0.83	1	0.17	0.17

FIGURE 7-3 NDepend report

Efferent Coupling value of 26 and an Afferent Coupling value of 0; therefore, the value is 1, or unstable. This makes sense—any time code changes, tests usually break (and if they don't, there could be issues with those tests).

Understanding these metrics for your code base can have dramatic effects on maintainability. For instance, assemblies with high Afferent Coupling should have a high degree of associated tests because, of course, with so much code dependent on that assembly, you want to guarantee it is reliable. Also, evaluating the long-term implications of Afferent Coupling could drive teams to decide to break assemblies into smaller, more flexible chunks of code.

Whereas high Afferent values belong to objects that do the breaking, assemblies with a high Efferent Coupling are subject to breakage. Again, having a healthy amount of code coverage for these assemblies will help teams spot troubles quickly. In a CI environment, monitoring these values over time can enable development teams to intervene sooner, before things get out of control. If you notice strong growth trends in coupling, teams can do any one or all of the following:

- Create tests right away based on the risks you have identified.
- Evaluate the long-term implications of any brittleness associated with that high coupling value.
- After running your tests, consider some refactoring to enable smoother changes in the future.

Much like NDepend for .NET, JDepend is an open source project for the Java platform that reports coupling metrics by package. JDepend can be run with Ant or Maven, and it produces reports in XML and HTML formats.

Architectural coupling metrics can effectively spot long-term maintenance issues for a code base by quantifying your assembly/package or object couplings. These metrics can provide insights into any associated risks in the face of change. What's more, monitoring these metrics on a regular basis in a CI environment effectively brings these risks to light *before* they become maintenance nightmares.

Maintain Organizational Standards with Code Audits

Coding standards facilitate a common understanding of a code base among a diverse group of developers. Just like the car maintenance market has been largely standardized so that you can buy a new headlight from your manufacturer or any number of third-party vendors, so too can a code base's "structure" become standardized, which permits various individuals to quickly assess behavior and modify it as needed. This makes your response in development faster, and keeps you from being dependent on one certain developer or team to make changes.

As mentioned earlier, while both human code reviews and pair programming can be effective in monitoring coding standards, they do not scale as well as automated tools. Not only do tools contain hundreds of rules (that are usually customizable), they can be run frequently and usually without intervention.

In a CI environment, a code analysis tool can be run *any time* a change is made to the project's repository. The tool can analyze an individual file when it is changed, or analyze the entire code base when structural or other system changes are made. What's more, due to the nature of CI, interested parties can be instantly notified of violations in architecture or coding. For instance, a popular code analysis tool for the Java platform PMD has more than 180 customizable rules in categories ranging from braces placement in conditionals to naming conventions, design conventions (like simplifying conditionals, etc.), and even unused code. In Java, if a conditional only has one statement following it, braces are optional. The code in Listing 7-1, for example, is completely legal in Java. Some organizations, however, find this code dangerous because later someone may forget to add braces when adding additional statements.

LISTING 7-1 Simple Conditional without Braces

```
if(status)
  commit();
```

The code in Listing 7-2 is completely legal; however, there is a subtle defect that could ensnare an unsuspecting developer who may think that a commit only occurs if status is true. Hint: The commit occurs no matter what. PMD, with its handy rule set, will find code that has the potential to cause these errors and signify them in a report.

LISTING 7-2 Simple Conditional with a Logical Defect

```
if(status)
  log.debug("committing db");
  commit();
```

Naming conventions are usually the first coding aspects defined by teams, since nondescriptive, terse variable names and methods can be somewhat difficult to comprehend (especially if the original author no longer works for the company). For example, the method shown in Listing 7-3 could use a better name, and the variables s and t are not very helpful in the larger context (you can figure out their type by examining the top of the method; however, if they were named more descriptively someone wouldn't be required to look back at the top of the method).

LISTING 7-3 A Poorly Named Method with Nondescriptive Variables

```
public void cw(IWord wrd) throws CreateException {
  Session s = null;
  Transaction t = null;
  try{
   s = WordDAOImpl.sessFactory.getHibernateSession();
   t = s.beginTransaction();
   s.saveOrUpdateCopy(wrd);

   t.commit();
   s.flush();
   s.close();
  }catch(Throwable thr){
   thr.printStackTrace();
   try{s.close();}catch(Exception e){}
   try{t.rollback();}catch(Exception e){}
   throw new CreateException(thr.getMessage());
  }
}
```

Once again, PMD comes to the rescue. Running PMD against this code would report rule violations for both the method name and those one-character variable names. By default, PMD's scanning lengths are set to 3; however, teams can modify these values for longer names if desired.

PMD can also facilitate the simplification of code. For example, the method shown in Listing 7-4, while syntactically correct, is rather verbose.

LISTING 7-4 Completely Legal Code, but Rather Verbose

```
public boolean validateAddress(){
   if(this.getToAddress() != null){
         return true;
   }else{
         return false;
   }
}
```

Once this method is flagged by PMD, it can be made more straightforward, as shown in Listing 7-5.

LISTING 7-5 A Simplified Method, Thanks to PMD

```
public boolean validateAddress(){
   return (this.getToAddress() != null);
}
```

PMD can be run via Ant or Maven and, like most every other inspection tool on the market, PMD produces an XML report that can be transformed into HTML. For example, the report in Figure 7-4 displays the violations for a series of .java files in a code base.

As mentioned earlier, PMD can also report complexity metrics like cyclomatic complexity, long methods, and long classes. Checkstyle is another open source tool available to Java developers, and it has extensive documentation and Ant and Maven runners capable of producing HTML reports. FxCop is a similar tool for the .NET platform with myriad rules and reporting capabilities. PyLint is available for Python.

By continuously monitoring and auditing code, your team can stay on track with architectural and coding guidelines. Issues are identified *early and often*, thus avoiding any long-term maintenance issues.

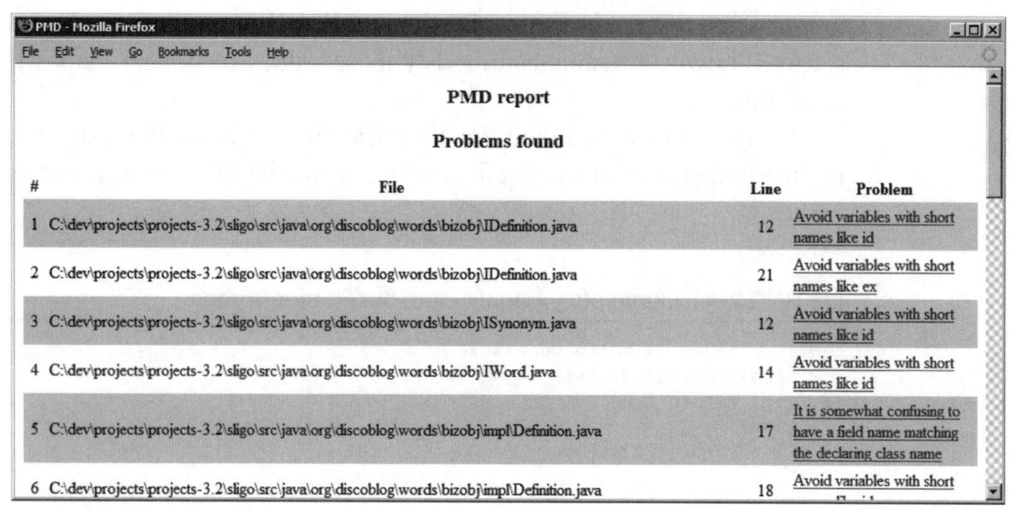

PMD report

Problems found

#	File	Line	Problem
1	C:\dev\projects\projects-3.2\sligo\src\java\org\discoblog\words\bizobj\IDefinition.java	12	Avoid variables with short names like id
2	C:\dev\projects\projects-3.2\sligo\src\java\org\discoblog\words\bizobj\IDefinition.java	21	Avoid variables with short names like ex
3	C:\dev\projects\projects-3.2\sligo\src\java\org\discoblog\words\bizobj\ISynonym.java	12	Avoid variables with short names like id
4	C:\dev\projects\projects-3.2\sligo\src\java\org\discoblog\words\bizobj\IWord.java	14	Avoid variables with short names like id
5	C:\dev\projects\projects-3.2\sligo\src\java\org\discoblog\words\bizobj\impl\Definition.java	17	It is somewhat confusing to have a field name matching the declaring class name
6	C:\dev\projects\projects-3.2\sligo\src\java\org\discoblog\words\bizobj\impl\Definition.java	18	Avoid variables with short

FIGURE 7-4 PMD report

Reduce Duplicate Code

Too often developers opt to copy and paste code rather than determining better ways to generalize, reuse, or abstract behavior. This problem of code duplication has existed since the first programs were written; moreover, researchers and developers alike have been working to eliminate the need to duplicate code for many years. Improvements to programming constructs—such as the introduction of procedural programming, object-oriented programming, and more recently, aspect-oriented programming—have all helped to reduce the need to duplicate code. However, the urge to copy and paste will always exist—and often, the problem is that the developer just doesn't realize he's doing it.

Copied-and-pasted code can occur in all areas of the system in one form or another, including

- Database logic, including stored procedures and views—for example, SQL
- Compiled source code—for example, Java, C, C++, and C#

- Interpreted source code—for example, ASP, JSP, JavaScript, and Ruby
- Build scripts—for example, make and Ant build files
- Data and configuration files—for example, ASCII, XML, XSD, and DTD

Michael Toomim, Andrew Begel, and Susan L. Graham[8] noted that "recent studies estimate that the Linux kernel (as of 2002) is 15%–25% duplicated,"[9] and "the Sun Java JDK is 21%–29% duplicated."[10] Code duplication is a real-life problem, even for popular software packages used throughout the industry.[11]

Duplicated code causes these problems:

- Increased maintenance costs due to discovering, reporting, analyzing, and fixing bugs multiple times
- Uncertainty about the existence of other bugs (duplicate code that hasn't been found yet)
- Increased testing costs for the additional code written

Using PMD-CPD

Several tools are available for finding duplicate code. PMD offers a Copy/Paste Detector (CPD) for C/C++, Java, PHP, and Ruby. The tool works fairly well, is simple to set up and use, and can generate output to XML, CSV, or text (ASCII). Listing 7-6 demonstrates using the CPD task with Ant.

---

8. See "Managing Duplicated Code with Linked Editing," at http://harmonia.cs.berkeley.edu/papers/toomim-linked-editing.pdf.

9. As referenced in the article "Analyzing cloning evolution in the Linux kernel," by G. Antoniol, M. D. Penta, E. Merlo, and U. Villano, in the *Journal of Information and Software Technology* 44(13):755–765, 2002.

10. As referenced in "CCFinder: A multilinguistic token-based code clone detection system for large scale source code," by T. Kamiya, S. Kusumoto, and K. Inoue, in *IEEE Transactions on Software Engineering*, 28(6):654–670, 2002.

11. See "Managing Duplicated Code with Linked Editing," at http://harmonia.cs.berkeley.edu/papers/toomim-linked-editing.pdf.

LISTING 7-6 Using CPD Ant Task

```
1      <property name="reports.pmd.dir"
            value="${reports.dir}/pmd-reports" />
2      <property name="reports.cpd.dir" value="${reports.pmd.dir}" />
3      <property name="cpd.output.type" value="text"
         description="csv,xml,text"/>
4      <property name="cpd.output.filename"
         value="cpd-results.${cpd.output.type}" />
5      <property name="cpd.output.dir" value="${build.dir}" />
6      <property name="cpd.outputfile"
         value="${cpd.output.dir}/${cpd.output.filename}" />
7      <target name="run-cpd">
8        <taskdef name="cpd"
             classname="net.sourceforge.pmd.cpd.CPDTask"
             classpathref="pmd.classpath" />
9        <cpd minimumTokenCount="20"
          outputFile="${cpd.outputfile}"
          format="${cpd.output.type}"
          ignoreLiterals="true"
          ignoreIdentifiers="true">
10         <fileset dir="${src.dir}">
11           <patternset refid="non.test.sources.pattern" />
12        </fileset>
13       </cpd>
14      </target>
```

- **Line 2**—Assigns the CPD report directory to the same directory where PMD reports are placed.
- **Line 3**—In this example, a text report is created. You can also create a comma-separated report or an XML report.
- **Line 9**—Invokes the CPD task. The attribute `minimumTokenCount` is used to determine how many tokens must match to be considered duplicated code. The `ignoreLiterals="true"` causes CPD to ignore string literals when evaluating a duplicate block. Likewise, the `ignoreIdentifiers="true"` does the same, but for identifiers (variables, methods).
- **Lines 10–11**—Specify the source code to check for duplication.

Using Simian

Another tool used to seek out copied-and-pasted code is Simian. Simian works with .NET 1.1 and later, and Java 1.4 and later. Listing 7-7 demonstrates how to use Simian in Ant.

LISTING 7-7 Using Simian in an Ant Task

```
1    <property name="reports.simian.dir"
         value="${reports.dir}/simian-reports"/>
2    <property name="simian.output.filename" value="simian-results.xml"/>
3    <property name="simian.output.dir" value="${build.dir}"/>
4    <property name="simian.outputfile"
         value="${simian.output.dir}/${simian.output.filename}"/>
5    <path id="simian.classpath">
6        <pathelement location="${lib.dir}/simian-2.2.17.jar"/>
7    </path
8    <target name="run-simian">
9        <delete dir="${reports.simian.dir}" quiet="true"/>
10       <mkdir dir="${reports.simian.dir}"/>
11       <taskdef resource="simiantask.properties"
             classpathref="simian.classpath"/>
12        <simian threshold="4" language="java">
13          <fileset dir="${src.dir}" >
14            <include name="**/*.java"/>
15            <exclude name="**/*Test*"/>
16          </fileset>
17          <formatter type="xml" toFile="${simian.outputfile}"/>
18        </simian>
19    </target>
```

- **Line 1**—Defines a property for the location of the Simian duplication report.
- **Lines 2–4**—Define a `simian.outputfile` property. The XML output file will be placed in the `build` directory.
- **Lines 5–7**—Create a Simian class path to load the Simian Ant task.
- **Lines 9–10**—Clean up any previous reports and prepare for a new duplication report.
- **Line 11**—Loads the Simian Ant task.
- **Line 12**—Invokes the Simian Ant task, with the duplication language to check set to `java`. The `threshold` attribute sets the minimum number of lines to be considered a match.
- **Lines 13–16**—Include the project source code; exclude any test code.

Simian comes with an XSLT style sheet to enable transformation of an XML report into HTML (see Listing 7-8).

LISTING 7-8 Generating a Simian HTML Report

```
1   <available property="simian.outputfile.present"
       file="${simian.outputfile}"/>
2   <target name="simian-report" if="simian.outputfile.present">
3      <xslt
          in="${simian.outputfile}"
          out="${reports.simian.dir}/Simian-Report.html"
          style="${config.dir}/simian/simian.xsl"/>
4   </target>
```

- **Line 1**—Checks for the existence of the Simian output file (XML) and sets the `simian.outputfile.present` property if the file exists.
- **Line 2**—Executes the `simian-report` target if the `simian.outputfile.present` has been set.
- **Line 3**—Generates the Simian report using the XSLT style sheet provided with the Simian distribution.

Figure 7-5 is a sample report that Ant and Simian generated for the code in Listing 7-7. Notice that the code in this example has 4.27% duplication, given the line threshold of 4.

Assess Code Coverage

There are different types of coverage measurements, but most tools focus on **line coverage** (also known as **statement coverage**). Line coverage simply indicates that a particular line of code was exercised. You obtain a test coverage measurement by exercising a code base with a test harness and capturing data that corresponds to code having been "touched" throughout the lifetime of the test process. The data is then synthesized to produce a coverage report. In Java shops, the test harness is commonly JUnit and the coverage tool is usually something like Cobertura, EMMA, or Clover. With .NET, NUnit may be the testing framework, and NCover and Clover.NET are commonly used as code coverage tools.

For example, if a method is ten lines long and seven lines of the method were exercised in a test run, then the method has a line coverage of 70%. The process works at the aggregate level as well: If a class

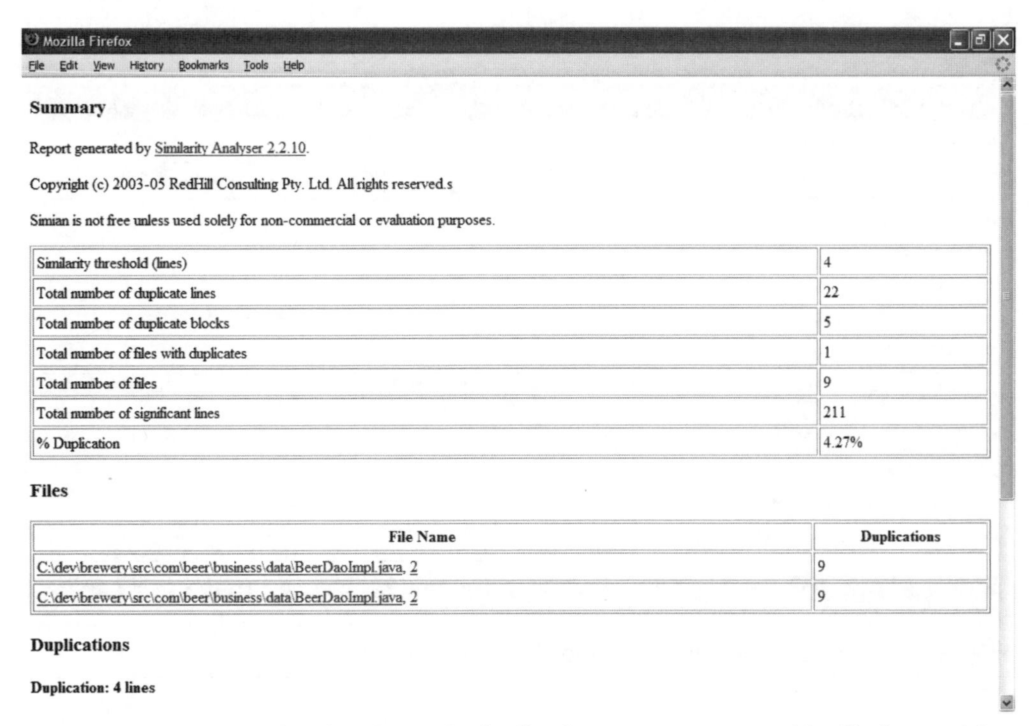

Mozilla Firefox

File Edit View History Bookmarks Tools Help

Summary

Report generated by Similarity Analyser 2.2.10.

Copyright (c) 2003-05 RedHill Consulting Pty. Ltd. All rights reserved.s

Simian is not free unless used solely for non-commercial or evaluation purposes.

Similarity threshold (lines)	4
Total number of duplicate lines	22
Total number of duplicate blocks	5
Total number of files with duplicates	1
Total number of files	9
Total number of significant lines	211
% Duplication	4.27%

Files

File Name	Duplications
C:\dev\brewery\src\com\beer\business\data\BeerDaoImpl.java, 2	9
C:\dev\brewery\src\com\beer\business\data\BeerDaoImpl.java, 2	9

Duplications

Duplication: 4 lines

FIGURE 7-5 Report showing the code duplication report generated by Simian and Ant

has 100 lines and 65 of them were touched, then the class has a line coverage of 65%. Likewise, if a code base comprises 10,000 noncommenting lines of code and 3,000 of them were exercised on a particular test run, then the code base's line coverage is 30%.

Some tools also offer reporting for **branch coverage** (sometimes referred to as path coverage). These tools attempt to measure the coverage of decision points, such as conditional blocks like `if` and `else`. As with line coverage reporting, if there are two branches in a particular method and both were covered through tests, then you could say the method has 100% branch coverage.

For example, in Maven environments, running EMMA requires two steps. First, you download the plug-in and place it into Maven's plug-ins directory. Second, you run the `emma` goal, which automatically compiles both the source code and the test code. EMMA then instruments the source code and runs the test code directly via the `test:test` goal. EMMA generates an HTML report like the one shown in Figure 7-6.

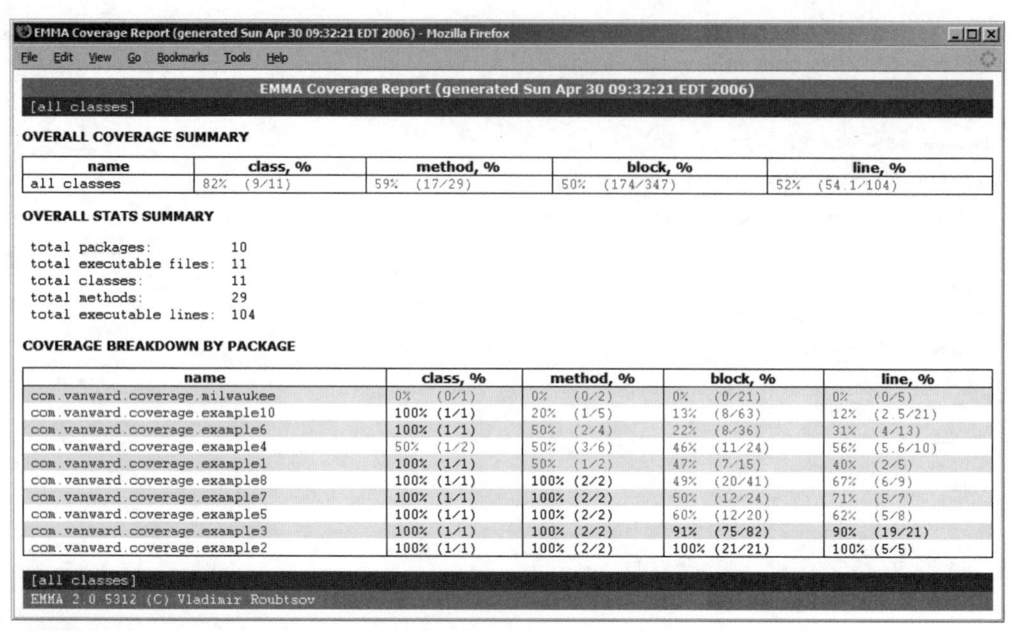

EMMA Coverage Report (generated Sun Apr 30 09:32:21 EDT 2006) - Mozilla Firefox

File Edit View Go Bookmarks Tools Help

EMMA Coverage Report (generated Sun Apr 30 09:32:21 EDT 2006)

[all classes]

OVERALL COVERAGE SUMMARY

name	class, %	method, %	block, %	line, %
all classes	82% (9/11)	59% (17/29)	50% (174/347)	52% (54.1/104)

OVERALL STATS SUMMARY

```
total packages:          10
total executable files:  11
total classes:           11
total methods:           29
total executable lines:  104
```

COVERAGE BREAKDOWN BY PACKAGE

name	class, %	method, %	block, %	line, %
com.vanward.coverage.milwaukee	0% (0/1)	0% (0/2)	0% (0/21)	0% (0/5)
com.vanward.coverage.example10	100% (1/1)	20% (1/5)	13% (8/63)	12% (2.5/21)
com.vanward.coverage.example6	100% (1/1)	50% (2/4)	22% (8/36)	31% (4/13)
com.vanward.coverage.example4	50% (1/2)	50% (3/6)	46% (11/24)	56% (5.6/10)
com.vanward.coverage.example1	100% (1/1)	50% (1/2)	47% (7/15)	40% (2/5)
com.vanward.coverage.example8	100% (1/1)	100% (2/2)	49% (20/41)	67% (6/9)
com.vanward.coverage.example7	100% (1/1)	100% (2/2)	50% (12/24)	71% (5/7)
com.vanward.coverage.example5	100% (1/1)	100% (2/2)	60% (12/20)	62% (5/8)
com.vanward.coverage.example3	100% (1/1)	100% (2/2)	91% (75/82)	90% (19/21)
com.vanward.coverage.example2	100% (1/1)	100% (2/2)	100% (21/21)	100% (5/5)

[all classes]

EMMA 2.0.5312 (C) Vladimir Roubtsov

FIGURE 7-6 EMMA coverage report for CruiseControl

Evaluate Code Quality Continuously

Now to the important part: How do we apply these measurements? You should use test coverage tools as part of a testing process in a CI environment, but *don't* overestimate what they can tell you. Remember that coverage reports are best used to expose code that hasn't been adequately tested. When you examine a coverage report, seek out the low values and ask why that particular code hasn't been tested fully.

QA can also use this information to fine-tune their functional testing. Knowing that certain sections of a code base are lacking in test coverage, QA can receive portions of an application in advance and focus their efforts in suspect areas.

Knowing this, development and QA teams can use test coverage tools in a CI environment to target manual functional testing.

Developer testing decreases the *risk* of defects in code; therefore, some development teams now require that unit tests be written alongside newly developed or modified code. CI helps ensure that this goal is met consistently throughout development, because these tests are run with every change.

Monitoring coverage reports helps development teams quickly spot code that is growing *without* corresponding tests. For example, running a coverage report in the beginning of the week shows that a key package in the project has a coverage rate of 70%. If later in the week that package's coverage has changed to 60%, you can infer that both

- The package grew in terms of lines of code, but no corresponding tests were written for the new code (or that newly added tests do not effectively cover the new code)
- And test cases were removed

Viewing the report regularly makes it easier to set goals and monitor progress, such as obtaining a certain coverage rate and maintaining ratios of test cases to lines of code. If you notice that tests routinely are not being written, you can take action by sending developers for training, mentoring, or pair programming.

The benefit of this is seeing trends in front of you. People can drift away from quality principles when deadlines are tight and the work is intense. Informed, proactive response to indicators is much better than pointing fingers later, when the customer discovers that "once in a lifetime" defect (which could have been exposed with a simple test months earlier), or the inevitable surprise (and anger) when management finds out some unit testing was overlooked.

Coverage Frequency

Because most code coverage tools instrument a code base with additional behavior for reporting purposes (i.e., the code has "listeners" that report when they've been executed), tests run slower than they do in noncoverage scenarios. This can have negative effects in a CI environment if the coverage process isn't well thought out. It may be most appropriate to run code coverage tools as part of a secondary, more heavyweight build.

If there are strategies for running tests at different stages (which map to test categorization), it makes sense, then, to create an additional strategy for the coverage process to run once a day as part of each categorical test run. For example, every time the repository changes, the unit tests are run. Using a secondary build or in regular intervals throughout the day, component tests are executed, and most likely once a day (usually during the evening) system tests are run. After the system test process is run, another series of tests can be run where coverage is turned on (i.e., unit tests run, then component tests, and then system tests). This process creates a series of reports the team can view the following morning.

Keep in mind that the three different reports have different perspectives, so be aware that uncovered code in one report may show high coverage in a different report. For example, the class Foo may have 0% coverage in the unit test report but may show high coverage in the system test report. Also, because the three coverage reports will be run, you must configure the build process to not overwrite, say, the unit coverage report that just got written with the component report that's coming next. Remember to do a move or to write each report to a unique location. Some tools, like Java's Cobertura, have a merge capability that lets you feed each into one master report.

In Listing 7-9, an Ant target is defined that merges the Cobertura coverage reports from three different test runs.

LISTING 7-9 The Cobertura merge Task in Action

```
<target name="merge-coverage" depends="all-coverage-run">
  <cobertura-merge datafile="${cobertura.all.ser}">
    <fileset dir="${base.dir}">
       <include name="${cobertura.comp.ser}" />
       <include name="${cobertura.unit.ser}" />
        <include name="${cobertura.sys.ser}" />
    </fileset>
   </cobertura-merge>

   <mkdir dir="${cov.report.dir}"/>
   <cobertura-report format="html"
         datafile="${base.dir}/${cobertura.all.ser}"
         destdir="${cov.report.dir}" srcdir="${src.dir}" />
</target>
```

Coverage and Performance

Here's an important point to remember, especially if you are running these processes at night: Consider whether these tests run at the same time as performance tests. This isn't very effective. Because the coverage process affects the test performance, we highly recommend you not run performance, stress, or load tests at the same time.

Listing 7-10 shows the JUnit task's `batchtest` element for running a series of component tests with coverage turned on. Note how a few tests (corresponding to load, stress, and performance categories) get excluded from the run. Much like you devise strategies for categorizing tests and their frequencies, think through your coverage report frequencies to obtain all of the benefits without any additional headaches from stressing out your computing resources.

LISTING 7-10 batchtest Element with Coverage Turned On, Excluding Tests

```
<batchtest todir="${testreportdir}">
   <fileset dir="test/component">
     <include name="**/*Test.*" />
     <exclude name="**/*StressTest.java" />
     <exclude name="**/BatchDepXMLReportPerfTest.java" />
     <exclude name="**/BatchDepXMLReportLoadTest.java"/>
   </fileset>
 </batchtest>
```

❑ ❑ ❑ ❑ ❑ ❑ ❑ ❑ ❑ ❑

Summary

In this chapter, you learned how to harness the power of CI—once again—by automating software inspections. No matter how mundane the anomaly, an inspection tool will consistently throw up flags on suspect code that more than likely will lead to bigger technical risks. Code inspections and reviews have proven to be an effective mechanism for discovering defects; however, by *continuously* performing this inspection process any time a change occurs (using CI), the time between the discovery and fix is consistently reduced.

As with testing, inspection can provide quantitative metrics of success to developers, management, the customer, and potential customers. Teams can quantify qualitative measurements by running inspectors on code to ensure quality thresholds are met, thus demonstrating the software's future performance in the user's environment.

Automated inspectors alone *will not* detect all problems, but by automating reviews and reporting before face-to-face code reviews, teams can concentrate on more interesting and complex analyses of code. Using automated software inspection tools puts the equivalent of *many* more eyes on the code. In performing continuous inspections, teams can see real benefits and timesavings. The inspection reports bring most routine violations to light, enabling more intelligent, speedy code reviews, improved decision-making capacity, and the best possible confidence as to the true health of a software system. Chapter 9 examines how you can utilize feedback from these inspectors to facilitate communication and rapid action.

Table 7-1 summarizes the practices covered in this chapter.

TABLE 7-1 CI Practices Discussed in This Chapter

Practice	*Description*
Reduce code complexity	Reduce cyclomatic complexity in your code base by leveraging automated inspectors such as JavaNCSS or CCMetrics to identify areas of your code with higher complexity. Run these inspectors from your automated build.
Perform design reviews continuously	Incorporate tools that can help determine packages/assemblies that are highly dependent on other packages and may lead to brittle architecture.
Maintain organizational standards with code audits	Run tools such as PMD or FxCop that report on coding standards violations from your automated build.
Reduce duplicate code	Reduce the amount of duplicate code in a code base by running tools such as Simian or CPD that pinpoint areas of higher code duplication based on custom thresholds. Use this information in targeted refactorings.
Assess code coverage	Leverage tools such as NCover, Cobertura, or Clover to identify line and branch coverage test code percentages. Use this information in determining areas that can use more tests.

Questions

The following questions will help you devise your own continuous inspection process.

- Do you perform unit testing sporadically, periodically, or continuously? How often do you run your full unit, component, and system test coverage review?
- Are you monitoring code complexity?
- Are you continuously performing automated design reviews with tools like JDepend and NDepend?
- Are you automating code audits with tools like PMD, Checkstyle, or FxCop?
- Are you monitoring code duplication?
- Are you able to assess code coverage? How are you reacting to the data?
- Do you know what percentage of your code has a corresponding test?
- Is your build properly configured to produce coverage reports?

Chapter 8
Continuous Deployment

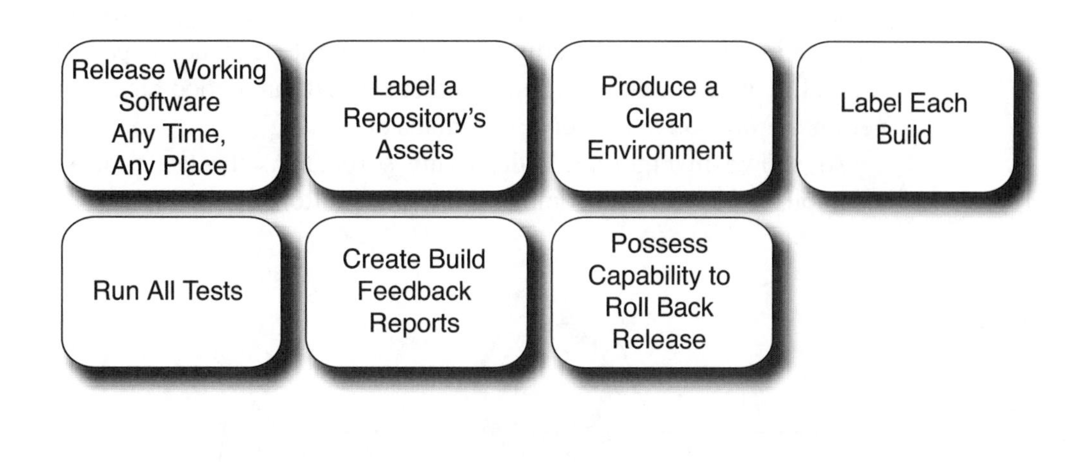

If you want a thing done well, do it yourself.
—ENGLISH PROVERB

If you are paid to write software, the organization that is paying you most likely expects you to provide *working* software to end users after a time span that is predictable and realistic. Therefore, it stands to reason that our industry would have figured out a rock-solid way to deliver high-quality, working software to end users on an expected schedule. But still we hear the stories of the "nightmare release" that went haywire, everyone was in a state of panic, lost sleep, got more gray hairs—and still may not have resulted with the end user getting a new release.

Creating working software efficiently is the reason for a professional software developer's existence. Without a successful deployment, the software doesn't even really exist. In today's world we create and release software much more frequently, so we have to get that process just as right as we get the development process. Continuous Integration then needs **Continuous Deployment,** a culmination of practices and steps which enable us to release working software any time, any place, with as little effort as possible.

This doesn't mean the process is easy, for though some of us have gotten it right, many of us haven't. Amazon, Google, and eBay are prime examples of organizations that release working software quickly. In fact, Tim O'Reilly reported that the lead developer of Flickr, the photo sharing Web site, indicated that, on a good day, they were *releasing* software every 30 minutes or so.[1]

As shown in Figure 8-1, deploying software is the last process accomplished by the one-command Integrate button.

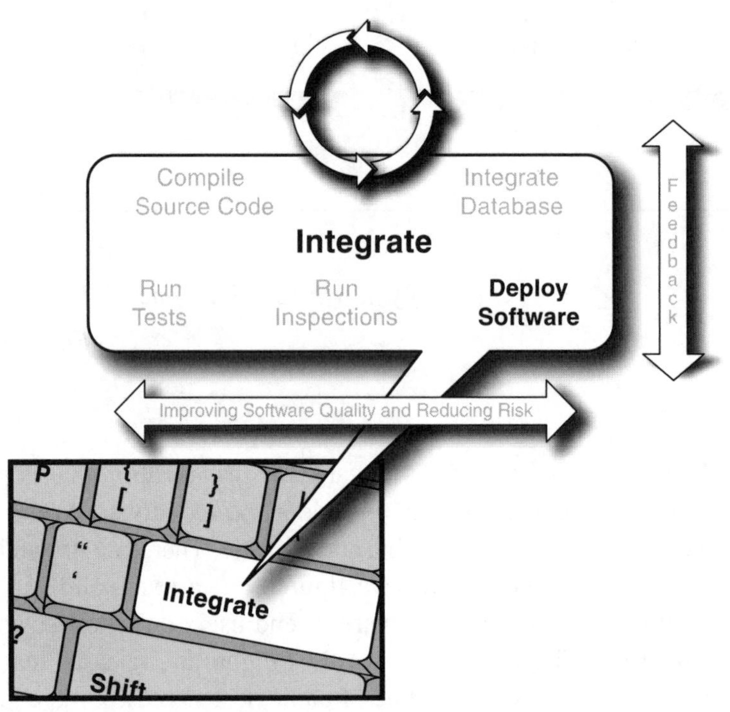

FIGURE 8-1 Integrate button—deploy software

1. See "What Is Web 2.0: Design Patterns and Business Models for the Next Generation of Software," at www.oreillynet.com/pub/a/oreilly/tim/news/2005/09/30/what-is-web-20.html.

Release Working Software Any Time, Any Place

Automated builds and repeatable builds. Automated tests and repeatable tests. Test categories and test frequencies. Continuous inspections. Continuous database integration. This string of tasks in creating an effective CI environment primarily enables one key benefit: releasing *working* software at any point in time, in any environment. As we said, if you can't release your software, then it's almost as if it doesn't exist.

What makes up a typical deployment? Regardless of platform, technology, or domain, deploying working software principally embodies six high-level steps.

1. *Label* a repository's assets.
2. Produce a clean environment, *free of assumptions*.
3. Generate and *label a build* directly from the repository and install it on the target machine.
4. Successfully run tests *at all levels* in a clone of the production environment.
5. Create build *feedback* reports.
6. If necessary, you can *roll back* the release by using labels in your version control repository.

Once your CI environment is established, these sometimes painful steps can become as easy as pushing the Integrate button. You still need to keep track of which of the delivered features were supposed to be delivered based on customer expectations (bill of materials), but you know that what *is* in there all works and constitutes working software.

The single command should be as simple as typing `ant deploy`.

Label a Repository's Assets

Creating a repository label facilitates the identification and tracking of assets, as it clearly delineates a group of files as belonging together. What's more, labels enable historical tracking of a group of files—and not just individual files, which may be on different versions at any given point.

For example, consider the files Foo.cs and Bar.cs in a repository, each on a different release version of your software (4.5 and 8.3, respectively). Both are related as one package, however, when they are grouped as a part of a repository label. As shown in Figure 8-2, 3_78 labels both Foo.cs (version 4.5) and Bar.cs (version 8.3) as belonging together.

Labeling repository versions is paramount in a disciplined software process, as it enables a smooth transition to newer versions of code by creating snapshots in time. These snapshots serve as a base for reporting—and in worst-case scenarios, rollbacks. These labels also allow parallel branches within a version control system, creating the capability to handle multiple development lines. The following demonstrates tagging a build for a particular release:

```
cvs -d:pserver:uname:passwd@cvs.ib.com:/cvsrepo rtag release_9 website
```

For example, having parallel branches with labels facilitates "bug fix" releases. If customers are using an application that was built off label `3_78` and the development team is working on a mainline (or trunk, the very latest version of any file in the CM system) of the repository, producing a point release from the trunk with bug fixes is risky, because there could be new features in this newer code or, even worse, new undiscovered defects. But by working off the `3_78` label, developers can add the required fixes and produce a stable build that doesn't necessarily contain new features that exist on the trunk.

Once a release has been labeled, generating that same release becomes quite simple. For example, via Ant, you can check out a labeled group of assets from CVS by specifying the label identifier (see Listing 8-1).

LISTING 8-1 Checking Out a Labeled Version from CVS

```
<cvs
cvsRoot=":pserver:${cvs.usern}:${cvs.passw}@${cvs.server.hostname}:
${cvs.server.path}" package="${cvs.module}" tag="${cvs.tag.id}"
dest="${cvs.module.dest}" command="checkout" />
```

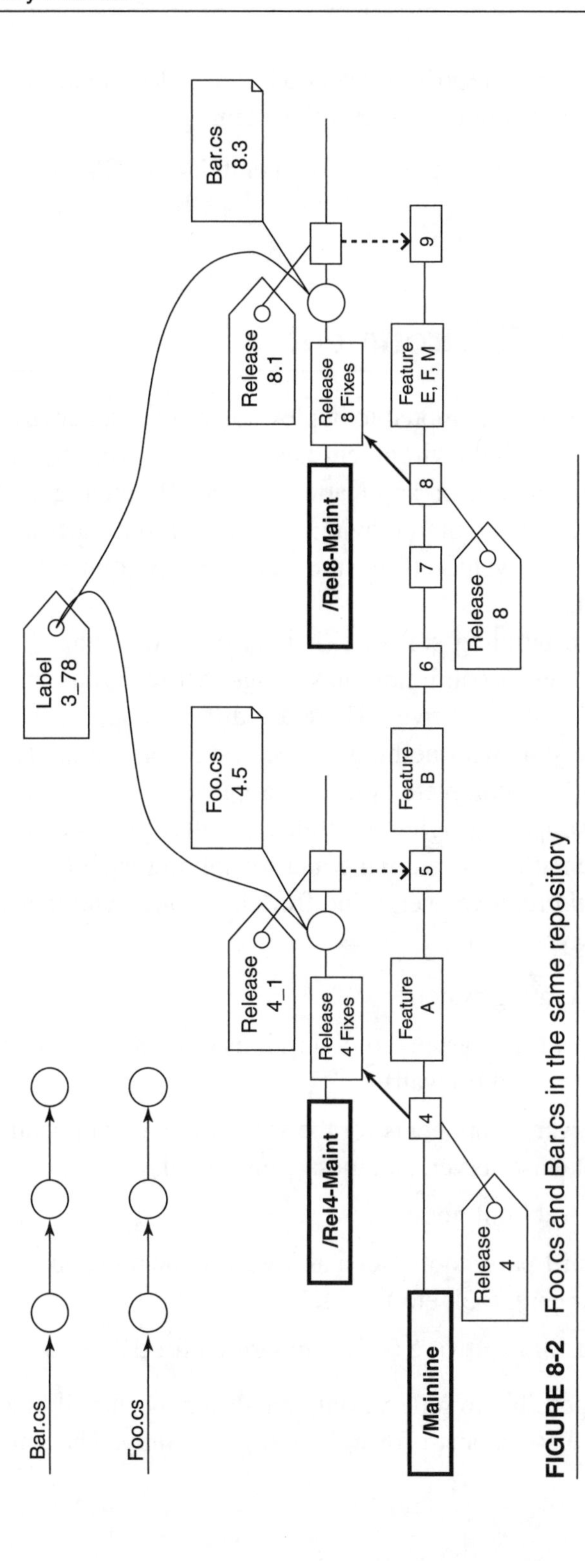

FIGURE 8-2 Foo.cs and Bar.cs in the same repository

Labeling a repository version can follow many different styles; however, the simplest follows this naming pattern:

> major release number '_' (or a point, if your CM system accepts them) minor release number (e.g., 2_89)

Produce a Clean Environment

Have you ever attempted to deploy software in an environment only to discover that the environment has a different version of the operating system, database, or application server? Producing a clean environment is a matter of removing and reapplying software, scripts, and configuration values to ensure that the environment is operating as expected.

When building software, it is critical to ensure that there are no leftover files or configuration settings that may make the software fail (or give a false positive). There are different approaches for this. The first is to start with nothing on the computer and apply a "layer" at a time until the complete system is applied. This is typically performed on a testing or staging machine. Ideally, you would automate the implementation of removing and reapplying each layer. For example, you would remove everything from a machine and then apply the following layers to it.

- Operating system
- Operating system configurations (e.g., network connectivity, users, and firewall)
- Server components for the software (e.g., application server, database server, and messaging server)
- Server configuration
- Third-party tools (such as Web frameworks, object-relational mapping tool, etc.)
- Custom software (software written for the user)

It's possible to remove only one layer when building the software, such as the custom software components only. The number of layers removed and reapplied will depend on the desired level of risk. If a software application relies on various operating system files, then it may be wise to clean the entire system more often. In any case, we recommend that all layers be removed at least a few times before releasing the software to end users.

Label Each Build

Creating a unique identifier for a build, **build labels,** follows two steps: First, the code in the repository requires a label (as just discussed); second, the actual act of building that code requires a unique label. These build labels create a common understanding of what version of code is in a particular environment; moreover, through build labeling, defects, features, and new requirements can be issued against that instance of a code base.

Note the difference, however, between a repository label and a build label. **Repository labels** signify that a group of files (usually uncompiled ones) are related. Build labels signify a binary output of a build as being unique. This could be a series of executables, a .jar file, a .NET assembly, or even a .zip file. The two naming schemes, however, are usually related, with build labels being slightly more specific in terms of build number and platform. Be sure that everyone knows and follows the conventions for your development project. For instance, if the repository label is `2_89`, a build of that snapshot of code could be `2_89.01`. If the build is targeting a specific platform, then additional information can be affixed, such as `2_89.hp-01`.

Not labeling a build makes it difficult to associate features, defects, or requirements to a binary artifact. For example, deploying an unlabeled build to a testing environment, such as QA, in essence creates a moving target. If the QA team finds a defect, then coordinating with the development team can be problematic. Without the ability to pinpoint when the problem occurred, it becomes difficult to identify what led up to the issue. If builds are labeled, however, problem reporting becomes a matter of specifying a build's unique identification.

Labeling a build is as simple as performing a full build and assigning an identification to it. For example, deploying a labeled version to a QA environment should be as easy as typing the following:

```
ant -Dbuild.id=2_89.01 -Denvironment=qa deploy
```

What's interesting about automating a deployment like this is that all of the other processes must be executed (compilation, database integration, testing, inspection, etc.) *before* the deployment is executed. Obviously, a compile is performed, but there are other key steps in the process, including a successful database rebuild and successful tests and inspections run. Moreover, there could be additional tests run after a deployment.

Run All Tests

While some stages of development may only require running certain groups of tests, before packaging a deployment build *all tests must run and pass.* It's that simple. Run all of your automated tests, from unit tests to functional tests. It can be done once on your build machine, but an important part of predeployment testing is to run all tests on your clean, reapplied environment, a clone of the targeted production environment. It is important to make sure one more time that no environmental issues will cause a failure or unintended performance. By running all tests before promoting to the next stage, you develop more confidence that you have *working software.* And even though we firmly believe in the power and necessity of automation in all sorts of processes, including testing, software is still a product which will be used by humans and, therefore, still needs to be tested by humans.

Create Build Feedback Reports

Generating automated build feedback facilitates a common understanding of what *exactly* is in a build intended for release, including the file differences in the build, the defects addressed, and the features

Don't Forget the Human Touch

You could say that even the most robust automated testing is still happening "from the inside." To be sure your product behaves as it should for the user, you must emulate user activities—look at it from the "outside"—before releasing the software.

I once had the opportunity to speak with a project manager at a large financial institution whose development team had fashioned a fairly rigorous automated development testing regimen. They had a high degree of testing at all levels, and they had built a fairly robust auto-deployment process via their build. However, they did notice that sometimes when the team deployed their application into company-wide production, glaring user interface-specific issues, such as pages with broken tables and missing images, would surface. It was particularly painful for this manager, as he would inevitably find out about the issues from *other* groups in the company who depended on this application. It turned out that this development team was focused on automation, but they got a little carried away: No one had ever actually sat down and worked through the behavior and appearance of their product. This team responded as they should, not by deprecating the automated testing, but by considering that the manual review could reveal things a "robot" would not know. Once they added the manual checks, issues with the UI largely disappeared.

Human testing requires 100% test success. If a test fails, there could be subtle issues in the environment or the code base that could spell disaster later, once the application is deployed.

98% Is Still an A, Right?

I once consulted for an organization that had a test-pass threshold of 98%. This strategy was put into place because of a perceived notion that the organization could never attain a pass rate of 100% due to various complexities in the code base and environment at any given point in time. Unfortunately, this strategy of permitting a pass rate with less than 100% created a situation of uncertainty between builds—they had no way of ascertaining which tests were failing between releases and whether they were the same failures or new ones. The CI approach requires that you *automate* a requirement for 100% test success; that way, you receive the data on which tests failed and why.

implemented. By capturing this information, interested parties can verify the presence or absence of desired aspects.

For example, when a release candidate is released to a QA team, ascertaining which defects have been addressed is of primary importance, because the team will need to verify that those defects have truly been fixed. Having a report clearly labeling the addressed defects quickly and effectively facilitates this process.

Another report which works in tandem with the defects addressed report is the file difference report, which is generated from the build. This report facilitates the understanding of what changes (as reported by your version control system) are present in the build. For example, Listing 8-2 shows how build tools like Ant can generate a list of the file differences in the build, with a CVS build difference report based on two dates or labels.

LISTING 8-2 Generating a Build Difference Report with Ant

```
<target name="diff-tag-to-tag">
  <delete dir="${cvs.reports.dir}" />
  <mkdir dir="${cvs.reports.dir}" />
  <cvstagdiff package="${cvstagdiff.package}"
      destfile="${cvstagdiff.destfile}"
      starttag="${cvstagdiff.starttag}"
      endtag="${cvstagdiff.endtag}" compression="true"/>
  <style in="${cvstagdiff.destfile}"
      out="${cvs.reports.dir}/tagdiff.html"
      style="${ant.home}/etc/tagdiff.xsl">
    <param name="title" expression="Ant Diff" />
    <param name="module" expression="ant" />
    <param name="cvsweb" expression="http://cvs.ib.com/viewcvs/"/>
  </style>
</target>
```

This Ant task will create an HTML report which describes the versions of any changed files present. With this report, interested individuals can trace changes back to versions. For example, imagine that the QA team reported a number of defects for the previous release candidate. On a subsequent release, the QA team reports an identical defect from the previous build that was said to have been "fixed." By collaborating with the development team, the QA team can examine the build difference report to verify that the changes related to fixing that defect are actually present.

Possess Capability to Roll Back Release

Ultimately, having the capability to *undo* a deployment is an important part of efficient development. There comes a time for many teams when they need to rapidly replace new defective code with some previous release that worked better. By using build labeling and repository labeling, this process only requires requesting the desired version.

For example, say that during a tight release schedule the QA team receives build 89_3.04, which was to have fixed a number of high-priority defects. After the deployment, however, QA quickly determines that this release candidate has a subtle yet showstopping defect that prohibits further testing. By rapidly rolling back to the previous build (89_3.03), QA doesn't necessarily lose precious testing cycles and can continue to test the previous release and issue defects against it.

Summary

Your project can benefit from continuously deploying working software. While every application, platform, and target domain has unique requirements, the process for effectively releasing working software at any time and any place is largely dependent on six steps. Labeling a repository version signifies a group of files as being related, while producing a clean environment reduces assumptions about existing assets that, when missing, can stump even the simplest of builds. Generating a labeled build produces a named binary that can be reported against, while ensuring that all tests run successfully can help give you more confidence that the software is working as intended. Build feedback reports facilitate a team's common understanding regarding features, defects, and requirements associated with a binary. Lastly, having the capability to roll back a release means that if something goes wrong, you can still provide users with the last working version.

Table 8-1 summarizes the practices covered in this chapter.

TABLE 8-1 CI Practices Discussed in This Chapter

Practice	*Description*
Release working software any time, any place	By running a fully automated build including compilation, all tests, inspections, packaging, and deployment, you have the capability to release working software at any time and in any known environment.
Label a repository's assets	Label the files for your project in your version control repository. Typically, this is performed at the end of a project milestone.
Produce a clean environment	Remove all files, configuration changes, servers, and anything else from your integration build machine and ensure you can rebuild back to a state where your integration build is successful. The more scripted this process is, the better.
Label each build	Label the binary artifacts of a build distribution in your version control repository.
Run all tests	Run all tests against the software. This includes unit, component, system, functional, and perhaps even performance, load, and other types of tests that ensure the software is ready to be delivered (to the next stage or even to production).
Create build feedback reports	List the changes that were made in the most recent build. This can be useful for other teams in the delivery process, such as QA.
Possess capability to roll back release	Something can always go wrong, so use your build labels to roll back any changes that shouldn't have been committed to the version control repository.

Questions

Are your deployments automated? How quickly are you able to get a release out into production? How quickly are you able to get the software into your development or test environment? Use these questions to determine your project's capability to continuously deploy software.

- Do you possess the capability to roll back a release?
- Are you labeling your builds in your version control system?
- Do you have a full set of automated tests that are followed by manual tests of the release candidate afterward?
- How does your team handle release fixes?

- Are your version control labels and build versions related?
- Does your build produce feedback reports?
- Are you able to deploy your software from the command line with a single command?
- Are you building your deployments from the version control repository?
- Are you able to configure your deployments for different environments? Does your software install and run properly on a "clean" machine clone of the user's environment?
- Do you have a bug tracking system, and can it generate reports?

Chapter 9
Continuous Feedback

Use Continuous Feedback Mechanisms

As a general rule, the most successful man in life is the man who has the best information.

—*Benjamin Disraeli (1804–1881)*

One day I was speaking with my coworker, Chuck, when the build failed on one of our projects. I knew this because I received a Short Message Service (SMS) text message on my mobile phone, a personalized sound clip played through my computer speakers, I received an e-mail, and the Orb on my desk changed to a red hue. I briefly interrupted my conversation with Chuck and rang the technical lead for the project, who said, "I just got it and I'm on it." I hung up the phone and continued my conversation without getting sidetracked. This is continuous feedback in action. I did have to interrupt Chuck for a moment, but this is an example of the relatively unobtrusive types of feedback mechanisms you can use with your CI system.

Feedback is a key output of the Integrate button. Without feedback, none of the other aspects of CI is useful. The reason you want fast builds and your builds to fail fast is feedback. Rapid feedback is at the heart of CI. For example, if you don't know that tests or inspections failed until several hours later in the day, you are unable to take immediate action and fix the problem before it propagates and causes other failures. The same goes for a database failure or a failed deployment. Feedback is necessary to take action, and it provides the real, current status of your integration build (see Figure 9-1).

Information on a software project is always changing. As the ancient Greek philosopher Heraclitus noted, "The only constant is change." We must communicate information to our customers, developers, management, or any other stakeholder on a project, and it is vitally useful when it is pertinent, concise, and up-to-date. While face-to-face communication may be the most effective, it is *not* very scalable. Making feedback *continuous* provides a team the capability to inform more people on more projects automatically; moreover, this information can be aggregated to detect trends across a project.

This chapter covers why and how to send the right information to the right people at the right time and in the right way.

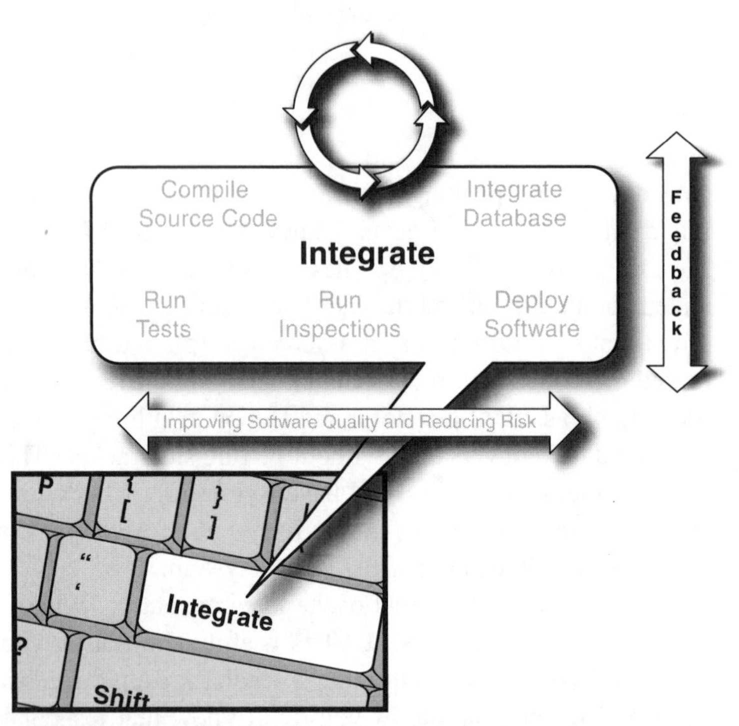

FIGURE 9-1 Providing feedback with the Integrate button

All the Right Stuff

Sending information to whoever, whenever, however is not what will achieve results. The purpose of feedback is to create a notification that most quickly and precisely stimulates action. You must send the *right information* to the *right people* at the *right time* and in the *right way*. In considering the right information, we first focus on the type of information we are sending and ensuring that it is accurate. Next, we discuss who gets the information, why they get it, and when they receive it.

Continuous Feedback and CI

Getting the right information to the right people at the right time and in the right way—CI is the best tool for making this feedback automated, targeted, and real-time (continuous).

Finally, in discussing the right way to send information, we'll discuss some of the communication mechanisms that can be employed with a CI system, which are known as **continuous feedback devices (CFDs).** CFDs typically notify project stakeholders of the success or failure of a build, but they also can notify them of other issues. For example, a CFD can notify specific parties that a threshold has been exceeded (e.g., code duplication has gone over a specified percentage).

Figure 9-2 illustrates this approach.

The Right Information

Continuous feedback doesn't *take* the action to improve the software, project members do—typically, software developers. The information may be useful to others, such as analysts, testers, and management, as well. Continuous feedback provides the means to structure the information, and you decide what portions are delivered to which project members upon certain events. You and the other recipients know both that the information is accurate and fresh and that you are taking the most effective action to solve an issue. Instead of waiting for stakeholders to notice they have questions and then putting them to you, *you*

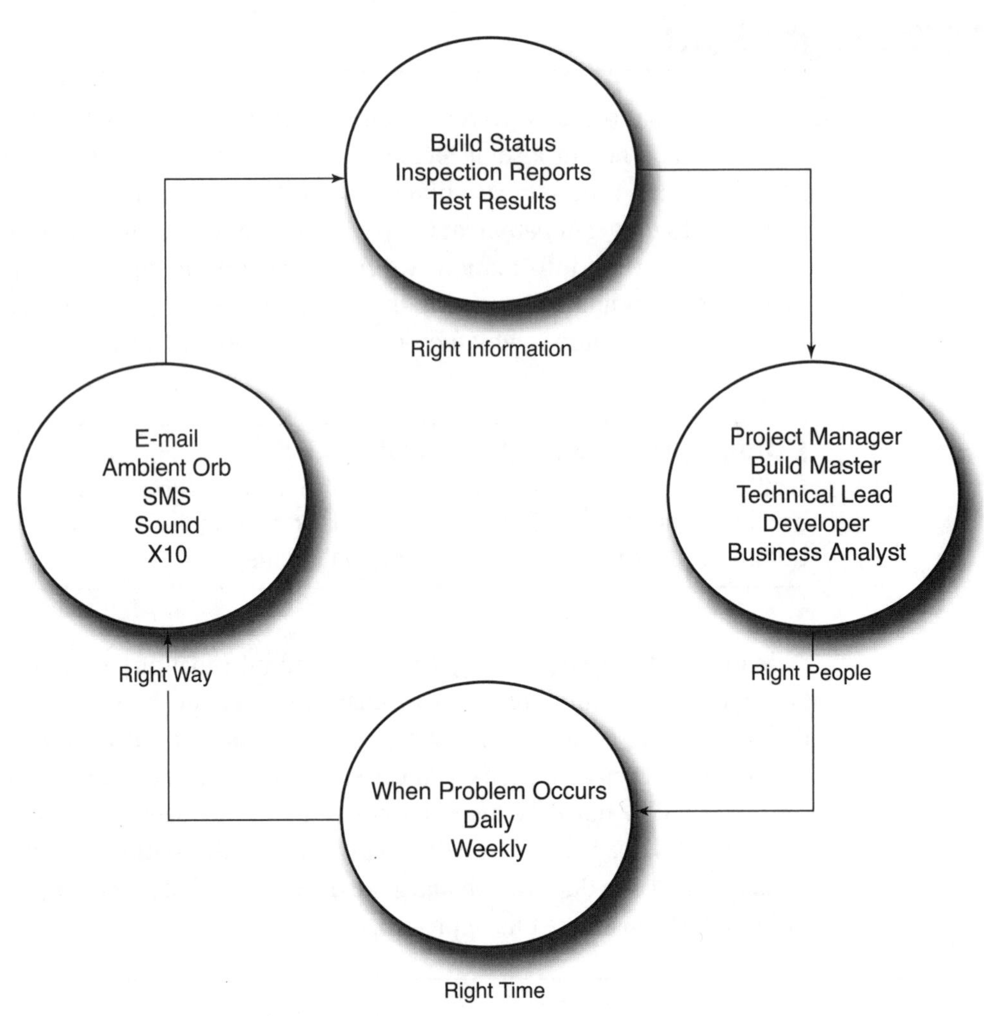

FIGURE 9-2 The right stuff for continuous feedback

can devise notifications for them on a particular concern and have the notices sent regularly and/or right when an issue develops.

As described throughout the book, you can leverage your CI system for work that you might otherwise have to do manually. Build status notification is a good example of information that is appropriate for a number of project roles. The ideal build status notification includes the results of all of the regression tests run against the application, the multitude of inspectors (e.g., static analysis tools) that report anomalies in the source code, and the results of a deployment. Some of this information does not always need to be continuous, but it should be on some type of schedule.

The Right People

Everyone needs to receive some type of feedback on the project, but not necessarily every item *every* time. With a little bit of planning, you can devise a strategy for distributing the type of information your CI system can generate. Sometimes a message simply informs members that everything is going fine, which is great, but you don't want a sea of "fine" messages burying a "not fine" message in its depths. Sending feedback to all project members too often will ensure that everyone begins to ignore the messages. Also, notifying a whole group about something that only one or two team members can fix creates undesirable bulk—what if all developers receive an error based on what a single developer just checked in? They may begin to see so many messages that they don't notice when one of them is in their area. It is important that your team doesn't learn to ignore messages from the CI build process altogether.

Beware of Information Overload

Sending feedback to everyone on a project usually only causes everyone to ignore the information.

CI helps get the right information to the right people, which is really the *right role.* On some projects, one person may serve multiple roles. Depending on your role, you may receive communications from the CI system in different ways.

- **Project Manager**—A project manager (PM) must often make decisions that center on resource allocation (people, hardware, and supplies), time, and costs. PMs are usually managing many tasks at once, so they need high-level, real-time feedback on software completion as it relates to time, cost, quality, and scope. A CI system can be most effective at providing much of this feedback because of its automated and continuous nature.

- **Architect/Technical Lead**—Technical leads and architects usually want to see the status of all builds because they're looking at the entire system. Of particular interest will be the results of the quality metrics, such as those from static and dynamic analysis tools (inspectors) that ensure adherence to the coding and architectural standards.
- **Developers**—Typically, developers will receive messages from the CI system on the code they just checked into the version control repository. Developers receive a variety of information from tests and inspections to the status of the most recent build. The group benefits only when the messages everyone receives from a continuous feedback mechanism (e.g., e-mail) are relevant to his or her own tasks.
- **Testers**—Testers will probably be most interested in communication relating to the automated tests and inspections. Their messages contain information about all code tested and inspected across the system. Depending on your team's approach to testing, this information can be used to learn about new features before they are "released" to the testing group.

The Right Time

Old news is not really news at all. Discovering that the build broke two days ago doesn't offer much help. Sending information that tells you what happened—such as fixing some code right away—is why continuous feedback insists on sending information at the *right time*. As many experts have already established, reducing the time intervals between the introduction, discovery, and resolution of a defect saves time and money. The more time that has passed since the defect was introduced, the less the parties responsible remember what happened or why; they may have applied a faulty principle elsewhere, may have built another component around it, or may target and "fix" the wrong part of the original code. Certainly as important as the wasted time and money are the chance for errors and the frustration in chasing bugs that don't even exist.

The Heart of Continuous Feedback

At the heart of continuous feedback is reducing the time between when a defect is introduced, discovered, and fixed.

CI is extremely effective in helping get the right information to the right people at the right time. Using a CI server such as CruiseControl enables the dissemination of information as soon as a build fails or succeeds, along with an available wealth of detailed information that contributes to that and other issues.

The Right Way

A CI system also provides the opportunity for sending information the *right way.* The right way is choosing the most appropriate communication mechanism, how to present this information, and to whom. There are various mechanisms to enable continuous feedback, such as e-mail, sound, visual devices, and text messages.

Certain communication feedback mechanisms inform better than others. Sometimes hanging poster paper on the wall that indicates the number of current defects is an effective communication device. However, this is a perfect example of information that very quickly can become dated, so this chapter focuses on using automation to communicate information in real time. The feedback typically dictates some type of action, so of course it is done in the right way to the right people, but they might have different preferences or needs for feedback.

Use Continuous Feedback Mechanisms

Just as you wouldn't use a hammer for every home improvement project, you won't use the same continuous feedback mechanism for every communication. This section introduces you to a variety of mechanisms that can provide continuous feedback: e-mail, text messaging, Ambient Orbs/X10 devices, Windows taskbar monitor, sounds, and others. It also discusses the use of wide-screen monitors.

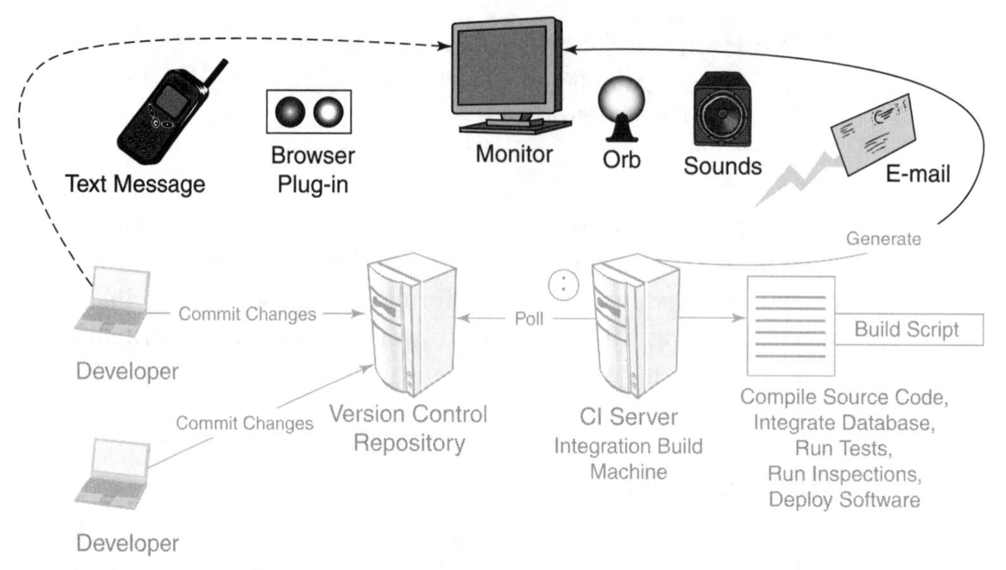

FIGURE 9-3 Continuous feedback mechanisms

Figure 9-3 shows the various feedback mechanisms you can utilize with a CI system.

E-mail

When considering e-mail as a feedback mechanism, you also should consider the following requirements, advantages, and disadvantages.

Requires: A CI server such as CruiseControl, an e-mail client such as Microsoft Outlook or Eudora, and an e-mail server (one that supports SMTP) such as James.[1]

Advantages: It pushes the information, asynchronously, to the right people.

1. "The Apache Java Enterprise Mail Server (a.ka. Apache James) is a 100% pure Java SMTP and POP3 Mail server and NNTP News server." From http://james.apache.org/.

Disadvantages: People don't always have immediate access to e-mail, and there's the potential of inundating ("spamming") project members with e-mails.

E-mail is the most common form of feedback for CI. A CI system can send an e-mail if the build succeeds or fails along with any details that you have specified. For example, I configure CruiseControl to send an e-mail in HTML that displays the status, the changes since the last build, the unit tests run, and the deployment files created. It also provides a link to the CruiseControl reporting application where I can see detailed information on the builds, including access to inspection artifacts and trend graphs. E-mail is a very useful form of feedback, but it does have its disadvantages. There is not an effective way to stay notified of trends in software without being inundated with e-mails that come every time something changes.

Listing 9-1 shows a CruiseControl config.xml file configured to send e-mails to the last person (@localhost) to check in files and the technical lead (pduvall@localhost) on the project using the `defaultsuffix` attribute of the `htmlemail` element.

LISTING 9-1 CruiseControl config.xml Configured to Send E-mail

```
...
<publishers>
  <currentbuildstatuspublisher
    file="buildstatus.txt"/>
  <htmlemail mailhost="localhost"
    xslDir="xsl"
     css="cruisecontrol.css"
     returnaddress="buildstatus@localhost"
     returnname="ABC Project Build Status"
     defaultsuffix="@localhost"
     spamwhilebroken="true"
     buildresultsurl="http://localhost:8989/cruisecontrol>
   <always address="pduvall@localhost"/>
   <failure address="pduvall@localhost "/>
  </htmlemail>
</publishers>
```

Figure 9-4 is a sample HTML message you can receive on the build status from a CI server. Notice also that the Inbox received three messages in just a couple of minutes; many people (including you) can get overloaded and begin to ignore this form of feedback.

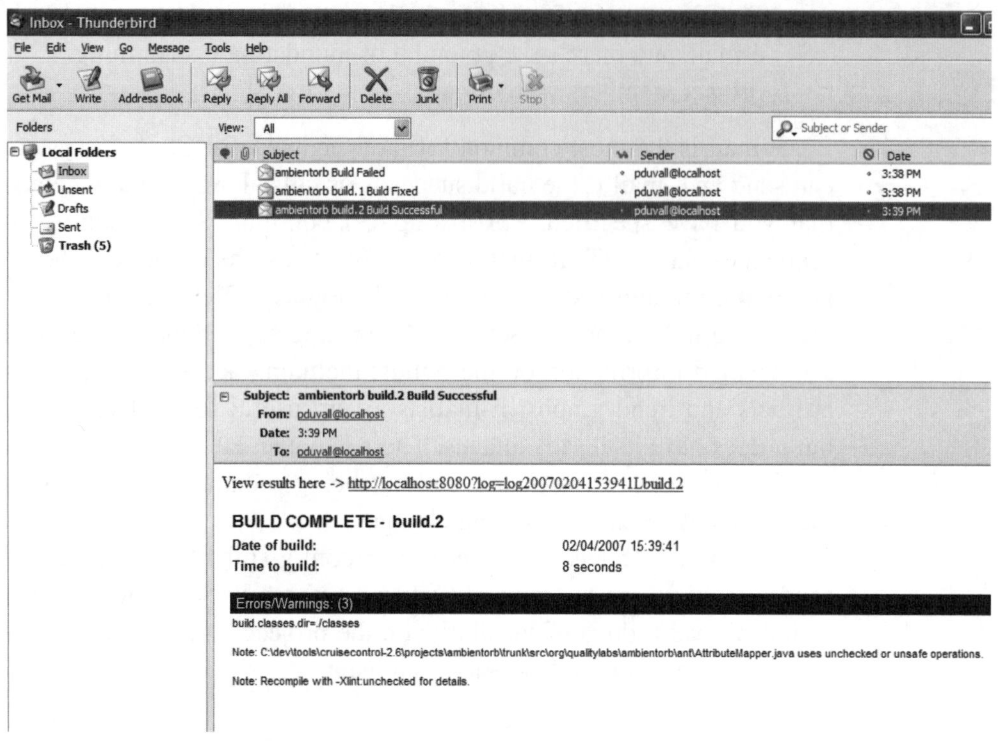

FIGURE 9-4 E-mail about build status

SMS (Text Messages)

Keep the following in mind when considering SMS as a feedback mechanism.

> **Requires:** A mobile phone with SMS capability, an e-mail server, and a tool capable of sending e-mail.
>
> **Advantages:** Can receive messages while away from e-mail.
>
> **Disadvantages:** Messages will be very short. Same disadvantages as mentioned earlier for e-mail.

It's easy to have a CI server using an e-mail server send an SMS text message to a mobile phone. All that's needed is a phone capable of receiving SMS text messages and a tool that will send the e-mail via an e-mail server. This is as simple as sending an e-mail in CruiseControl. Listing 9-2 demonstrates sending a text message from CruiseControl when the build fails.

LISTING 9-2 Sending a Text Message from CruiseControl When the Build Fails

```
<publishers>
  <email mailhost="smtp.mydomain.com"
    returnaddress=buildstatus@mydomain.com
    defaultsuffix=@mydomain.com
    returnname="Project Build Status"
    spamwhilebroken="false"
    buildresultsurl="SMS">
    <failure address="7035551212@mobilephone-emailaddress.com"
       reportWhenFixed="true"/>
  </email>
</publishers>
```

Here's a short explanation of Listing 9-2 as well as some other options you can use with SMS.

- `smtp.mydomain.com` should be replaced with your SMTP server. You may also need to specify credentials to send e-mail through your SMTP server; in this case, use the `username` and `password` attributes.
- The `returnaddress` attribute identifies the return e-mail address that appears in the e-mail's from field.
- The text `@mydomain.com` in the default suffix attribute should be replaced with your domain name.
- This uses a `<failure>` child element to always send failure messages to a specified e-mail address. The value `7035551212@mobilephone-emailaddress.com` should be replaced with the e-mail address you would like your build failures to be sent to. The `reportWhenFixed` attribute is set to `true` to send a follow-up e-mail to indicate when a build has been fixed.
- CruiseControl permits the use of the `xslfile` attribute, which eliminates the need for `css` and `xslDir` attributes.

You may want to receive a text message every time the build succeeds or fails. However, I prefer to receive a text message only when the build fails, and then once when the fixed build succeeds. We have many builds per day, and I do not want a flurry of text messages when no action is required (i.e., a successful build).

Ambient Orb and X10 Devices

Visible devices are great as notifiers because you can set them anywhere (some don't even need to be connected to a computer), and team members can simply look at a device to determine the build status.

Ambient Orb

We recommend using an Ambient Orb because it can be customized to display lots of different colors to show you different things. It is more expensive than a typical X10 device, so your team has to value its greater capability. When considering an Ambient Orb as a feedback mechanism, bear in mind the following.

Requires: Ambient Orb, special subscription with Ambient Devices,[2] a script capable of sending HTTP `get` messages, a build script (such as Ant), and a network connection (or 9-pin serial connector)

Advantages: At-a-glance, nonbinary information; cool factor.

Disadvantages: Cost, presents no detailed information, and need to be within visual range to notice need for action.

We refer to the Orb as a "glanceable device" because you can simply glance at it and determine the status of your project—without receiving 20 e-mails indicating different thresholds the project may have exceeded, and without receiving details that you are not prepared for or want yet. Everyone on the project can glance at the Orb and get the status of the latest build and/or quality metrics (if you have added customizations). I set up the Orb in our project development room so that it displayed different colors based on the build status. For example, if the build has been failing for more than 30 minutes, it is a deeper red.

Benefits of using an Orb is that it can be placed anywhere, and it is not binary, like e-mail or an X10 device (discussed next). The Orb contains a pager-like device that is a part of a wireless network. From a build script, such as Ant, an HTTP `get` message can be sent to the

2. See www.ambientdevices.com.

device's Web server component. Orbs can be a bit pricey, but they have proven very useful on projects. There is, of course, a "cool factor," and we think it shows that we're very serious about quality, we want immediate notification of a problem, and we also believe in creating a fun and visual work environment.

Listing 9-3 demonstrates an Ant target that executes the `ambientorb`[3] task and changes the Orb color based on the success or failure of your build. Figure 9-5 shows the Ambient Orb.

LISTING 9-3 Registering ambientorb Ant Task to Notify Ambient Orb

```
<target name="registerOrb" if="is.integration.machine">
<taskdef classname="org.qualitylabs.ambientorb.ant.OrbTask" name="orb"
classpathref="orb.class.path"/>
 <orb listener="org.qualitylabs.ambientorb.ant.OrbListener"
    deviceId="AAA-99A-AAA"
    colorPass="green"
    colorFail="red"
    animationFail="heartbeat"
    animationPass="none"
    commentPass="The+build+passed"
    commentFail="Build+Failure!!"/>
</target>
```

FIGURE 9-5 Ambient Orb on a desk

3. The Ambient Orb Ant task is available at www.qualitylabs.org/projects/ambientorb.

X10 Devices

X10 devices are not as flexible as the Ambient Orb in several ways, but they are a great option when you don't have the budget for an Ambient Orb. When thinking about implementing an X10 device as a feedback mechanism, consider the following.

> **Requires:** Device capable of receiving X10 messages and a home automation kit (e.g., FireCracker).
>
> **Advantages:** Cool factor, "glanceable," and access to any electrical device.
>
> **Disadvantages:** Binary information: the device is either on or off. Just like the Orb, you must be within visual range to notice that action needs to be taken. X10 devices are not useful to the visually impaired.

An X10 device is another "glanceable" device with two distinct differences: There are literally hundreds of different X10 devices to choose from, and there are only two visual modes with an X10 device, either on or off (you configure which mode indicates what). The effect is similar to the Ambient Orb; we value a central, simple notification to improve quality, and we rather like using something a little more fun to do it. The X10 device is a relatively cost-effective solution to notify all project members in visual range of the latest build status.

Listing 9-4 shows a CruiseControl config.xml file configured to turn on X10 device(s) A2 and turn off X10 device(s) A3 using a CM17A computer interface on COM1 whenever the build succeeds or fails. This example demonstrates how to control two lava lamps as homemade traffic lights (red and green).[4]

LISTING 9-4 CruiseControl config.xml File Configured to Trigger X10 Devices

```
<publishers>
  <!-- Successful Builds: Turn on Green Lava Lamp / Light -->
  <x10
    port="COM1"
```

4. Quick Start instructions are provided at http://cruisecontrol.sourceforge.net/main/configxml.html#x10.

```
    houseCode="A"
    deviceCode="2"
    onWhenBroken="false"
    interfaceModel="CM17A"/>
  <!-- Failed Builds: Turn on Red Lava Lamp / Light -->
  <x10
    port="COM1"
    houseCode="A"
    deviceCode="3"
    onWhenBroken="true"
    interfaceModel="CM17A"/>
</publishers>
```

By default, the device's "on" signal is sent when the build fails. The device's "off" signal is sent when the build succeeds/passes. If you want the opposite, that is, on when successful and off when broken, set the `onWhenBroken` attribute to false. The CI server sends an X10 message to the devices each time, but if it's the same as before, the lamp won't change state.

Any Time, Any Place

One time while having lunch at a conference in Denver, I received a text message on my mobile phone indicating that the build on one of our projects back in Virginia had failed. I called the technical lead on the project, and he briefed me on the nature of the problem. After some troubleshooting, they found out that one of the JUnit tests had failed because one of the component interfaces had changed. It really gave me peace of mind to know that an automated system was building, testing, inspecting, and deploying software (among other activities) and letting me know if anything was wrong, even while I was away from my office and not able to access e-mail.

Windows Taskbar

CCTray will monitor your CruiseControl.NET builds and report on the status using the Windows taskbar. This way you don't need to open or wait for an e-mail to know the status of the build—you just look at the icon located on your desktop. Figure 9-6 shows the CCTray Windows

FIGURE 9-6 CCTray build status message from Windows taskbar

taskbar icon and the latest build status (which appears in hover text). The CCTray installation, provided in the CruiseControl.NET installation, is simple to set up and configure using a Windows installer.

This is useful because team members can simply look in their Windows taskbar to determine the build status. Consider the following when thinking about implementing a message from the Windows taskbar as a feedback mechanism.

Requires: Windows operating system and CruiseControl.NET or CruiseControl.

Advantages: Real-time, unobtrusive feedback.

Disadvantages: This is only available for Windows systems.

Sounds

Sound is another item that can add a bit of fun to the workplace, and it's useful if you're within earshot. When considering implementing sound as a feedback mechanism, bear in mind the following:

Requires: A sound card and speakers.

Advantages: It's able to reach many people at the same time and makes the process fun.

Disadvantages: Typically, the sound only plays once. You must be nearby to hear the sound. If you are wearing headphones (that aren't connected to the computer from which the sound is played), you may not hear it. People who have difficulty hearing may not be aware of it.

I enjoy using different sounds based on the build status. This can be integrated into other CFDs as well, such as the Windows system tray or e-mail. I've used e-mail rules to play a certain sound depending on the subject of the e-mail. For example, when a build fails, it plays a sound byte from the movie *Office Space* saying “We’ve got sorta a problem here.” If the build succeeded, it plays “Houston, we are go for launch” from the movie *Apollo 13.* On some of our projects, the development group works in the same room as the build machine. Using the same sounds, the build machine announces success or failure from its speakers. Listing 9-5 demonstrates an Ant delegating build script that provides this functionality. This delegating build script is called by the CruiseControl configuration file (config.xml).

LISTING 9-5 Register Sounds with CruiseControl

```
<project name="project-delegating-build" default="run-cc-build">
      <target name="run-cc-build" depends="registerSounds ">
      ...
      </target>
      <property name="sounds.dir" location="PATH_TO_SOUNDS"/>
      <target name="registerSounds" if="use.sounds">
            <sound>
            <fail source="${sounds.dir}/failure/problemhere.wav"/>
            <success source="${sounds.dir}/success"/>
            </sound>
      </target>
</project>
```

A bit of explanation is in order.

- You will register the build sounds in your delegating-build.xml, and make sure the `<sound>` task is invoked at the beginning of your script.
- The `<fail>` element will play a specific sound file from the build failure sounds directory.
- The `<success>` element will play a specific sound file from the build success sounds directory.
- You need to replace the `PATH_TO_SOUNDS` value with the location of your sounds directory.
- You can enable and disable the use of build sounds from your CruiseControl config.xml file by setting the value of the `use.sounds` property.

Again, we really believe in incorporating gadgets, noises, and notification styles that make environments more fun and personalized while conducting the business of continuous feedback. We believe these devices demonstrate how seriously the team takes their work, not the opposite.

Wide-Screen Monitors

You can use a wide-screen monitor to provide high visibility to what your project team considers important. What's more, the information is automated. When thinking about implementing a wide-screen monitor as a feedback mechanism, consider the following.

> **Requires:** A network connection and video projector or large-screen monitors.
>
> **Advantages:** Automated, real-time "actionable" information.
>
> **Disadvantages:** Some upfront costs depending on the type of information you are automating.

Alistair Cockburn uses the term **information radiators** to describe communication mechanisms that "radiate" information. When he first conceived this idea, this meant posting a large item that everyone nearby could see (called BVCs—big visual charts). They originally used colors and large writing, but we can step way beyond that technologically. BVCs are not effective for distributed development groups, and they require repetitious manual updates to keep information fresh. Since CI can generate much of this information, you can leverage the reports generated from the CI server for much of this.

I can't count how many times I've heard conversations at work that begin, "Did you receive my e-mail?" or "I checked the latest version of the file into CVS the other day," or "Did you check the latest project schedule?" In my experience, communication is typically the number one challenge on software projects. The typical problem is not that we don't communicate; problems arise when we don't communicate in the right way.

Information radiators make project schedules, metrics, build results, and other information visible to all project members, and they are updated automatically. When people view them, and for what information, is up to them. Be sure to focus your design the same as you do with your outgoing single notifications (e-mail and text messages): Include some key data and set it to update as needed. Otherwise, the wide-screen monitor is the same sea of information in a different form.

Additional Feedback Devices

There are many other types of devices and mechanisms you can use to communicate; just make sure the information is informative, concise, timely, and fun. The purpose is for someone to take action on the information *as quickly as possible.* You may want to change CFDs from time to time to keep your environment from getting stale. Here are some other ideas of CFDs you can use on projects.

- **Browser plug-in**—There is a useful plug-in[5] for the Firefox Web browser that displays the build status using red and green indicators (similar to the Windows taskbar).
- **Instant Messenger**—Notify project members on the build status via one of the instant messenger applications such as AIM or Yahoo.
- **RSS**—Publish the results of your builds using Really Simple Syndication (RSS). An RSS XML file is updated for every build. You can use a reader to get these updates rather than having to check your e-mail. Many CI servers provide support for RSS.
- **Widgets**—There are various widgets created for the Windows and Mac platforms that monitor CruiseControl servers and report the build status.

5. See www.md.pp.ru/mozilla/cc/ for more information on the Firefox plug-in for CruiseControl.

❑ ❑ ❑ ❑ ❑ ❑ ❑ ❑ ❑ ❑

Summary

In this chapter, you learned how to harness the power of CI by automating feedback on a continuous basis based on established thresholds. Sending the right information to the right people at the right time and in the right way can drastically cut the time between when a problem or risk is introduced and when it is fixed. This will help improve software quality and reduce risks as they occur.

Questions

Here is a handy list of considerations to help you develop continuous feedback mechanisms in your development environment.

- Have you automated your feedback processes?
- Is your feedback incorporated into your CI system so that feedback does not need to be sent manually?
- Are the right people getting notified? Are too many people being notified too often?
- Is the feedback timely? Are project members receiving the feedback as soon as a problem is identified?
- Are you sending the appropriate amount of information to project members?
- Is your team distributed geographically? Are you automating your information radiators?
- Are you making feedback fun? Have you incorporated devices such as sounds or the Ambient Orb into your feedback processes?

Epilogue:
The Future of CI

I've found there are typically two key complaints from those who have been practicing CI for a while.

- How can I prevent broken builds?
- How can I get my builds to run faster?

I will address each of these concerns here, although I don't expect we'll find a "perfect" solution to these concerns for some time.

Although the practice of CI provides faster feedback in smaller increments, it is still a rather reactionary practice. Some people choose to perform manual sequential integrations because they always want to keep the build in the green. I expect to see more tool support for running successful integrations on a separate machine, using a queue, before the source code changes are committed to the version control repository.

Imagine if the only activity the developer needs to perform is to "commit" her code to the version control system. Before the repository accepts the code, it runs an integration build on a separate machine. Only if the integration build is successful will it commit the code to the repository. This can significantly reduce broken integration builds and may reduce the need to perform manual integration builds. At the time of publication, we are starting to see tool support[1] for this approach, and we expect to see much more in the coming years.

1. See Borland's Gauntlet (www.borland.com/us/products/silk/gauntlet/), JetBrains' TeamCity (www.jetbrains.com/teamcity/), and Microsoft's Team Foundation Server (TFS) (http://msdn2.microsoft.com/en-us/teamsystem/). At publication time, Microsoft doesn't provide "out of the box" support for CI, but it supports scheduled builds instead.

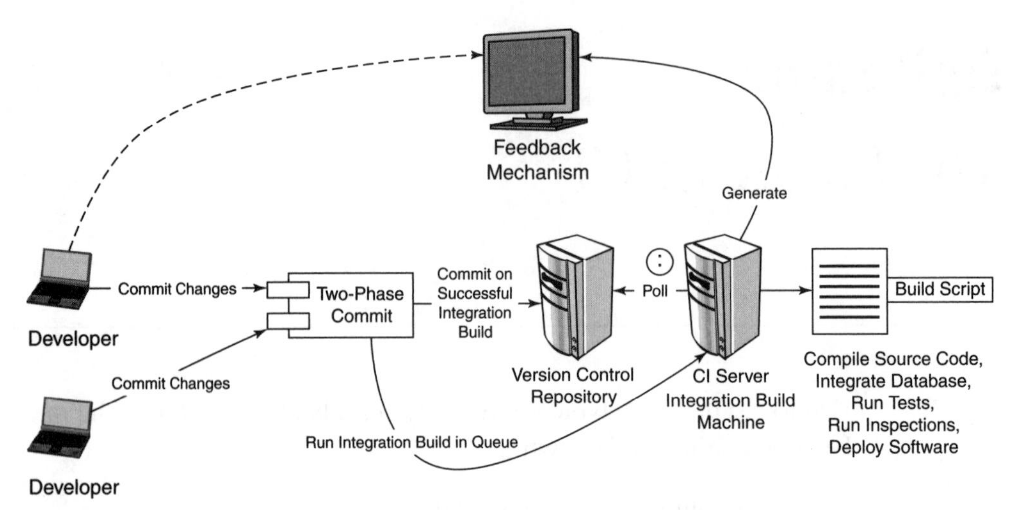

FIGURE E-1 The future of CI—automated queued integration builds

Figure E-1 demonstrates this automated queued integration approach. A developer commits her code changes, and a process intercepts requests to commit and runs an integration build on the integration build machine in a queue to ensure that there are no conflicts with other changes being committed. If the integration build is successful, the code is committed to the repository. If a developer attempts to commit code while an integration build is occurring, the server will place it in the queue until the first integration build is successful.

I also figure we'll see more version control system vendors provide CI features. It seems logical that since a version control system is always running, and an effective CI system requires a version control system, you could use it to prevent broken code, tests, or even inspections from ever entering the shared code base.

An alternative approach to preventing broken builds is to provide the capability for a developer to run an integration build *using the integration build machine and his local changes* (that haven't been committed to the version control repository) along with any other changes committed to the version control repository.[2] When this technique is practiced by all developers, it can lead to significantly fewer broken

2. Zutubi calls this a "personal build" and is provided by their CI server, Pulse.

builds because you integrate all your changes and run an integration build on a separate machine before committing your changes to the repository.

The other area for improvement in practicing CI is providing more rapid feedback by running faster builds. Chapter 4 covers techniques and possible solutions, but I expect to see more capabilities in the areas of parallelization and other capabilities to leverage additional hardware and software resources to speed up builds.

Appendix A
CI Resources

This appendix provides information about tools and resources for CI categorized under the following topics.

- Continuous Integration Web sites/articles
- CI tools/product resources
- Build scripting resources
- Version control resources
- Database resources
- Testing resources
- Automated inspection resources
- Deployment resources
- Feedback resources
- Documentation resources

Continuous Integration Web Sites/Articles

Automation for the people: Continuous feedback

- http://www-128.ibm.com/developerworks/java/library/j-ap11146/

This IBM developerWorks article covers different feedback mechanisms that can be used in a CI environment.

Automation for the people: Continuous Inspection

- http://www-128.ibm.com/developerworks/java/library/j-ap08016/

This IBM developerWorks article looks at how automated inspectors like Checkstyle, JavaNCSS, and CPD enhance the development process and when you should use them.

Automation for the people: Remove the smell from your build scripts

- http://www-128.ibm.com/developerworks/java/library/j-ap10106/

This IBM developerWorks article covers build smells using examples in Ant.

Continuous Integration

- www.martinfowler.com/articles/continuousIntegration.html

Martin Fowler introduces the principles and practices of CI.

Continuous Integration

- www.stickyminds.com/BetterSoftware/magazine.asp?fn=cifea&id=58

An article in *Better Software Magazine* on CI, by Jeffrey Frederick.

Daily Build and Smoke Test

- www.stevemcconnell.com/bp04.htm

Lest we think that the practice of CI is new or was created out of thin air, here's another very influential software leader, Steve McConnell, discussing daily builds and smoke tests in *IEEE Software*, Vol. 13, No. 4, July 1996.

IntegrateButton.com

- www.integratebutton.com

This is the book's companion Web site, maintained by the authors, that is dedicated to information about CI, including videos, examples, a blog, and much more.

Realizing continuous integration

- http://www-128.ibm.com/developerworks/rational/library/sep05/lee/

This IBM developerWorks article, by Kevin Lee, introduces the concept and practices of CI.

CI Tools/Product Resources

AnthillPro

- www.urbancode.com/products/anthillpro/

A commercial build management server that provides CI as a feature. Also see Appendix B.

Apache Continuum

- http://maven.apache.org/continuum/

The Web site for the Apache Maven project. Also see Appendix B.

Bamboo

- www.atlassian.com/software/bamboo/

A commercial CI server, but freely available for open source projects. Bamboo provides build metrics, an easy-to-use UI, and integration with Atlassian tools such as JIRA.

BuildForge

- http://www-306.ibm.com/software/awdtools/buildforge/enterprise/

BuildForge is a heavy-duty commercial build management tool that provides high-performance, distributed build, test, and deployment functionality.

Continuous Integration Server Matrix

- http://damagecontrol.codehaus.org/Continuous+Integration+Server+Feature+Matrix

This matrix gives an overview of both commercial and open source CI servers on the market. It provides many criteria to use in determining the best server.

CruiseControl

- http://cruisecontrol.sourceforge.net

CruiseControl, written in Java, is one of the first CI servers and has been available since 2001. Also see Appendix B.

CruiseControl.NET

- http://ccnet.thoughtworks.com

Written in C#, this CI server is based on the Java version of Cruise-Control and is open source and freely available as well. Also see Appendix B.

Gauntlet

- www.borland.com/us/products/silk/gauntlet/

Guantlet provides a feature called "sandboxing," which isolates source code changes in a branch until the integration build is successful. Jet-

Brains' TeamCity provides a similar feature and is a positive step in the evolution of CI, as it can prevent broken builds from entering a version control repository.

Hudson

- http://hudson.dev.java.net

An easy-to-use and freely available CI server provided as a WAR file.

Luntbuild

- http://luntbuild.javaforge.com/

Luntbuild is a build management server that also provides CI. Also see Appendix B.

ParaBuild

- www.viewtier.com/products/parabuild/index.htm

ParaBuild is a commercial automated software-build management server.

PMEase QuickBuild

- www.pmease.com/

QuickBuild is a professional version of Luntbuild.

Sin

- http://sin.tigris.org/

The Sin (its formal name is Continuous Integration for Subversion) approach to CI helps prevent the corruption of a version control repository using defensive "checkin branches" to verify correctness before accepting (i.e., merging) changes into the mainline. Sin requires .NET and a Subversion repository.

Other CI Tools and Product Resources

Name	*Web Site*
Bitten	http://bitten.cmlenz.net/
BuildBeat	www.timpanisoftware.com/
BuildBot	http://buildbot.sourceforge.net/
CM Crossroads	www.cmcrossroads.com/
ElectricCommander	www.electric-cloud.com/
Gump	http://gump.apache.org/
Pragmatic Automation	www.pragmaticautomation.com/
Pulse	www.zutubi.com/products/pulse/
TeamCity	www.jetbrains.com/teamcity/
Tinderbox	www.mozilla.org/tinderbox.html

Build Scripting Resources

Ant

- http://ant.apache.org

Ant is easily the most popular build scripting tool for Java development teams. If you're on a Java project, it is worth spending time learning its features. Most CI servers support Ant.

Groovy

- http://groovy.codehaus.org/
- www.javaworld.com/javaworld/jw-10-2004/jw-1004-groovy_p.html
- http://www-128.ibm.com/developerworks/library/j-pg12144.html

Groovy is a dynamic language for the Java platform that you can use to script your Ant XML scripts. You can script your build process by using Groovy's programming constructs.

Maven

- http://maven.apache.org

A project management and build tool. Also see Appendix B.

NAnt

- http://nant.sourceforge.net/

NAnt is the port of the Java-based Ant tool to the .NET platform.

Rake

- http://rake.rubyforge.org/

Rake is the build-scripting tool for Ruby-based applications. If you are using Rake, you can also utilize the power of Ruby when scripting your builds.

Version Control Resources

ClearCase

- www.ibm.com/software/awdtools/clearcase/

A commercial software configuration management tool with many advanced features.

Concurrent Versions System (CVS)

- www.nongnu.org/cvs/

An open source, freely available version control tool.

MKS

- www.mks.com/

A commercial version control tool.

Subversion

- http://subversion.tigris.org/

Subversion is a freely available, open source, version control tool developed by CollabNet.

Other Version Control Resources

Name	*Web Site*
AccuRev	www.accurev.com/
Alienbrain	www.alienbrain.com/
Perforce	www.perforce.com/
PVCS	www.serena.com/Products/professional/vm/home.asp
SnapshotCM	www.truebluesoftware.com/
StarTeam	www.borland.com/us/products/starteam/index.html
Surround SCM	www.seapine.com/surroundscm.html
Synergy CM	www.telelogic.com/corp/products/synergy/index.cfm
Visual SourceSafe	http://msdn.microsoft.com/vstudio/Previous/ssafe/default.aspx

Database Resources

Hypersonic DB

- www.hsqldb.org/

HSQLDB is a lightweight (100K footprint), in-memory database written in Java that is freely available. It is great for managing test data for your application during developer testing.

Mckoi

- www.mckoi.com/database/

Mckoi is another open source (under GPL license), lightweight SQL database for Java. It is great for teams that want to use a "developer database sandbox" for development. A little work is required to get your SQL to adhere to Sybase's and Oracle's SQL, but it is possible.

MySQL

- www.mysql.com

MySQL offers a suite of powerful databases that originally started as an open source relational database system capable of running on all major operating systems, including Linux, UNIX, and Windows. Today, it has grown into an industry RDBMS leader. The Community Edition is freely available under GPL license.

Oracle

- www.oracle.com/technology/database/index.html

A well-known, enterprise-class relational database management system capable of running on all major operating systems, including Linux and Windows. Oracle Express Edition offers the best of both worlds for developers: It is free to download, develop, deploy, and distribute, and it is a lightweight version of the Oracle product line including Standard and Enterprise Editions.

PostgreSQL

- www.postgresql.org/

PostgreSQL is a powerful, open source relational database system capable of running on all major operating systems, including Linux, UNIX (AIX, BSD, HP-UX, Mac OS X, SGI IRIX, Solaris, and Tru64), and Windows.

Testing Resources

AgitarOne

- www.agitar.com/products/

Agitar's AgitarOne is a commercially available product that automatically generates test cases for Java code.

DbUnit

- http://dbunit.sourceforge.net

DbUnit is an open source JUnit extension that puts a database back into a known state between test runs.

Fit

- http://fit.c2.com/

Fit is an open source tool that facilitates communication between the business clients who write requirements and the developers who implement them. Fit is available for Java, .NET, Ruby, and Python.

FitNesse

- http://fitnesse.org/

FitNesse is an open source tool that enables Fit testing via a wiki. FitNesse is available for .NET, Java, and Ruby.

Floyd

- www.openqa.org/floyd/

Floyd, an open source testing tool for the Java platform, simulates a browser for testing Web-based applications.

HtmlUnit

- http://htmlunit.sourceforge.net/

HtmlUnit is an open source Java testing framework for testing Web-based applications.

JUnit

- http://junit.org

JUnit is an open source unit-testing framework for Java.

JWebUnit

- http://jwebunit.sourceforge.net/

JWebUnit is an open source Java framework that facilitates creation of acceptance tests for Web applications.

NDbUnit

- www.ndbunit.org/

NDbUnit is an open source .NET library for putting a database into a known state. NDbUnit can be used to increase repeatability in tests that interact with a database by ensuring a consistent database state across test executions.

NUnit

- www.nunit.org/

NUnit is an open source unit-testing framework for all .NET languages.

Selenium

- www.openqa.org/selenium

Selenium is a Fit-style (table-based test cases), in-browser functional testing tool for Web applications. It works great for development teams that desire automated regression system testing of their Web applications, and it is easily incorporated into your CI system. A useful open source companion tool, Selenium IDE, makes test script creation simple by allowing testers to record their actions while using the application (some basic HTML/JavaScript knowledge is required).

SQLUnit

- http://sqlunit.sourceforge.net

SQLUnit is an open source testing framework for verifying database stored procedures.

TestEarly.com

- www.testearly.com/

TestEarly.com is a blog dedicated to building quality into software early in the development lifecycle. Some of this book's authors are regular contributors on this site.

TestNG

- www.testng.org

TestNG is an open source testing framework for the Java platform. Inspired by JUnit and NUnit, it introduces some new features that make it quite powerful for testing from component to system level.

utPLSQL

- http://utplsql.sourceforge.net/

utPLSQL is an open source testing framework for verifying programs written in Oracle's PL/SQL language.

Watir

- www.openqa.org/watir

Watir is an open source functional testing tool, written in Ruby, for automating browser-based tests of Web applications.

xUnit Test Patterns

- http://xunitpatterns.com/

This is the Web site for the *xUnit Test Patterns* book, by Gerard Meszaros.

Automated Inspection Resources

Checkstyle

- http://checkstyle.sourceforge.net

Checkstyle is a Java-based coding standard adherence and inspection tool. Since version 3, the types of checks have grown beyond the typical coding standard adherence. Currently, Checkstyle includes checks for various types of inspections such as design, code complexity, and code duplication.

Clover

- www.cenqua.com/clover/

Clover is a commercially available code-coverage tool for both Java and .NET.

Cobertura

- http://cobertura.sourceforge.net/

Cobertura is an open source code-coverage tool for Java.

EMMA

- http://emma.sourceforge.net/

EMMA is an open source code-coverage tool for Java. EMMA's reports are slightly different than those of Cobertura.

FindBugs

- http://findbugs.sourceforge.net/

FindBugs is a Java-based inspection tool to find bugs in your Java code based on bug patterns. Incorporate this tool into your build process and generate the report. You'll be surprised at what you didn't know about programming in Java.

FxCop

- www.gotdotnet.com/Team/FxCop/

FxCop is a code analysis tool for .NET that analyzes assemblies for conformance to the .NET Framework Design Guidelines.

JavaNCSS

- www.kclee.de/clemens/java/javancss/

JavaNCSS is an open source tool that determines the lengths of methods and classes by examining Java source files.

JDepend

- www.clarkware.com/software/JDepend.html

JDepend scans Java class files and generates design-quality metrics for each package.

NCover

- http://ncover.org

NCover is an open source code-coverage tool for .NET.

NDepend

- www.ndepend.com/

NDepend analyzes .NET code and generates design-quality metrics, such as afferent and efferent coupling, instability, and a host of other interesting metrics.

PMD

- http://pmd.sourceforge.net

PMD is an open source static-code analyzer for the Java platform that supports coding standard adherence.

Simian

- www.redhillconsulting.com.au/products/simian/

Simian is a tool that identifies duplication in Java, C#, C++, Ruby, and just about every other language available today. It can even spot duplication in plain text files.

SourceMonitor

- www.campwoodsw.com/sm20.html

SourceMonitor is freeware inspection tool (metrics) for programmers. It supports C/C++, Delphi, HTML, Java, C#, and Visual Basic programming languages. Analyze your code and learn how to improve it; if you are unsure what certain metrics mean, you can refer to the extensive documentation describing the metrics used by the tool. You can parse the XML reports to HTML so that you can incorporate this into your build process.

Deployment Resources

Capistrano

- http://manuals.rubyonrails.com/read/book/17

Capistrano is a utility for deploying Ruby on Rails Web applications.

Feedback Resources

Ambient Devices

- www.ambientdevices.com/
- www.qualitylabs.org/projects/ambientorb/

Ambient Devices offers several products. Chapter 9 mentioned how you can use the Ambient Orb as a "glanceable" information radiator.

An Ambient Orb Ant task is available at Quality Labs to make it easier to interface with the Orb.

GoogleTalk

- www.google.com/talk/

With some work, you can incorporate a Jabber message to be sent from your CI system (e.g., CruiseControl) to your instant-message client.

Jabber

- www.jabber.org/

Incorporate open source instant messaging as a part of your CI system's feedback. Jabber is compatible with GoogleTalk.

X10

- www.x10.com/

You can use X10 to control any electrical device that uses radio frequency. This site contains information on starter kits you can use to grow your project's or organization's feedback mechanisms.

Others

Name	*Web Site*
Apache Java Enterprise Mail Server ("Apache James")	http://james.apache.org/server/index.html
Gaim	http://gaim.sourceforge.net/
Lava lamps	www.lavalites.com/

Documentation Resources

Doxygen

- www.stack.nl/~dimitri/doxygen/

Doxygen is an open source documentation system for C/C++, Java, Objective-C, Python, and IDL (Corba and Microsoft flavors) and, to a lesser extent, PHP, C#, and D. This program allows you to generate documentation in various formats such as LaTeX, RTF, PostScript, PDF, HTML, and UNIX man pages. Perhaps the best aspect of Doxygen is using GraphViz to generate UML-style diagrams to help visualize your source code.

Javadoc

- http://java.sun.com/j2se/javadoc/

Java includes a standard tool for generating API documentation in HTML format. Various "doclets" exist that allow you to generate different formats as well as check your Javadoc comments for irregularities.

NDoc

- http://ndoc.sourceforge.net/

NDoc is an open source documentation tool for .NET (namely, .NET assemblies and the XML documentation files generated by C#). This tool will help you generate your documentation in the standard Microsoft ways such as .chm, HTML Help 2, and MSDN online style Web pages.

Appendix B
Evaluating CI Tools

A craftsman who wishes to practice his craft well must first sharpen his tools.

—CHINESE PROVERB

Raoul (not his real name) was part of a small team brought in to help subdue a struggling J2EE project for a large development team. His role in this effort was lead integrator, responsible for ensuring that sixty or so development environments were consistent with one another as well as with the test and production build environments. The first task was to hunt down the source code and other build artifacts used to create the development environments. He searched in various version control repositories and networked file systems; then one team member offered, "I think Carl has a pretty good copy of the application server configuration on a diskette in his drawer."

With the source artifacts in hand, Raoul's next challenge was to create an automated build process for the development environments. The test and production build process was stable but was written as a set of UNIX shell scripts that would check out the code, invoke compilers, copy JARs, and so on—but unfortunately, all of the development environments were Windows machines, each with whichever JVM, application server version, and editing tools the developer had installed.

Raoul pointed out to the project's configuration manager the frustration and loss of productivity that everyone was suffering at integration time. "We're already on top of it," Raoul was told. "We're going to requisition and install UNIX emulation software on the workstations so that they can run the UNIX build scripts." With a lot of reconfiguration work and an equal amount of prayer, this rickety approach would probably work, at least for those developers who had configured their workstations similarly enough to the UNIX environments.

Raoul mustered some political and rhetorical skill (which isn't much, he tells me) and convinced the project managers to reverse their course and instead institute a common Ant-based build mechanism. Ant and Java are platform-independent, after all, and they could even use Ant scripts to automatically set up consistent development environments, saving the developers many hours of time.

The moral of this story is that tool selection matters. True, there is more than one way to do most things, but some ways will leave you scarred and bleeding. Fortunately, barring any "roll your own" type approaches, it's hard to make a big mistake choosing tools made to implement your development environment. Most of the tools that are available are mature and well suited to the task of CI.

This appendix is devoted to helping you select appropriate CI tools. I wish I could tell you which tool is the perfect choice for you, but choosing tools is highly dependent on your environment, the size of your project, and the functionality you want to get out of your automated builds. Which is the better tool for driving nails, a hammer or a nail gun? I'd expect to get a different answer depending on whether I had asked a roofer on a construction job or a hobbyist building a bird house. That being the case, the first section in this appendix elaborates on the factors to consider when choosing tools to implement CI for your development group.

The second and third sections give an overview of the tools currently available. Though space prevents giving complete instructions on their use, I'll discuss enough information to really give you the "flavor" of the tools from installation to their use. I cover tools used to support the two most common application development platforms: Java and .NET. If you work in another language, such as Ruby, C, Perl, or PHP, don't despair—there are CI tools for a wide range of languages and development styles. A quick search of the Internet should turn up what you need for these platforms.

Keep This Appendix Up to Date

Since the tools we cover in this appendix are in a rapidly changing market, we recommend that you visit the book's Web site, www.integratebutton.com, to keep up-to-date with the latest scripts, tools, and research.

This appendix covers build and scheduling tools, but not version control tools, because it's likely that your version control system has been chosen for you. If not, there are plenty of fine online resources and books to help you choose. If you're on an active project that doesn't use a version control tool yet, put this book down right now and put one in place. Done? Good. Let's get started.

Considerations When Evaluating Tools

Choosing automation software is a matter of finding the best fit for your environment and development process. The best tool is the one that saves you and the rest of the development team the most pain and serves you the longest. Tool comparison conversations can often transcend the practical and escalate into what sounds like a religious debate. There were times where you'd read a discussion about the relative merits of CruiseControl and Anthill and you might be reminded of the ongoing Ford versus Chevy debate (though I haven't seen any disparaging window decals on the software topic yet).

Also, bear in mind that your choice of tools needn't be a lifelong commitment. If it becomes one, it indicates that the tool works well with you and you with it. I've worked on a couple of projects where I changed the build scheduling tool in midstream. In both cases, it only took an afternoon to do. Of course, if you've invested significant effort and money in one of the heavy-duty distributed build tools, it may be a different story. For most of us, though, one of the many open source tools will work just fine, and switching between them is easy.

Let's look at the various factors that should influence your decision. These points are helpful to take into account while contemplating how to set up your development environment. Again, this isn't a decision that will require weeks of research and has deep finality to it. After a day or two, you should be up and integrating continuously, and you can make adjustments as you go along.

Functionality

Naturally, the most important criterion in choosing a tool is whether it does what you need it to do. This section describes the valuable essential and extended functionality offered by build and build-scheduler tools.

Build Tools—Essential Functionality

The following are essential functionality for build tools.

- **Code compilation**—No surprise here: Compiling source code is the main ingredient in building software. For efficiency, compilation should be performed conditionally based on whether source code or dependencies have changed.
- **Component packaging**—After compiling the source code and formatting any other artifacts that need to be included, software typically needs to be bundled into deployable components such as Java JAR files or Windows EXE files. The build tool you choose should understand how to package the necessary components for your environment and do so only when the contents of the package have changed.
- **Program execution**—The build tool should have good support for invoking programs in its target platform as well as for invoking any program that has a command-line interface.
- **File manipulation**—Creating, copying, and deleting files and directories are typical build functionality that the tools should support.

Build Tools—Extended Functionality

Extended functionality for build tools includes the following.

- **Development test execution**—Beyond simply compiling the software, the most common activity is running the suite of automated developer tests for the software. Though you can integrate your build tool with your testing tool via command-line execution if necessary, the better your build tool integrates with your unit test tool, the better off you are.
- **Version control tool integration**—If your build scheduler tool delegates version control activities to your build tool, or if you have other version control activities that would benefit from automation, look for support for your version control system within the build tool. Again, command-line-based integration is always a fallback option if necessary.
- **Documentation generation**—If you work in a programming language that supports embedded documentation, such as C# or Java, it's very useful to have your build tool automatically generate the API documentation when the build is run.
- **Deployment functionality**—If you plan to run functional tests or in-container unit tests during your automated build, the build must first deploy the application to a test server. This functionality may be provided from your build tool or may be provided as a plug-in by the server vendor or the server's user community.
- **Code quality analysis**—As Chapter 7 makes clear, you can gain great insight into the stability and maintainability of your code by running various types of automated inspectors. Look at which analysis tools are bundled with your build tool or are available as plug-ins.
- **Extensibility**—It's uncommon to need to write your own plug-ins for a build tool; most challenges you'll run into aren't unique and have already been solved for you. However, in some cases, you may want to extend the build tool itself; for instance, if you want to seamlessly integrate a new test or reporting tool. A well-documented extensibility API is a must in this case. Just don't forget to contribute your plug-in back to the user community. You, your plug-in, and the community will be better off for it.
- **Multiplatform builds**—Most CI servers are designed to run on a single build machine. This, of course, means that all the build

activities will take place on the build server platform. For most applications, this is fine. However, if you're developing software that must be built and tested for multiple platforms, things get a little trickier. The best option in this case may be to purchase one of the commercial tools that orchestrate build processes across multiple servers.

- **Accelerated builds**—A key to CI is the capability to run the complete build cycle quickly. Some experts advise keeping the complete build time less than ten minutes[1] for this reason. If your build cycle is many hours long due to the sheer volume of your code (this is rare), you may want to examine some of the tools that are able to distribute build steps among multiple processes on multiple build servers.

Build Schedulers—Essential Functionality

Essential functionality for build schedulers includes the following.

- **Build execution**—The core functionality of a build scheduler is the execution of the automated build on a periodic basis. There are some subtle differences between how different tools determine when to execute a build. Some tools are polling-driven. These tools poll your version control repository periodically (usually every few minutes) and execute a build when they detect that a change has been made. Other tools are schedule-driven. These tools check your version control repository on a predetermined schedule based on an interval or an explicit schedule.

  CI purists will argue that schedule-driven tools aren't true CI servers, since they are often configured for daily builds and usually don't handle short-interval configurations well. From a technical standpoint I agree, and I personally prefer polling-driven tools, but remember that the best tool is the one that helps you do your job most effectively. If you find you work best with an hourly build, it won't be held against you, but it isn't CI by definition.

1. See Kent Beck's *Extreme Programming Explained, Second Edition.*

Finally, some tools are **event driven,** meaning that a build is triggered automatically when a change is made to the artifacts in your version control system. Though this may sound preferable, there's little practical difference between event-driven builds and polling-driven builds. Furthermore, an event-driven tool will almost certainly require some amount of monkeying around with your version control system, whereas a polling-driven tool will not.

- **Version control integration**—Naturally, it's important that you choose a tool that integrates with your version control system. Most tools support the most popular version control systems, and it's unlikely that you won't find a tool that works with yours. You'll want to pay attention to how the tool interacts with your tool. Does the tool always fetch a complete set of files for each changed build with no option to configure this behavior? This approach may be unsuitable if your project is large and you're trying to run near-continuous builds. Another helpful feature to look for is how well the tool identifies the changes that went into the build. At a minimum, the tool should identify which files changed and the version numbers of the changed files.
- **Build tool integration**—This is another component that you choose for integration with your version control system, and most tools support most popular version control systems. Just watch how the tool interacts with your version control platform.
- **Feedback**—Feedback is essential to CI. All of the tools listed in this appendix support at least e-mail feedback, which may be sufficient, but there are other options you might wish to consider, such as feedback by instant message, text message, or some other device. See Chapter 9 to learn more about some of our favorite feedback devices.
- **Build labeling**—In most cases, you'll want the tool to mark the artifacts that contributed to a given build. This is called either labeling or tagging, depending on your version control system. Most tools provide some sort of ascending counter that is appended to the label format that you provide.

Build Schedulers—Extended Functionality

Extended functionality for build schedulers includes the following.

- **Interproject dependencies**—Depending on your configuration management strategy, if you have interproject dependencies you may want to execute dependent project builds when a depended-upon project is rebuilt.
- **User interface**—Strictly speaking, there's no reason to require a user interface for a build scheduler tool. The core functionality runs as a daemon checking for version control changes, running builds, and sending feedback. However, it is useful to have a user interface that allows you to alter the configuration, check the current build status, and download artifacts. All tools provide this in some fashion, usually as a Web application interface. Some tools, such as Luntbuild, are distributed as Web applications. Other tools, such as CruiseControl, take a different approach with the user interfaces provided as optional elements. Whatever the approach, a well-designed user interface will save you time and effort when working with the tool.
- **Artifact publication**—At the very least, the end result of a successful build is a deployable component. If you're leveraging the real power of CI, the results will also include documentation, test results, quality analysis results, and other metrics. All tools provide some level of publication functionality by providing a directory to hold published artifacts. More sophisticated tools format developer test results and other reports automatically for easy review.
- **Security**—Finally, some tools provide authentication and authorization to allow you to specify who may view results and make configuration changes. Usually, given the collaborative spirit of CI, this isn't necessary, but if you are supporting multiple development groups or have unique security requirements, this may be important. Remember, though, that enabling security increases the support burden. Each time someone joins or leaves your development team, you will need to update the tool's security database.

Compatibility with Your Environment

By **compatibility,** we're talking about how well the tool integrates with the other elements of your software development process. When evaluating a build tool, check whether it includes a compiler for the language you work in. Does it support your version control system? These are the essential considerations. Looking further, you may wish to examine the following issues.

- **Does the tool support your current build configuration?** Let's say you're working on a Java project that's still using JDK 1.2 and the deprecated elements therein (perhaps you are on a government project). Will the tool run on this Java release, or can you configure that JDK to be used for compilation and execution? Most tools can be configured to build for any arbitrary platform, but this is something you want to check.
- **Does the tool require installation of additional software in order to run?** In the best case, you can drop the new tool into place and get right to configuring it. In other cases, you may be required to install some additional software before you can start. For example, most of the Java build schedulers we examine later in this appendix require a Web server with a servlet container. Some tools may require installation of a new execution environment, such as Python or Ruby, in order to run. You should consider the additional effort required to set up and support any additional software required. Typically, the burden is fairly low for these additional elements, but sometimes the less you're required to change, the better.
- **Is the tool written in the same language as your project?** The more the tool developers have had to walk in your shoes and experience the same environment-related hassles that you have, the better their tool will deal with those issues. With open source software, you'll have the opportunity to run the tool in a debugger if necessary. Also, as you become a master in the ways of CI, you might extend the tool in interesting and useful ways and contribute back to the tool community.

Reliability

Basically, what you're looking for here is the maturity of the tool. Unless you want to spend your time being a toolsmith, you want a tool that's been around the block a few times; one that's been beat up a lot and has become battle-hardened as a result. It's safe to say that a release 3.0 tool is likely to be more reliable than the Beta release of a different tool.

Other important indications of maturity include the size of the user and development communities. Support for noncommercial software generally comes from its users, so the larger the user community, the easier it is to find answers to your questions. Check out the support mailing list archives for the tool. Are they very active? For open source tools, how many developers are contributing to the project? How active is recent development? How many times has the tool been downloaded? Furthermore, if the tool has a long and storied history, it's a good indication that it will continue to be around for a while longer.

Longevity

Whereas with reliability we are considering a tool's past and present, with longevity we're concerned with the tool's future. I'd be willing to bet that none of the tools described later in this appendix will still be around 1,000 years from now, but then again you don't want to choose a tool that goes belly-up next month.

Again, look for evidence of a healthy user base and an established development group. Is the tool used by a large and thriving community, or is it being sold off the back of a wagon as a "miracle" solution that is supposedly still a "well-kept secret?"

Though counterintuitive to some, longevity is a compelling argument for choosing an open source tool. With open source, it's the tool's user community that keeps the tool vital. A good tool with unique value stays in use, and a tool with nothing special to offer goes out of fashion very quickly. With commercial products, the lifecycle depends on the economic viability of both the product and its vendor. We've all seen cases where a sleek, well-designed commercial product has turned into unusable bloatware due to the pressure to continually add features. This is not to say that choosing a commercial tool is necessarily a bad decision. Some commercial tools offer features that can't be found in any of the open source offerings. Just keep in mind that your CI server will become your close companion, and you'll want it to stick around for a long time before having to say good-bye.

Usability

Finally, the easier a tool is to configure and use, the better. You may need to experiment with a few tools to figure this out. Typically, the only variation in usability you'll find between tools is in configuring new projects, which only needs to be done once per project. CruiseControl is my tool of choice, and I typically hand-code the XML configuration file that it requires (though a separate configuration GUI application is available for this purpose). Writing XML is certainly less user-friendly than the Web interfaces provided by most other tools, but I find the difference in configuration time much less important compared to the advantages in using CruiseControl for my projects.

So now that you know the various facets to consider when evaluating CI tools, consider which are the most important for your CI scenario. Let's take a look at the tools that are currently available.

Automated Build Tools

Choosing an automated build tool is fairly straightforward. If you're building Java software, you'll probably use Ant or perhaps Maven if you want the project management features that it offers. If you develop for .NET, you'll most likely use NAnt or MSBuild.

This section provides an overview of these automated build tools. This isn't meant to be an exhaustive list of all possible build tools; for instance, we won't cover the build tools bundled with IDEs or GUI-centric stand-alone build tools.

Before proceeding, we should give a tip of the hat to **make,** the granddaddy of all build tools and still going strong. Invented in 1977 at Bell Labs, make introduced us to dependency checking and incremental builds. Though the tools that followed are better suited for Java and .NET projects, make (or one of its many variants) is a viable option for building software written in many languages, most notably C or C++. Now, with that acknowledgment out of the way, let's start our tool survey.

Ant

Distributor: Apache (http://ant.apache.org)

Platform: Java

Requires: JDK 1.2 or later

At the time of this publication, Ant is the most widely used build tool for Java. Its functionality is extensive, covering all the features listed earlier in the appendix. Because the use of Ant has been covered earlier in this book, I'll simply reiterate that Ant builds are defined using an XML configuration file (build.xml) and are run from the command line or through integration with other tools such as IDEs and build scheduler tools.

Ant was originally released by Apache for its own use in 2000 and is one of the most widely used Java tools in the world. It is well documented and rock solid in terms of reliability. Simply put, Ant should probably be your first thought when choosing a build tool for a Java project. The only compelling alternatives to Ant—Maven and some commercial tools covered later—work at a higher level than Ant and often use Ant's functionality "under the hood."

Maven 1

Distributor: Apache (http://maven.apache.org/maven-1.x/)

Platform: Java 2

Requires: JDK 1.4 or later

Apache Maven is an open source tool that works at a level above typical build tools. On its Web site, Maven is described as a "software project management and comprehension tool." With very little configuration, Maven is able to build your software project, run your developer tests, produce a number of useful source quality reports, and generate a Web site to contain the output of all of these steps.

Installing Maven is straightforward. An installer is provided for Windows platforms; on other platforms it's a simple matter of extracting the distribution, setting a `MAVEN_HOME` environment variable, and adding Maven to your path. Integration is also provided for the following IDEs: IntelliJ IDEA, Eclipse, JBuilder, and JDEE.

To configure a project to use Maven, you first write a project.xml file in the project's root directory that describes your project. A very simple example can be seen in Listing B-1. The information in project.xml defines what is known as the Project Object Model (POM). The POM describes a wide range of information about the project, from basics such as the layout of the project's directory structure up to higher-level information such as subscription information for the developer and user mailing lists.

LISTING B-1 A Simple project.xml Example

```
1  <project>
2    <id>helloworld</id>
3    <name>Hello World</name>
4    <version>1.0-SNAPSHOT</version>
5    <organization>
6      <name>Continuous Integration Book</name>
7    </organization>
8    <description>Our Hello World project</description>
9    <build>
10     <sourceDirectory>src/java</sourceDirectory>
11     <unitTestSourceDirectory>src/test</unitTestSourceDirectory>
12     <unitTest>
13       <includes>
14         <include>**/*Test.java</include>
15       </includes>
16     </unitTest>
17   </build>
18 </project>
```

One of the key advantages of Maven is that, whereas with a build tool such as Ant you are required to explicitly describe what you want your build to do, Maven provides very sensible defaults for how a project should be built and what artifacts should be produced. This isn't to imply that Maven is inflexible; you can easily customize your POM to override and extend Maven's default behavior. Maven includes plug-ins that are used for everything from building J2EE artifacts to running additional reports. You can also extend Maven by writing your own plug-ins or through scripting.

Another interesting aspect is how Maven handles dependencies, including the JARs required to build your project and those required internally by Maven for its own functionality. Instead of including your own library of JARs within your project, you declare the JARs as project dependencies, and Maven handles the task of downloading the JARs from a central repository to a cache on the machine on which Maven is installed.

Maven is used by invoking a `goal` from the command line. Maven goals are analogous to targets in other build tools. For instance, calling `maven clean` from the command line will remove all build output and other generated artifacts. Calling `maven build` will build the project and run its JUnit test suite. One of the more interesting goals is `site`, which will build your project, test it, run reports, and publish to a project Web site. This is the default project reports summary page generated from the project.xml shown in Listing B-1.

It's important to understand that Maven is designed to produce a single build artifact per project, be it a JAR, WAR, or EAR. If your project is built from multiple JARs and other files, each of these requires its own separate Maven project, with the interproject dependencies declared as necessary. Maven 2 makes it much easier to aggregate multiple build artifacts under a single Maven project.

Most Java build scheduler tools provide Maven integration in addition to Ant integration. There is also a separate Maven subproject named Continuum, discussed later, to provide build scheduling. If you've decided to use Maven, be sure that the build scheduler tool you pick is one that supports it.

Overall, Maven is very worthy of consideration, provided that you are comfortable with giving up the absolute control that you get with a lower-level build tool and buy into its view of dependency management. Maven certainly provides a lot of functionality for a relatively small amount of configuration overhead.

Maven 2

Distributor: Apache (http://maven.apache.org)

Platform: Java

Requires: JDK 1.4 or later

Maven 2 continues Maven 1's tradition of a commonsense and easy-to-use project management framework. Ease of use is achieved by providing a common project structure and enforcing a uniform build system. Furthermore, Maven 2 supplies standardized project information, guidelines for best practices, and a transparent route to migrating Maven 1 features.

Maven 2 has significant improvements over its predecessor. It seems much faster and the new distribution is also much smaller in size. Other enhancements include improved dependency management (support for transitive dependencies), defined build lifecycle, improved plug-in architecture, and unified project definition.

Setting up and running Maven 2 is straightforward. Start by downloading the latest binary distribution from http://maven.apache.org/download.html. You can easily create a skeleton project with the very basic structure and the minimum number of files. Just run

```
mvn archetype:create -DgroupId=my.group.id -DartifactId=my-artifact-id
```

and Maven 2 will create a project conforming to a standard directory layout. You can now add your own Java classes and build the project by typing `mvn clean package`.

One of the features that makes Maven 2 so versatile is the availability of high-impact, open source plug-ins. The set of core Maven 2 plug-ins in Apache covers common tasks such as compilation and deployment, packaging (EJB, JAR, RAR, WAR, and EAR files), reporting, tools, and IDE project generation. Maven 2 is also supported by the Mojo project at Codehaus. Mojo provides many plug-ins, ranging from assembler and AspectJ to xml and xdoclet. Using a plug-in can be as simple as declaring it in the POM file. The tool is smart enough to locate the plug-in on the Internet, download its binaries to a temporary location on the local drive, configure the plug-in, run the appropriate goal, and report its results. Very useful—and just four lines of code made that possible.

Maven 2 provides support for IDEs as well. Codehaus, the host of Mojo, distributes Mergere for Eclipse and Mevenide for NetBeans. Both plug-ins provide the capability to open a Maven 2 project file (POM) inside the IDE and run Maven goals seamlessly from the IDE.

Having heard all the benefits of this new tool, should you consider Maven 2 as your build system? It depends. If you have a large enterprise project with a number of Ant scripts, migrating the scripts and changing your project layout can be quite time-consuming. Maven 2 provides ways to call Ant targets from the POM file, which could potentially ease the migration; however, a certain level of planning will be necessary. If, on the other hand, you're starting a new project, the key features such as standardized project layout, dependency management, automatic project documentation, and the availability of highly usable third-party plug-ins should put Maven 2 on top of your list of choices for a build system. Many CI servers, including CruiseControl, provide support for Maven 2. Figure B-1 shows a project site generated by Maven.

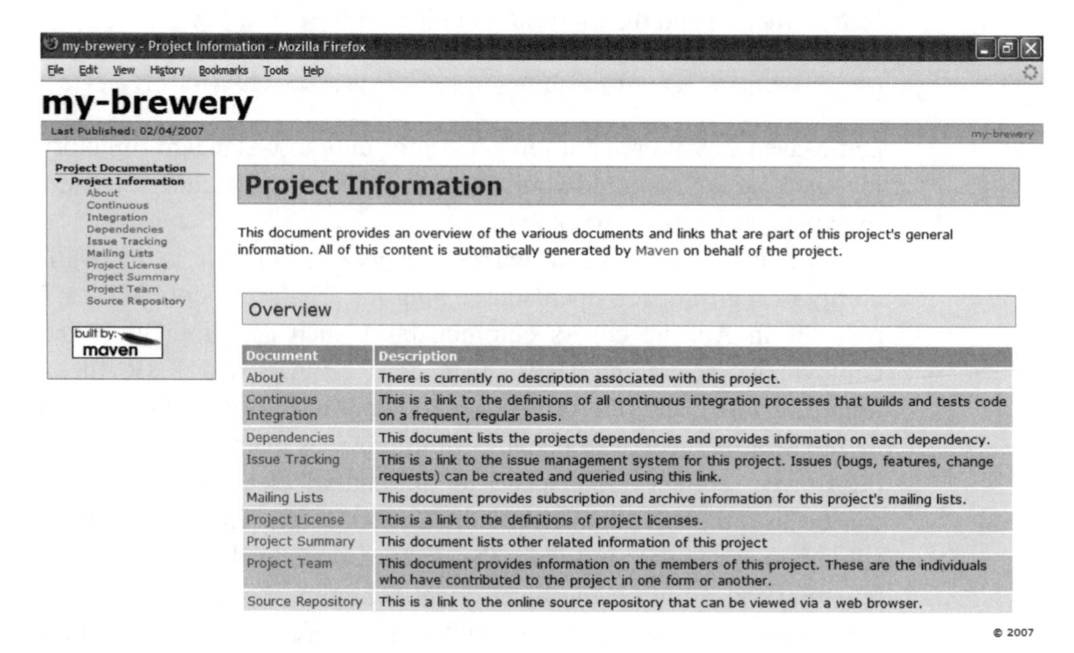

FIGURE B-1 Project site generated by Maven

NAnt

Distributor: SourceForge (http://nant.sourceforge.net)

Platform: Microsoft .NET

Requires: Microsoft .NET Framework 1.0 and later or Mono (1.0 and 2.0 profile)

NAnt is an open source automated build tool for Microsoft .NET projects. As its name implies, NAnt is very similar to Ant in configuration and operation. Like Ant, NAnt uses an XML build file to define how projects are built. Listing B-2 shows an sample build file that compiles a single C# source file. Build files should be named with a `.build` extension.

NAnt provides functionality as `tasks` that are called from `targets` defined in your build files. NAnt includes tasks for compiling programs written in C, C++, C#, J#, Visual Basic.NET, and JScript.NET. Other tasks supplied with NAnt provide functionality for managing files, creating AssemblyInfo files, registering .NET services, running NUnit unit tests, and accessing CVS version control repositories.

LISTING B-2 A Simple NAnt Build File

```
1  <project name="Hello World" default="build" basedir=".">
2    <target name="clean">
3      <delete file="HelloWorld.exe" failonerror="false" />
4    </target>
5    <target name="build">
6      <csc target="exe" output="HelloWorld.exe">
7        <sources>
8          <include name="HelloWorld.cs" />
9        </sources>
10     </csc>
11   </target>
12 </project>
```

Builds are run from the command line by invoking NAnt and passing a target name as an argument. For example, to run the `clean` target in the example in Listing B-2, you would enter `nant clean` on the command line. Build files may also declare a default target to run when no target name is provided. Line 1 in Listing B-2 declares the target `build` as the default.

NAnt has been available since 2001. Though it is still in the Beta phase of release, it is widely used and very robust. It should be noted that beginning with Visual Studio 2005, Microsoft has entered the fray with its own XML descriptor-based build tool named MSBuild. Both NAnt and MSBuild should be considered good choices for automating your .NET project builds.

Rake

Distributor: RubyForge (http://rake.rubyforge.org/)

Platform: Ruby and other development platforms

Requires: Ruby 1.8 or later

Rake is Ruby's make; however, it's unique in that Rake files are essentially Ruby scripts rather than XML or some other grammar. Consequently, employing Rake is incredibly simple. Much like Java's Ant, Rake has the notion of *tasks,* which can have dependencies on other tasks; furthermore, Rake comes with a series of tasks out of the box, such as running developer tests, generating RDocs, and a plethora of file utilities. Interestingly enough, Rake's powerful build language can support building other languages, such as Java.

For example, Listing B-3 shows a Rake file that runs all unit tests defined in the `tests/unit/` directory.

LISTING B-3 Sample Rake File That Runs Unit Tests

```
require "rake/testtask"

task :default => [:unit-test]

Rake::TestTask.new(:unit-test) do | tsk |
 tsk.test_files = "tests/unit/**/*Test.rb"
end
```

Note how the second line defines the `default` task as the `unit-test`, meaning that if Rake is invoked via the command line without any arguments, the `unit-test` task will be run.

Creating Rake task dependencies is easy; in fact, you can see this in action in Listing B-3. The `default` task has an implicit dependency on `unit-test`. Within task definitions, you can also define dependencies. For instance, it probably makes sense to run all unit tests before generating source code documentation; consequently, the Rake file in Listing B-4 adds an RDoc generation task that has a direct dependency on the `unit-test` task.

LISTING B-4 Sample Rake File with Dependencies

```
require "rake/testtask"
require "rake/rdoctask"

task :default => [:unit-test]

Rake::TestTask.new(:unit-test) do | tsk |
 tsk.test_files = "tests/unit/**/*Test.rb"
end

Rake::RDocTask.new(:rdoc => [:test]) do | tsk |
  tsk.rdoc_files.include("./src/ruby/*.rb")
end
```

Obviously, for those developing applications in a Ruby environment, Rake is the way to go. As mentioned previously, Rake doesn't prohibit building non-Ruby applications.

Build Scheduler Tools

Looking at the variety of build scheduler tools and their popularity, it's plain to see that CI has gained a lot of popular acceptance. In this section, we examine the most popular of these tools for Java and .NET projects. As indicated, we will not cover all of the different tools on the market. However, we do cover the most well-established tools in this arena (as well as some interesting newcomers), but new tools are arriving on the scene all the time. These general-purpose tools are designed to run on a single build server and easily handle most projects. This accounts for the majority of tools in this appendix. You'll find both open source tools and commercial tools in this category. For each tool, we tell you whether it's open source or commercial, then list the system prerequisites and the supported build tools and version control systems.

AnthillPro

Distributor: Urbancode (www.anthillpro.com/)

Platform: Java

Build tools: Ant, GNU Make, Maven, NAnt, and command line

Version control systems: AccuRev, ClearCase, CVS, MKS, Perforce, PVCS, StarTeam, Subversion, and Visual SourceSafe

Requires: JDK 1.4 or later

Urbancode created Anthill OS in 2001 as a freely available tool for build management. Based on the success of this product, they provide a commercial product called AnthillPro. AnthillPro builds upon the functionality provided by Anthill OS, providing additional features, more flexible configuration, and a revised user interface. The main dashboard is shown in Figure B-2. Urbancode offers an evaluation edition available for download from its Web site, so you can try it for yourself.

AnthillPro adds a number of capabilities beyond those offered in Anthill OS. First, AnthillPro provides adapters for several additional version control providers. Another key differentiator is that AnthillPro provides support for Maven and GNU Make, as well as providing integration with Ant. For some, the most useful addition may be the authentication and authorization features. This new functionality allows administrators to control who is allowed to view and edit configuration options, as well as who can access build artifacts. Because it provides a tool for comprehensive build management, not just CI, it provides features for multiple build types (other than just an integration build during the development cycle), project dependencies, and several other features.

Installation essentially consists of extracting an installation JAR from the command line. AnthillPro is very flexible when it comes to configuration, allowing users to configure different JVM profiles and Ant installations to be used for builds. Like Anthill OS, AnthillPro is also schedule-driven. New schedules may be defined as simple intervals or as `cron` expressions.

Configuring AnthillPro can be daunting for new users—the increased flexibility is embodied in a vast array of options that can be confusing. As often occurs with tools with an increased set of func-

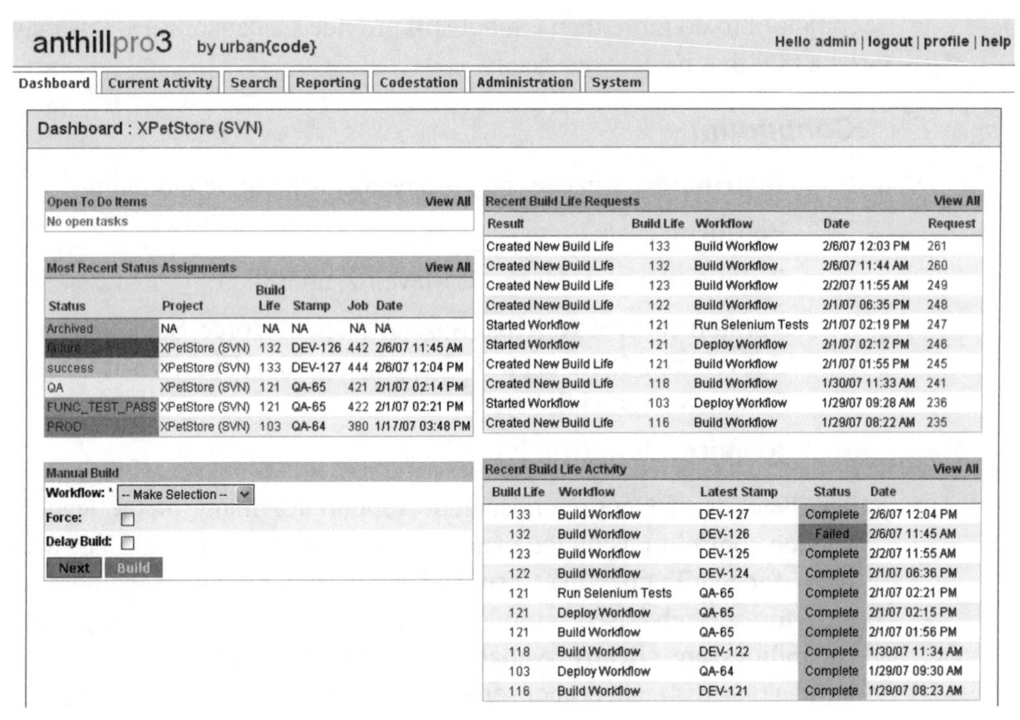

FIGURE B-2 AnthillPro dashboard

tionality, this can make configuration difficult, though it shouldn't take long to become accustomed to the tool.

Creating a new build in AnthillPro takes several steps. First, you add a new project, which identifies the project's version control repository and the labeling strategy to use. After creating the project, you choose which version control branches of the project to build. Often this will just be the main branch (also called the trunk), but this feature can also be used to provide different configurations—for example, for a development branch, a release branch, and a bug fix branch. Each branch lets you configure multiple "build life(s)." Each build life can define its own schedule, publishing strategy, and build process. For instance, you might configure an hourly incremental Ant build throughout the day for compilation and testing, with a full Maven site publication performed once a night for full system testing.

AnthillPro provides a lot of flexibility for those who require it, but the increase in settings is fairly steep from Anthill OS. If you're looking for a tool to do more than CI, but still provide CI capabilities, this may be a tool that meets your needs.

Continuum

Distributor: Apache (http://maven.apache.org/continuum/)

Platform: Java 2

Build tools: Ant, Maven 1, Maven 2, and Shell

Version control systems: Bazaar, CVS, Perforce, StarTeam, and Subversion. There is partial support for ClearCase, Visual Source Safe, and file systems.

Requires: Java JDK 1.4 or later

The benefits of Continuum include support for many of the leading version control tools on the market, such as Subversion and CVS, with plans for StarTeam, ClearCase, and Perforce. Continuum includes an easy-to-use Web-based setup and user interface. Remote management capabilities are already available via XML-RPC and SOAP. Continuum, along with most other servers, provides various feedback mechanisms such as e-mail and instant messaging (IRC, Jabber, and MSN). Should Continuum not come up to speed fast enough, other Java-based CI servers such as CruiseControl have already included support for Maven 2. Be sure to check out the latest Maven 2 with Continuum advancements online. Figure B-3 illustrates an example of configuring a Continuum project for Ant.

CruiseControl

Distributor: ThoughtWorks (http://cruisecontrol.sourceforge.net)

Platform: Java 2

Build tools: Ant, Maven 1, Maven 2, and NAnt

Version control systems: ClearCase, CM Synergy, CVS, MKS, Perforce, PVCS, Snapshot CM, StarTeam, Subversion, Surround SCM, and Visual SourceSafe

Requires: Java JDK 1.3 or later

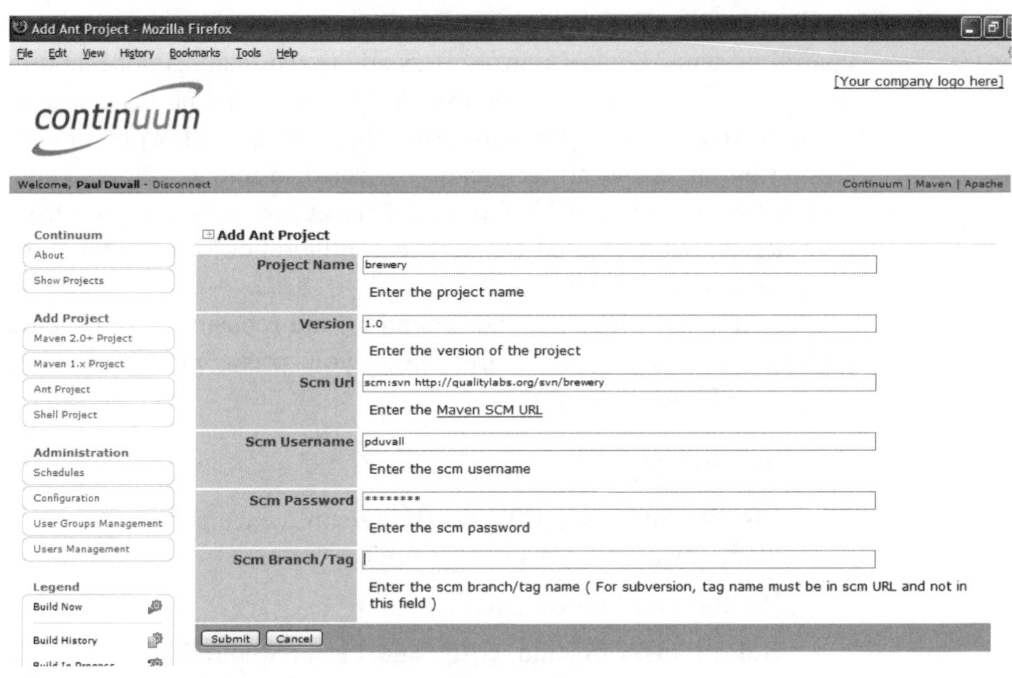

FIGURE B-3 Configuring an Ant project using Continuum

The open source product CruiseControl is by far the most widely used CI server for Java. Unlike the other general-purpose Java build scheduling tools in this appendix, which are packaged as monolithic Web applications, CruiseControl is packaged as several complementary components, such as the main CruiseControl service, an optional reporting Web application, and an optional Swing configuration GUI.

CruiseControl is typically set up to run as a background process, with the Java Web application providing the front-end and reporting interface. Refer back to Chapter 1 for an overview of configuring CruiseControl. New users often find the initial setup challenging, at least compared to the tools that provide a Web-based configuration interface. You will probably find that using the Swing configuration GUI will help reduce the time required for configuration. Even so, allow yourself extra time to review the configuration reference and online resources that exist to help you get started. Understanding the config.xml file is crucial to configuring CruiseControl properly.

Beyond its efficient engine and support for a wide range of version control systems, CruiseControl offers additional features not found in some of the other tools. If you use CruiseControl to automate several projects, you can configure it to run multiple threads, allowing for concurrent builds. Build artifacts can be pushed to remote servers using FTP or Secure Copy (SCP) if desired. CruiseControl also offers a JMX interface that can be used for remote configuration or automation of the CruiseControl service itself.

Given its functionality, wide adoption, and robustness, you should probably consider CruiseControl one of your prime candidates when adopting a CI for Java projects.

CruiseControl.NET

Distributor: ThoughtWorks (http://confluence.public.thoughtworks.org/display/CCNET)

Platform: Microsoft .NET

Build tools: MSBuild, NAnt, and Visual Studio .NET

Version control systems: ClearCase, CVS, MKS, Perforce, PVCS, SourceGear Vault, StarTeam, Subversion, Synergy, and Visual SourceSafe

Requires: Microsoft .NET Framework version 1.0, 1.1, or 2.0

Like CruiseControl for Java, CruiseControl.NET is the most widely used CI server for .NET projects. I have to say that I found installation and configuration quite easy to perform. Especially helpful were the sample configuration files that are provided with the installation. These examples demonstrate most of the common build and version control configuration options. Granted that I've been using CruiseControl for some time and configuration of CruiseControl.NET is very similar, I was still impressed when I was up and running with CruiseControl.NET literally within minutes of installation.

CruiseControl.NET can be used to run NAnt and MSBuild tasks, but it can also be used to automate simple builds using Visual Studio .NET (though this requires installation of Visual Studio components on the build server). CruiseControl.NET build status information and build artifacts can be accessed via the optional Web application. Installation of the Web application was likewise hassle-free. Figure B-4 shows a sample build result Web page.

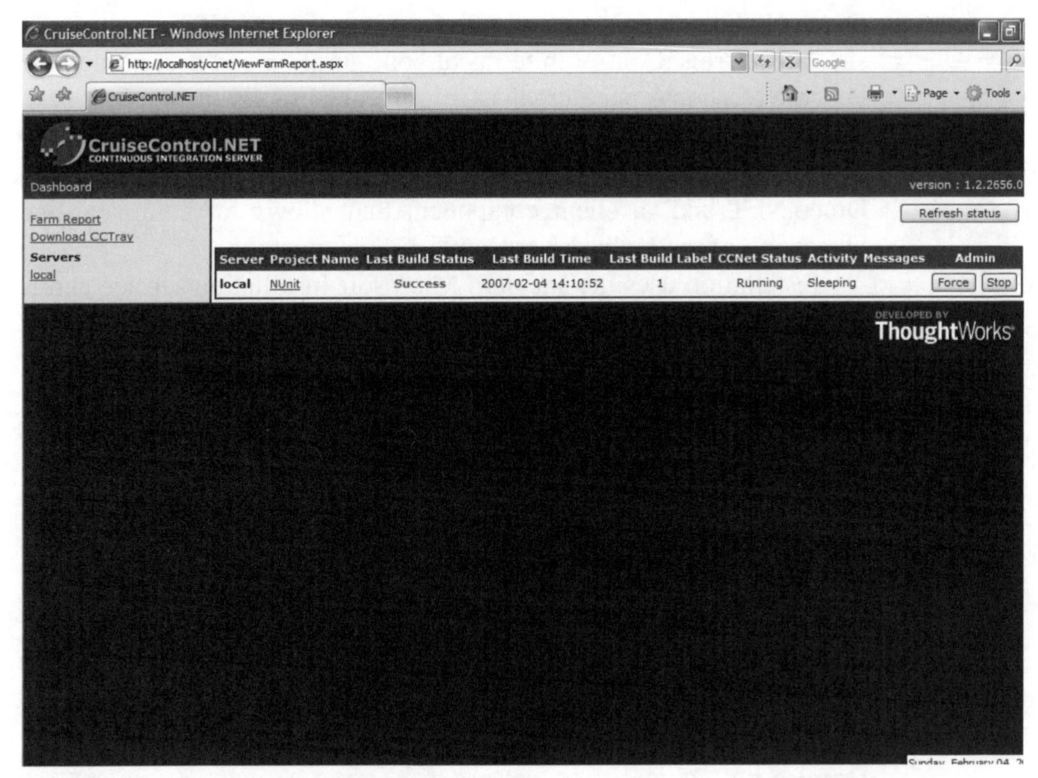

FIGURE B-4 CruiseControl.NET dashboard

Released in 2003, CruiseControl.NET hasn't been around as long as its Java counterpart. Despite its relative youth, however, CruiseControl.NET is a very reliable tool and its documentation and user support are excellent. If you're planning to implement CI for your .NET projects, I strongly recommend using this tool.

Draco.NET

Distributor: SourceForge (http://draconet.sourceforge.net/)

Platform: Microsoft .NET

Build tools: NAnt and Visual Studio .NET

Version control systems: CVS, Subversion, and Visual SourceSafe

Requires: Microsoft .NET Framework version 1.0 or 1.1

Draco.NET is another open source CI server for the .NET set. It's very similar to CruiseControl in terms of configuration and use; in fact, the Draco.NET home page credits CruiseControl as its inspiration. Like CruiseControl, the core service and the Web front end are distributed as separate components, in this case as Windows installers. To this, Draco.NET adds a client component that allows for command-line invocation of the build server from a remote machine.

Installation uses the standard Microsoft Installation service and is very straightforward. Similar to CruiseControl, builds are configured using an XML descriptor file, in this case named Draco.builds.config. Listing B-5 shows a simple example. Documentation on configuring Draco.NET is contained in a help file included with the distribution, but it is fairly brief. Fortunately, Draco.NET includes extensive examples in its default configuration file. Even so, configuring builds and the optional Web front end can be a tricky trial-and-error process; be sure to allow yourself extra time to set up the tool. Draco.NET is typically used to control NAnt builds of .NET projects, but you can also directly invoke Visual Studio .NET build functionality if Visual Studio is installed on the build server.

LISTING B-5 Sample Draco.builds.config File

```
1  <draco xmlns="http://www.chive.com/draco">
2    <pollperiod>600</pollperiod>
3    <quietperiod>60</quietperiod>
4    <timeoutperiod>3600</timeoutperiod>
5    <rootsourcedir>Source</rootsourcedir>
6    <mailserver>mail.5amsolutions.com</mailserver>
7    <fromaddress>draco@5amsolutions.com</fromaddress>
8    <builds>
9      <build>
10       <name>HelloWorldNET</name>
11       <notification>
12         <email>
13           <recipient>etavela@5amsolutions.com</recipient>
14         </email>
15         <file>
16           <dir>C:\Draco\Output</dir>
17         </file>
18       </notification>
19       <nant>
20         <buildfile>nant.build</buildfile>
21         <targets>build</targets>
22       </nant>
23       <cvs>
```

```
24          <cvsroot>:pserver:anonymous@localhost:/cvsrepo</cvsroot>
25          <module>HelloWorldNET</module>
26        </cvs>
27      </build>
28    </builds>
29  </draco>
```

Though not as widely used as CruiseControl.NET, Draco.NET has a significant number of users. Despite some glitches along the way, installation and configuration are reasonably manageable. If you're setting up CI for .NET for the first time, though, you'll probably be happier starting with CruiseControl.NET due to its usability and more extensive documentation.

Luntbuild

Distributor: SourceForge (http://luntbuild.javaforge.com/)

Platform: Java 2

Build tools: Ant, Maven, and command line

Version control systems: AccuRev, ClearCase, ClearCase UCM, CVS, Perforce, StarTeam, Subversion, and Visual SourceSafe

Requires: JDK 1.3 and later, Java Servlet container

Luntbuild is another popular open source Web-based CI server for the Java platform. As one would expect, installation consists of deploying the Luntbuild WAR to an existing Java Server engine on the build server.

The Web-based user interface can be somewhat confusing and counterintuitive. Luntbuild does offer more flexibility than other Web-based CI servers if you are willing to overcome the usability hurdle. Figure B-5 is an example of configuring a scheduler using Luntbuild.

Luntbuild is a relatively recent addition, having been first released on SourceForge in 2004, but nevertheless is robust and has a good-sized user base. Its usability does leave something to be desired. Perhaps as Luntbuild matures the interface will improve. In the meantime, I would recommend sticking with the tried-and-true CruiseControl unless having a Web interface for configuring builds is important to you.

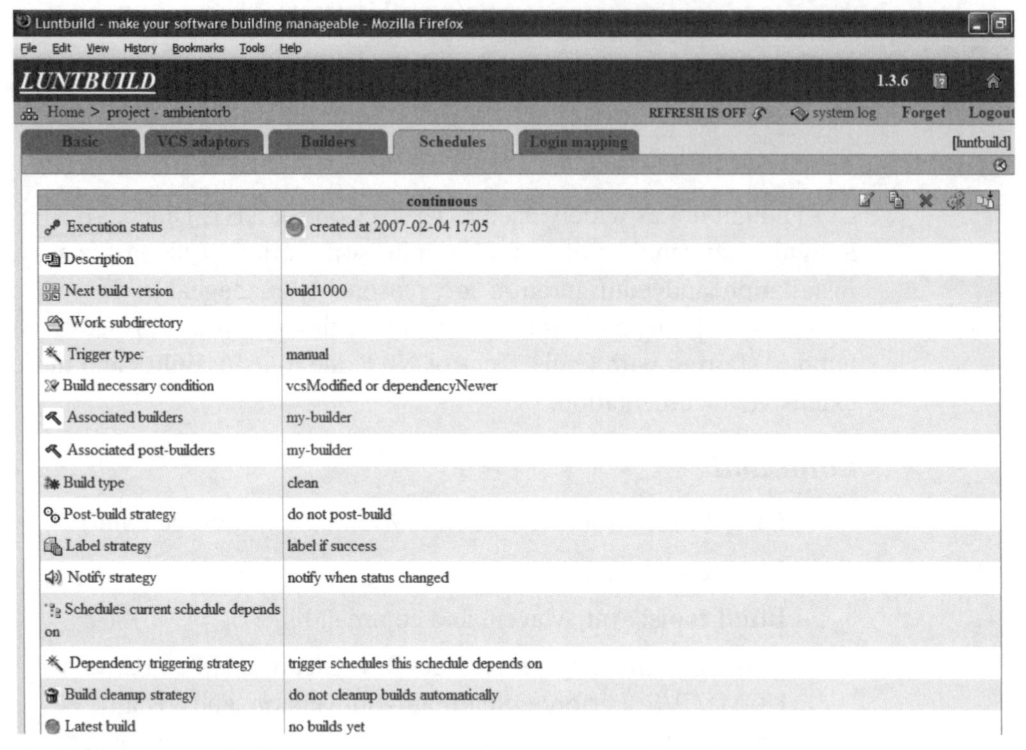

FIGURE B-5 Luntbuild

Conclusion

CI has entered the mainstream and has the tools and user community to prove it. Now that you're ready to join those of us who have benefited from the CI approach, you can choose the tools that provide the best match for you, your project, and your team. Though we've tried to provide you with as much information as possible to inform your decisions, you should use this appendix as a starting point in your investigations. Be sure to explore the wealth of information about these tools that you can find online in their documentation, FAQs, and mailing lists. With all this information in hand, you should be able to make your CI implementation a productive one.

Bibliography

Ambler, Scott W., and Pramod J. Sadalage. *Refactoring Databases: Evolutionary Database Design*. Boston: Addison-Wesley, 2006.

Antoniol, G., M. D. Penta, E. Merlo, and U. Villano. "Analyzing cloning evolution in the Linux kernel." *Journal of Information and Software Technology*, 44(13):755–765, 2002.

Beck, Kent, and Cynthia Andres. *Extreme Programming Explained, Second Edition.* Boston: Addison-Wesley, 2005.

Berczuk, Stephen P., and Brad Appleton. *Software Configuration Management Patterns: Effective Teamwork, Practical Integration.* Boston: Addison-Wesley, 2003.

Booch, Grady. *Object Solutions: Managing the Object-Oriented Project.* Menlo Park, CA: Pearson Education, 1996.

Cusumano, Michael A. "Software Development Worldwide: The State of the Practice" (with Alan MacCormack, Chris Kemerer, and Bill Crandall), *IEEE Software,* November–December 2003, vol. 20, no. 6, pp. 28–34 (Invited). www.pitt.edu/~ckemerer/CK%20research%20papers/SwDevelopmentWorldwide_CusumanoMacCormackKemerer03.pdf

Cusumano, Michael A., and Richard W. Selby. *Microsoft Secrets: How the World's Most Powerful Software Company Creates Technology, Shapes Markets, and Manages People*. New York: Free Press, 1995.

Duvall, Paul. "Automation for the People: Choosing a Continuous Integration Server." http://www-128.ibm.com/developerworks/java/library/j-ap09056/.

Duvall, Paul. "Automation for the People: Continuous Inspection." http://www-128.ibm.com/developerworks/java/library/j-ap08016/.

Duvall, Paul. "Automation for the People: Remove the Smell from Your Build Scripts." http://www-128.ibm.com/developerworks/java/library/j-ap10106/.

Fowler, Martin. "Continuous Integration." Available online at www.martinfowler.com/articles/continuousIntegration.html.

Fowler, Martin, Kent Beck, John Brant, William Opdyke, and Don Roberts. *Refactoring: Improving the Design of Existing Code.* Reading, MA: Addison-Wesley, 1999.

Fowler, Martin, and Pramod Sadalage. "Evolutionary Database Design." Available online at www.martinfowler.com/articles/evodb.html.

Hunt, Andrew, and David Thomas. *The Pragmatic Programmer: From Journeyman to Master.* Boston, MA: Addison-Wesley, 2000.

Kamiya, T., S. Kusumoto, and K. Inoue. "CCFinder: A multilinguistic token-based code clone detection system for large scale source code." *IEEE Transactions on Software Engineering*, 28(6):654–670, 2002.

McConnell, Steve. *Software Project Survival Guide.* Redmond, WA: Microsoft Press, 1998.

O'Reilly, Tim. "What Is Web 2.0: Design Patterns and Business Models for the Next Generation of Software." www.oreillynet.com/pub/a/oreilly/tim/news/2005/09/30/what-is-web-20.html.

Sierra, Kathy. "Why 'duh'... isn't." http://headrush.typepad.com/creating_passionate_users/2006/09/why_duh_isnt.html.

Toomim, Michael, Andrew Begel, and Susan L. Graham. "Managing Duplicated Code with Linked Editing." http://harmonia.cs.berkeley.edu/papers/toomim-linked-editing.pdf.

VanDoren, Edmond. "Cyclomatic Complexity." www.sei.cmu.edu/str/descriptions/cyclomatic.html.

Venners, Bill. "Refactoring with Martin Fowler: A Conversation with Martin Fowler, Part I." www.artima.com/intv/refactor.html.

Wake, William C. "Java Coding Conventions on One Page." www.xp123.com/xplor/xp0002f/codingstd.gif.

Watson, Arthur H., and Thomas J. McCabe. "Structured Testing: A Testing Methodology Using the Cyclomatic Complexity Metric." http://hissa.ncsl.nist.gov/HHRFdata/Artifacts/ITLdoc/235/title.htm.

Wilcox, Glen. "Managing Your Dependencies with JDepend." www.onjava.com/pub/a/onjava/2004/01/21/jdepend.html.

Index

A

B

C

D

E

F

G

H

I

J

L

Q

R

S

T

U

V

W

X

THIS BOOK IS SAFARI ENABLED

INCLUDES FREE 45-DAY ACCESS TO THE ONLINE EDITION

The Safari® Enabled icon on the cover of your favorite technology book means the book is available through Safari Bookshelf. When you buy this book, you get free access to the online edition for 45 days.

Safari Bookshelf is an electronic reference library that lets you easily search thousands of technical books, find code samples, download chapters, and access technical information whenever and wherever you need it.

TO GAIN 45-DAY SAFARI ENABLED ACCESS TO THIS BOOK:

- Go to **http://www.awprofessional.com/safarienabled**
- Complete the brief registration form
- Enter the coupon code found in the front of this book on the "Copyright" page

If you have difficulty registering on Safari Bookshelf or accessing the online edition, please e-mail customer-service@safaribooksonline.com.